Texas Ranger

NUMBER FIFTY
The Centennial Series
OF THE ASSOCIATION OF FORMER STUDENTS,
Texas A&M University

Texas Ranger

Jack Hays
in the Frontier Southwest

By
James Kimmins Greer

Texas A&M University Press
College Station

F
391
H44
G74
1993

Texas Ranger: Jack Hays in the Frontier Southwest is an adaptation of *Colonel Jack Hays: Texas Frontier Leader and California Builder*, originally published in 1952 by E. P. Dutton & Company, Inc., New York.

The paper used in this book meets the minimum requirements
of the American National Standard for Permanence
of Paper for Printed Library Materials, Z39.48-1984.
Binding materials have been chosen for durability.

∞

Library of Congress Cataloging-in-Publication Data

Greer, James K.
    Texas Ranger : Jack Hays in the frontier Southwest / by James
Kimmins Greer. — 1st ed.
        p. cm. — (The Centennial Series of the Association of Former
    Students, Texas A&M University ; no. 50)
    Includes bibliographical references and index.
    ISBN 0-89096-567-6. — ISBN 0-89096-572-2 (pbk.).
    1. Hays, John Coffee, 1817–1883.   2. Texas Rangers — Biography.
3. Frontier and pioneer life — Texas.   I. Title
F391.H44G74   1993
976.4'05'092 — dc20   93-4302
    [B]   CIP

CONTENTS

ILLUSTRATIONS

MAPS

PREFACE

IN TEXAS, John Coffee Hays was a soldier, surveyor, Ranger, officer in the Mexican War, and explorer. Tennessee and Mississippi were already part of him. He was one of the key men who maintained the Republic of Texas and then helped make it into a state. Yet he left San Antonio for the Gila River country to head an Indian agency, and went on to California, where he was a sheriff, federal surveyor general, and town developer before he entered his long period as gentleman ranchman and capitalist, to say nothing of his influence in politics and his exemplary life.

The heroic individualism and the courage of the Texas Rangers have long been a tradition. Jack Hays's name heads the list of those who created the tradition. Captain of the Rangers at twenty-three, his most eminent successors were from seven to seventeen years older when they assumed that position, nor did they remain in active service as long.

A leader should be judged by what he accomplishes in his locale with what he has. In fighting Indians, Hays rarely engaged less than ten and occasionally forty times his own number, but was never defeated. The unchallenged statement has been made that he "fought more than forty engagements when he was protecting San Antonio and southwest Texas against robbers and savages." The number probably was larger, yet no one knows just how many encounters he had with the Comanches and the Mexican marauders. Without question, Jack Hays was the most spectacular and successful Indian fighter of Texas history.[1] He was equally successful against border bandits and then won national distinction in the Mexican War.

In relating the conflicts along the frontier and the battles of the Mexican War, I have attempted to thin the haze of war. The

[9]

opinion that Indians and bandits came to have of Hays is summed up in a frontier expression: "They tore into the woods as if Jack Hays, himself, were after them."

The chief guardian of the Texas frontier until 1849, John Coffee Hays served the people "long and well . . . never led them in defeat." Hays so reduced the Comanches, the principal barrier to settlement, that Santa Anna, perhaps the greatest Comanche war chief, later stated that no Indian could properly pass below a line established by Hays. The Texas account of Rip Ford, Hays's regimental adjutant, records: "The people of southern and western Texas can truthfully say that but for the watchfulness of Colonel Hays and his eminent and illustrious acts in their behalf, there is no telling when their regions would have been settled."

Nelson Lee, who spent eighteen adventurous years in Texas, factually told his editor in 1858 that

> I entered [1841] my second campaign as a Texas Ranger by joining Jack Hays at San Antonio. . . . In the imaginations of most persons Hays undoubtedly figures as a rough, bold giant, bewhiskered like a brigand, and wielding the strength of Hercules. On the contrary, he was a slim, smooth faced boy not over twenty years of age [actually 24], and looking younger than he was in fact. In his manner he was unassuming in the extreme, a stripling of few words, whose quiet demeanor stretched quite to the verge of modesty. Nevertheless it was this youngster whom the huge-framed brawny-armed campaigners hailed unanimously as their chief and leader when they had assembled together in their uncouth garb on the grand plaza of Bexar. . . . young as he was, he had already exhibited abundant evidence that, though a lamb in peace, he was a lion in war.

Lee could have added that among the Texas Rangers were "doctors and lawyers, and many college graduates." Hays possessed the prerequisites of a Texas Ranger captain: judgment, boldness, speed, and youth. While he could outride them, he could also use his fists, Bowie, or Colt better than any in his command.

Hays was humane as well as valiant. While war was his apparent element, he fought relentlessly because he wanted a quick ending. He had a clear eye and a fast hand, but was not a gun-

[10]

man. He did not wear long hair, chase the red men on posters, nor wait until he could see the whites of a reporter's eyes before going into action. In peace his virtues were noble.

Until the publication of *Colonel Jack Hays: Texas Frontier Leader and California Builder* (1952, 1987), from which this book is adapted, there had been no previous study of Hays, although many brief biographical sketches had appeared. These were not adequate even for their purpose, as the authors invariably fell into numerous errors of fact, copied each other's mistakes, or neglected many activities of his life. The best of these efforts furnished an excellent apologetic statement: "The exploits of Jack Hays in Texas, if told in detail, would fill several volumes. . . ."[2]

Hays's associates and other contemporaries have been used as collaborators in telling his story, which is shaped from his papers and other bibliographical sources. Condensation has been necessary at most points; nearly every paragraph could be elaborated from the material collected. Objectivity has been sought; stock depictions have not always been accepted; no testimony has been suppressed.

Since the American future can only emerge from the American past, it is hoped that *Texas Ranger: Jack Hays in the Frontier Southwest* will aid in stimulating readers to understand their heritage and meet the problems confronting them.

J. K. G.

PUBLISHER'S PREFACE

IN 1952 James Kimmins Greer first published a rousing biography of the life of famed Texas Ranger John Coffee (Jack) Hays, entitled *Colonel Jack Hays: Texas Frontier Leader and California Builder.* In 1987, Texas A&M University Press published a revised edition of that account, which the *New York Times* described as an "excellent, well-documented biography of one of the frontier's most colorful individuals."

Continuing interest in the Texas Rangers and one of their most outstanding members has led Texas A&M University to release this abridged version of Greer's biography of Hays. *Texas Ranger: Jack Hays in the Frontier Southwest* makes available again the tale of the first half of Hays's life: his career as a Texas Ranger—standing off bands of Indians single-handedly, leading his volunteers against fifteen-to-one odds, commanding his small forces as the sole bulwark between Texas and the Mexican army, and operating behind enemy lines in the Mexican War to lead in the desperate fighting that resulted in the capture of Monterrey.

Jack Hays, Texas Ranger, rides again.

Texas Ranger

I

THE ALAMO HAS FALLEN!

LIEUTENANT HARMON HAYS was at last back on his plantation near Little Cedar Lick, Tennessee. Peace had come to the United States after General Andrew Jackson had broken the power of the Creek confederacy at Horseshoe Bend and defeated the British at New Orleans. In the quiet of his country home Harmon remembered those strenuous campaigns, and he recalled with gratitude the kindness of his commander, General John Coffee. It was not unfitting, therefore, that when a son, their second child, was born to him and his wife Elizabeth, on January 28, 1817, the parents named him John Coffee Hays.[1]

Among the neighbors who came to view the baby was Harmon's aunt, Rachel Donelson Jackson. As she stood beside the bed, looking at the tiny boy, Rachel remarked that he was a handsome baby, not red like most newcomers to this planet. Another visitor added that the mother would continue to be as beautiful as ever; then Grandfather Robert Hays, who was permitted a glimpse of the child, left the room with the observation that he was going to call the young fellow "Jack." It was an affectionate nickname that stuck to the end of his life.[2] Other babies came in rapid succession, five in the next nine years.

Meanwhile life in and around Little Cedar Lick was glorious for young Jack. There was excellent fishing, game in the woods nearby, and a log-cabin school which served until the boy could enter Davidson Academy in Nashville.

More important than any schoolmaster's lessons to the impressionable lad, however, was the conversation of his parents and their friends. Since the social life of the neighborhood centered about the Hermitage, the Hays boys heard a never-ending flow of talk about planting, horse racing, military affairs, and politics. No person can say how much General Andrew Jackson influ-

[15]

enced the bright, retentive mind of Jack, but certain it is that the boy, before reaching the age of twelve, listened to Old Hickory often and profited by what was said.

His brown hair, quick, piercing hazel eyes, fair complexion, slightly aquiline nose, firm mouth, and steady chin were even now beginning to reveal qualities which were to hold the regard of others. Partly, no doubt, from his charming mother and partly from his magnetic father, Jack inherited and acquired elements of individuality that made him from early boyhood an unusual person. People gravitated to him, whether he talked with them or remained silent, for he was reliable, faithful, and transparently honest.

Jack enjoyed sprinting, cross-country races, riding calves and unbroken colts, which exercises gave him a wiry frame and endurance. Perhaps the diversions he remembered best of all were the neighborhood rifle matches and those pleasant hours when he gathered with the crowd at the Hermitage racetrack to watch somebody bet on the bobtail nag and somebody else bet on the bay. Thus environment accustomed him to riding and skill in the use of weapons before he was a dozen years of age. From his elders and through his acquaintance with a few friendly Cherokees he absorbed much Indian lore, and he grew into a mannerly and studious youth.

One morning in 1832 a neighbor came running to the school and whispered hurriedly to the master. The Hays children were sent home immediately only to learn that their father was seriously ill. Several days later he died. People said, "It was the fever. Such a large, strong man to waste away in such manner!" A few weeks later Jack's mother, too, died. It rained the day neighbors buried her beside her husband. During the brief ceremony in the family cemetery, Jack stood near the casket, bareheaded in the cold drizzle, and felt the rain trickle down his neck and back and send chills along his spine. His older brother, William, stood only a few feet away. Between them were Sarah, James, Mary Anne, Harry Thompson, and Robert, other members of the bereft family.[3] That night all seven children slept at the home of Stockley Hays, his father's oldest brother.

On the next day the kin assembled. A death in the Hays family or in that of their close relatives was always followed by a gathering of the clan and a few of their most intimate friends. There Jack was told that his uncle Robert Cage, planter from Yazoo County, Mississippi, wished three of the children to make their home with him. He and Sarah, the youngest sister, and Robert, the youngest brother, were to be as Uncle Robert's own children. For a moment the boy was silently rebellious at the idea of separation from the others. His uncle, able to surmise something of the fifteen-year-old lad's thoughts, hastened to say that Robert, only five years old, needed his brother Jack—the one appeal which was unchallengeable.

The Hayses were of Scotch-Irish descent. Induced by a combination of famine and politics, Jack's great-grandfather John, of Ireland, sailed with his family and a numerous party of immigrants to the English colonies in 1740. Jack's grandfather Robert was born to Martha Thompson Hays, a Virginian, the second wife of his great-grandfather. Robert grew up in the Rock Bridge section of Virginia. Too young to participate in the Seven Years War, he became a lieutenant in the North Carolina Infantry during the Revolution and was later an original member of the North Carolina Society of the Cincinnati.[4]

In 1785 Robert Hays settled on Little Cedar Lick, Wilson County, Tennessee, and prospered in his new environment. Through marriage with Jane Donelson, daughter of Colonel John and Rachel Stockley Donelson, he became a brother-in-law of John, William, Stockley, and Samuel—sons of Colonel John Donelson.[5]

Colonel Robert Hays erected Fort Haysboro, later called Haysboro. Here in the pioneer home Harmon A. Hays, sixth child of the colonel's and father of John Coffee Hays, was born. At the first assessment of real estate in the Nashville area, the list of principal property-holders included John Donelson and Robert Hays, and ten years later Colonel Hays was being spoken of as a "wealthy citizen."[6] A historian has written: "Colonel Robert Hays, who was brother-in-law to [Andrew] Jackson . . . was not only a prominent and wealthy pioneer, but a close friend and associate of the more wealthy and prominent land speculators, William Polk and William Blount." [7]

Harmon Hays served with Sam Houston in the Creek War in Alabama and was in Coffee's dragoons, becoming a second lieutenant in May, 1814.[8] It was he who was selected to face the center of the British advance at New Orleans.

Harmon married Elizabeth Cage, a member of a notable Virginia family,[9] and soon thereafter resigned his army commission. Some of her people lived in Nashville; some removed to Mississippi. Jack had heard these incidents and others from his relatives, especially from his grandaunt Rachel Jackson. Aunt Rachel was wonderfully kind to children and particularly so to this namesake of her niece's husband.

In the neighborhood there had been children's parties on weekends when he became ten, and, by the time he had entered his teens, his aunts and grandaunts were insisting upon his attendance at dances. With a little practice young Jack danced himself into the hearts of the girls and his popularity became assured.

Together with good breeding, Jack Hays inherited a tradition of leadership and public service. Many of the families that had intermarried with the Hayses also had contributed substantially to the life of Tennessee, Mississippi, and Louisiana. This made him ever conscious of his heritages and traditions of honor and civic duty.

When Robert Cage and the three Hays children arrived at the Cage plantation, the novelty of change somewhat buoyed up the youngsters. The well-meaning uncle mentioned business as a career and suggested that Jack begin by going to work in a store, to which the boy countered by saying that he had hoped to attend West Point. At length after being unable to convince his uncle of the desirability of a military career, the lad "very peacefully left home." [10]

Now wholly on his own, Jack decided to learn surveying and hired out as chain boy while still only fifteen.[11] He continued in that capacity during the first summer, but soon he conceived the idea of trying for promotion, saving his money, and going

to school. Land speculators and ex-soldiers, having learned that
the boy-surveyor had acquired a practical knowledge of surveying, paid him liberally to locate numerous tracts of land for
them.[12]

Surveying in Mississippi was often dangerous. While locating
claims near a Choctaw hunting section, Jack and a companion,
George Work, were warned by a white trapper that the Indians
were becoming irritated by the presence of the surveyors; hence
the boys decided early one morning to reconnoiter the country
over which they proposed to work. Hays had a single-shot pistol,
but George was unarmed when unexpectedly they met several
mounted Indians who seemed to be watching the trail the boys
were traveling. When the Indians charged, the lads wheeled
their horses and rode for their lives.

One Indian, much better mounted than his companions or
the boys, soon came closer and fired at Work, the shot killing
the horse and throwing the rider. Hays raced back to his companion and shouted, "George, take my horse and lasso the first
Indian that comes up!" While George was mounting, Jack ran
to some projecting rocks and took position behind them. When
the leading pursuer came rushing along the trail, Work tossed
a noose over him as he passed. As the Indian jerked his horse to
a halt, Jack took deliberate aim and fired. While the red man's
frightened horse was bounding forward and throwing his dead
rider to one side, Hays was running toward the animal. He leap-
frogged into the Indian's saddle, and, slapping his hands hard
upon the horse's rump, he and Work raced out of danger.[13]

After surveying for two years, Jack had saved enough money
to afford a year's study in Davidson Academy at Nashville. He
was known there as the fastest runner in the school. To include
the small boys in their sport, often dashes were run with each
of the entrants carrying a little boy on his shoulder. This handi-
cap race—one of the most amusing of all their sports—was always
won by Jack over larger and stronger boys, who did not have
his speed.[14] Close application to his studies together with hard
play, however, finally overtaxed his strength. Becoming ill during the long, cold winter, he decided to return to the milder

coastal climate of Mississippi.[15] He reasoned that he might visit
in Yazoo County and also do enough surveying there to be
independent.

Hardly had Jack reached his uncle's plantation when news
came of the siege of the Alamo and Travis's appeal for aid. In
the same post was brought the inspiring intelligence which
hastened his departure: Texas declared itself an independent
republic on March 2, 1836. This was successively followed by
the calamitous reports: the Alamo fell on March 6, its defenders
slaughtered and their bodies burned; Fannin surrendered his
entire command at Goliad and his soldiers had been executed;
Texans were fleeing toward Louisiana in advance of Santa
Anna's army. Jack Hays's patriotism was aroused. He decided
to cast his lot with the Texans.

In preparation for the venture, Hays bought a good knife and
the best brace of pistols he could find. Most of the remainder
of his funds he expended for a fine horse and a few articles of
camping equipment. The last of the money he made surveying
in the swamps of Mississippi he felt would be sufficient to get
him to Texas.[16]

After Jack had prepared to start on his journey, he dreaded
the parting from Sarah and from Robert, who was now nine. As
he could not bear the thought of their sad faces if he bade them
good-by, he eased his conscience by writing a note to them in
which he promised that if fortune smiled upon him, he would
have them join him before many years had elapsed. He also
composed a note of farewell to his aunt, expressing his gratitude
to her and to his uncle, and next morning before dawn he pinned
the notes to his pillow, saddled his horse, and rode quietly away.

At New Orleans young Hays joined a group composed of
volunteers from Kentucky, Mississippi, and Louisiana. There
were ninety[17] in this heterogeneous crowd who traveled to
Nacogdoches, the nearest town in Texas and the gateway to
the new Republic. He found Nacogdoches crowded with
debtors, volunteers, and refugees from justice—many of them
desperate characters. Hays had serious trouble with one of this
last type of transients, a bully whose practice was to select in-

offensive-looking men, insult them, and then shoot or pistol-whip them.

Suddenly he became aware of young Hays at the end of the bar. After deciding that a fight with the quiet, slender youth would contribute to his growing fame as a bloodthirsty man, the barroom bully shambled to where Jack stood, paused, and looking straight at his intended victim, knocked the drink from his hand. Jack did not utter a word; his eyes flashed resentment. The man reached for his gun. "Then, with a movement as quick as lightning, he [Hays] presented a pistol and fired. . . . the desperado was a corpse when his body touched the ground."[18] Hays was "completely exonerated" before he resumed his journey toward Washington-on-the-Brazos, where the independence of Texas had been declared.

Upon leaving Nacogdoches, he had heard of the victory of Sam Houston and the Texans over Santa Anna's army at San Jacinto on April 21. High with hope, Jack rode away from Washington to Isaac Donahoe's on Clear Creek, two miles from the site of later Hempstead. Donahoe was an old friend of his uncle Abner Cage, and Jack had brought letters from relatives to Donahoe. As one of the colonists of "The Father of Texas," Stephen F. Austin,[19] Donahoe had prospered and had become well-known. Hays learned from him where the Texas troops were. A new nation had been born and Jack Hays, the nineteen-year-old Cedar Lick lad, found life exciting and fortune beckoning.

II

SOLDIER-SURVEYOR

JACK HAYS celebrated May Day by hastening to join the army
of the Republic, commanded by General Thomas J. Rusk. Assigned to a spy company, he was ordered in almost his first
important duty to assist in burying the remains of General James
W. Fannin's three hundred and fifty men. What the nineteen-
year-old volunteer learned during this assignment gave him
a realistic conception of the Texas Revolution and the problems
confronting the infant Republic. When volunteers therefore
were furloughed while money was being raised to pay and discharge them, Hays chose to remain in service, regardless of
compensation.

His duties with the army having been concluded, he visited
President Houston at Columbia and presented his letters of
introduction. Houston, after talking with the young volunteer,
advised him to join a company of Rangers being enlisted for
service on the southwestern frontier by Captain Erasmus
("Deaf") Smith, Houston's former chief of scouts. These Rangers under the orders of Colonel H. W. Karnes were to carry out
the Republic's policy from the settlements to the Rio Grande.
Hays decided to follow Houston's advice.

By early December, the young Ranger found himself one of
the first recruits in a battalion of two hundred and eight mounted
men. He had enlisted for a minimum of twelve months, with
pay of thirty dollars a month and subsistence for himself and
his horse. He was to furnish his own horse, rifle, pistols, and
other equipment, which were subjected to the inspection of
an army officer.[1]

San Antonio, then usually called Bexar—an old place, endowed by nature with many charms—commanded a profitable trade with several villages along the Rio Grande; but this commerce had to traverse a region heavily infested with bandits. This municipality of ancient Bexar was still a vast territory, though San Antonio, Goliad, and Refugio were the only settlements in the wide area occupied by wild animals and even wilder Indians. The Comanches claimed the region as their hunting grounds and had driven out the Apaches, though one of their disaffected chiefs, Lipan, had established his band upon the Medina River. This tribe, known as Lipans, became bitter enemies of the Comanches. In this section were remnants of Alabamas, Delawares, and Cherokees who were also suffered to remain there by the lordly Comanches.

Mexico claimed the territory as far north as the Nueces, and the disputed country between that stream and the Rio Grande was inhabited thinly, but nearly wholly, by Mexicans who sympathized with their kinsmen and were unfriendly toward the Republic. Outlaws swarmed daily into the Rio Grande Valley. The Comanches dominated all.

Hays was one of Smith's company of twenty Rangers that camped below Bexar on the San Antonio River late in December, 1836—the first military force sent by the Republic to San Antonio. An estimate of five Anglo-Americans in the little outpost probably would have been an exaggeration. Here for four weeks the company remained in camp while horses were being rested, equipment supplemented, and the men trained in the fundamentals of frontier warfare.

In this camp Hays passed his twentieth birthday. He, looking more youthful than his years, stood five feet nine inches in height, was broad-shouldered and erect, and weighed a little less than a hundred and fifty pounds. His hair was reddish brown and his eyes hazel, and his nose gave a slight Roman cast to his features. He was always well armed and was seldom without one or more fine horses. All of the privates were on the same level, but Jack's modest, simple manners and his relish for humor soon established him a favorite among his comrades. Matters moved smoothly along until the necessity for fresh grazing forced Captain Smith to move his company to the Medina in mid-February. But on the 25th they returned to San Antonio to help bury with military honors the ashes of the Alamo defenders.

On the anniversary of the fall of the Alamo, Smith led his little company back toward Laredo on the Rio Grande. As the town was still held by the Mexicans, he declared his intention to raise the flag of independence on the church spire and had reached the Chacon, five miles from Laredo, when a force of forty cavalry arrived to oppose him.

The enemy, coming up at a run, surrounded the Rangers and demanded their surrender, all the while bitterly reviling the Texans and promising them a hard fate.[2] As his men were outnumbered and mostly inexperienced, Deaf Smith ordered them to make a defensive fight. The result was ten enemy dead, as many wounded, several prisoners, and twenty of the Mexican mounts captured. Only a few Texan troopers had been wounded, but when Smith learned that Laredo was now being occupied by a force superior to his own he returned to San Antonio very proud of his men's conduct.[3]

This expedition marked the first appearance of the Texas Rangers west of the Nueces and initiated the renewal of the partisan conflict between Mexico and the Republic of Texas. During this campaign Jack Hays's adeptness at discovering the enemy's position and quickly reporting the facts brought him promotion to a sergeancy.[4]

Sergeant Hays and three men usually patrolled a beat of between forty and fifty miles, and once while on one of these rounds, he was told by a Mexican rancher that on the opposite side of the river a dozen Mexican bandits were in hiding. Hays decided at once that he would try to capture these outlaws without sending back to headquarters for assistance. He laid his plans carefully and just before sundown placed his men in ambush as a reception committee for the Mexicans. At dusk the mounted marauders forded the stream and came on cautiously toward where the Rangers lay. Unfortunately one of the boys accidentally discharged his pistol and precipitated the fight. In the clash that followed, one Texan was wounded, but three dead Mexicans lay sprawled in the cactus.

Seeing the fate of their companions, four of the Mexicans wheeled their horses and raced toward the river with Hays and another Ranger spurring in close pursuit. The remaining five enemy horsemen suddenly tried to block the Texans, but the Sergeant, bringing up his last loaded pistol in a quick shot, toppled the nearest outlaw from the saddle and forced the others to flee. Toward the open country the bandits spurred and flogged their ponies, since a dash to the river would have slowed them down. As the race continued, a fugitive's horse fell, and its rider was thrown and lay still. Hays, having slowed his mount, swung from his saddle, swooped up a pistol from the man's holster, and spurred forward in the chase. By this time Sergeant Hays's companion was alongside him, and the two pressed the three remaining bandits so closely that they took refuge in the hills. Hays and his men then quickly separated and attacked vigorously from front and rear. This medicine was effective. The bandits surrendered—one of them the notorious Juan Sanchez. Before they were hanged, the prisoners revealed the whereabouts of the remainder of the gang, who subsequently were captured.

In May President Houston furloughed all except six hundred of the army, most of whom he discharged soon afterwards. Frontier defense now became the main problem of the militia and a few companies of Rangers.[5] Meantime much land near San Antonio was being awarded to colonists and to veterans, and these awards had to be surveyed. Many claims also were made on the remote frontier streams, necessitating more surveying.

Since surveyors worked heavily armed or under the protection of a military escort, it was quite natural for a surveyor to divide his time between frontier patrol and surveying. Hays was only one of the many who followed both professions[6]— surveying and soldiering—when San Antonio began to swarm in 1838 with holders of headright certificates, bounty warrants, surveyors seeking employment, and adventurers. Surveyors by the wholesale invaded the Indian country, thereby inaugurating a long struggle for the establishment of civilization against Comanche resistance. Sometimes Hays commanded an escort for a party of surveyors, but more often he led his own surveying group.[7]

Hays applied for and received an appointment as Deputy Surveyor of Bexar District under R. C. Trimble. The first field notes that he recorded described land later known as a part of Alamo Heights. During a further assignment he was in charge of a party of four who were making a survey on Comal Creek when he suddenly became aware that numerous Indians were watching them work. Without seeming conscious of the danger, the surveyors kept busy until nightfall. As only one of the group had a horse, there was little chance for escape; so the party made camp.

At night the red men camped uncomfortably near and formed a cordon about the surveyors. As Hays lay watching the Indians' smoldering fire, he discovered they were Cherokees who were in Comanche territory and supposedly friendly to the whites. But he decided to investigate their puzzling actions. Moving away from his sleeping companions, he sat down for several minutes, then rolled over on his stomach, and began crawling toward the spot of light in front of him. Soon he realized that more than two dozen Indians had first encircled and then had crawled in very close to his camp. As he completed his check of the siege ring and became convinced it was too tight, he decided there was only the alternative of bluffing through by continuing their work on the morrow or by making a dash to escape.

Back at camp at dawn, he told the men to carry on as usual. In compliance with orders after an early breakfast they set to work industriously. As Hays and his party moved along throughout the day, the Indians followed. But when several braves shifted between the white men and some timber ahead, Hays, sensing the seriousness of the move, signaled a flank-run to the timber.

For a mile and a half even the fleetest of the red men could not overtake the Rangers. At last, however, the boy chainman, who had been allowed to set the pace, became exhausted. Hays ordered the only mounted Ranger to bring aid from a distant camp of surveyors. He himself elected not to leave the boy. The others chose to follow his example.

At this change of procedure the Indians stopped running, made signals of friendship, and advanced slowly to where the surveyors awaited them. But when they had arrived within a few paces, the Cherokees suddenly surrounded the whites and shouted that the Texans now were prisoners. Hays could understand only part of the Cherokee language, but with the Indians was a Negro who did a fair job of translating. The captors asked for the Rangers' guns, but Hays refused to give them up. Since the Indians were unsuccessful in this demand, they marched the party to a nearby creek to decide the fate of the surveyors. The Negro said that the Cherokees had been fighting the Comanches, had taken many scalps, but now were leaving that section of the country. Although the captives were kept under heavy guard, they were permitted to keep their guns, since Hays had threatened to send as many as possible to the Happy Hunting Grounds if they attempted to take them forcibly.

About two o'clock the Indians made their decision: if Hays would write a statement that they were friendly Indians, the surveyors would be liberated. He wrote the testimonial; he and the others signed it, and the surveyors were released. The strange aftereffect of this experience was that one of the Hays party became very much frightened when he saw the Indians hang and clean the Comanche scalps. His mind raced to conclusions. Shortly afterward his hair turned gray, and he sickened and died a few days later.[8]

Evidently Hays was not intimidated by his risks, since he was back surveying on the Rio Frio and other distant points in June.[9] The Comanches resented his presence, but he continued to work, although some of the parties which had left San Antonio had been almost entirely destroyed and others had been wiped out completely.[10]

Hays was one of twenty men with Colonel Karnes who participated in a fight with the Comanches on the Arroyo Seco in August. One hot day while the company rested by this small stream, two hundred mounted Comanches swept boldly toward them. There was barely time for the troops to place the horses behind shelter of the creek bank and to scatter themselves in the chaparral brush. Aware of their enormous odds, the Indians sought to flush the troops out of cover so that they could ride them down. Round and round the red men circled, filling the air with whistling arrows and showering the platoon with deadly missiles. But Hays, using frontier tactics, split the charging horsemen by singling out their chief and bringing him down. This halted the rush beyond rifle range, but the warriors wheeled their mounts for another try. The return onset, signaled by a barrage of arrows, was likewise disastrous to the Indians. Again persistent, the courageous Comanches formed for a third attack, though their spirit was flagging, the death of their leader having sapped their zeal. Their final effort, also launched with arrows, was merely an attempt to shield themselves as they picked up their dead and wounded. Victory would prove too costly; they galloped away. In this engagement twenty of the red men were killed and as many more were wounded. The clouds of arrows had killed nearly every horse of the Rangers, no light loss in a land where good American horses were not too plentiful.

While the Rangers sought remounts to take the place of those lost in the recent encounter, Hays busied himself with surveying. Indians still made efforts to prevent him from working on the Leon when he led a combined force of surveyors and Rangers to run three compasses.[11] In 1838, though he worked only a part of the year, he located seventy-six certificates. His cousin, Captain A. C. Cage, was one of eight killed in a party of eleven who fought a finished fight with one hundred and eighty Comanches.[12]

Whites and redskins alike now recognized that Ranger Jack Hays was skilled in the battle tactics of Indians. He learned early to recognize one of the Comanches' prized maneuvers: charge the palefaces, but recoil before their counteroffensive;

let the center of the Indian line continue to fall back until the white men are between two wings; then have flanking warriors meet pincerlike at the rear of the enemy. Hays mastered this simple battle strategy and used it many times successfully.

Part of Hays's rapid development on the frontier was due to his friendship with friendly Lipans and Delawares. A chance meeting with Flacco,[13] promising young headman of the Lipans, influenced both their lives. After this meeting, the Lipan watched Hays's every move in an effort to be like him. He thought his white friend possessed some sort of charm that enabled him to accomplish deeds of bravery and perform extraordinary feats in encounters. In his search for the young frontiersman's spell, the Lipan rose to power as war chief of his tribe.

From Flacco, Hays learned many of the finer points of trailing. He also talked much with him concerning variations in the tribal features and appearance and in methods of fighting. The Comanche was customarily an open-field fighter; the Apache attacked almost always from ambush. Comanches were free-booters of the plains, who swarmed along their war trails in the light of the moon, with every moonlight night a special time to raid the white settlements. These "horse Indians" cared little for distance, mesquite country, or stony mountains.

Flacco was tall and erect, with well-shaped limbs. He gave an impression of bounding elasticity. His forehead was better developed than was the average Indian's. His circlet of eagle feathers was set back so that it revealed his black eyes and gave to his bearing a fierce alertness coupled with strength and agility. His facial expression contained more magnanimity than did that of Buffalo Hump of the Comanches, another war chief of Hays's acquaintance. Flacco's general appearance was suggestive of the hawk and the panther.

The chief of the Lipans dressed more richly than Buffalo Hump. Flacco's fine string of beads, numerous armlets, and wrist bands were of pure silver, while those of the Comanche chief were of brass. One wide belt crossed Flacco's chest and supported the quiver swung on his back; a wider belt bore the hunting knife and held the breechclout in place. The Lipan wore leggings of white buckskin which came to his knees and were attached by thongs to his waistbelt. Wide fringes behind and neat figures executed in black and red paint set off the leggings. His moccasins, attached to the leggings, were of the same material and were decorated with fringes and beads. Buffalo Hump often wore only a breechcloth and moccasins in addition to his brass rings and a single string of beads.

While surveying occasionally beyond Bexar, Hays became friendly with some Delawares and promised one of their headmen that he would go on a trapping excursion with a detachment of them. John Caperton, a contemporary of Hays at San Antonio, used to tell this story of one of the forays.

The hunting party which Hays finally joined numbered seventeen Delawares. They went to the Pecos River on foot in order to be free from caring for horses while trapping and also to be rid of a temptation to the Comanches. By planning to ascend the river into New Mexico, they hoped to avoid their enemy who ravaged the plains.

Soon after they had reached the Pecos and had organized in pairs, one Delaware tribesman stumbled into camp and told of having been surprised by a passing band of over a hundred Comanches. When they killed his companion, the young Delaware had raced away and had hidden. In their fury, thoughts of trapping were forgotten as the Delawares voted to pursue the Comanches, who were en route to Chihuahua. If successful, however, the Delawares must overtake their enemies before they had crossed the Rio Grande, for neither Hays nor the Indians were permitted to enter Mexico without violating President Houston's policy. Hays had cast his lot with the Delawares in this excursion, and now felt he could not refuse to pursue the Comanche raiders.

The decision having been made, the Delawares took the trail with a swinging, never-tiring trot from which Jack wearied at the end of the first few miles. If it were only a sprint up to several hundred yards, he did not doubt that he could lead their entire tribe; if it were a run of from two to five miles he believed he could defeat any in this band. Now on the trail only pride in his own race prevented him from asking for pauses while he caught his wind. Hour after hour his only outward revelations of fatigue were the tightening of his hand on his rifle, which he carried at low trail, or the closing of his eyes for seconds while he mechanically pumped strides behind the man in front of him in the Indian file.

Rays of autumn's retreating sun slanted down with summer intensity at midday. Water holes were far apart, and the Indians stopped only briefly to eat or sleep, while the everlasting pounding of feet set Hays to wondering how much longer he could endure. At last he reached the point where screaming muscles and depleted wind somehow restored themselves. He had run farther than he had ever run before—surprising to himself.

At last at noon one day the trailers stopped at a spring, took a drink of water, ate a few bites of dry, cold meat, then resumed the steady pace. Only when dusk found them at another spring did the leader gesture a stop. After resting a few minutes, the Indians drank, ate again, and moved away from the trail to lie down and fall asleep instantly. For a long while Hays was too tired to sleep, but heavy eyes overcame tired muscles and finally he sank into a deep slumber.

It seemed that only minutes had elapsed when a light hand on his shoulder brought him upon his feet with his knife in hand. But instant awareness held the blow he had almost delivered as a Delaware said softly that the moon was rising and the Rio Bravo[14] was far away. They must travel while the "horse Indians" still slept.

After the first two miles Hays's stiffness vanished, and dog-trotting along the trail in the light of the moon became momentarily exhilarating. Soon he ran automatically, unaware of time or distance. The second day and the second night were a repetition of the first. As the cool false dawn of the third day broke, the leader halted the column, and the Indians conferred. Pursuit was ended. Frequently a head was raised from the whispering huddle to throw a quick glance ahead toward the enemy camp near the river. Hays now could notice the odor from the smoke of a flameless campfire. The hurried council determined to surround the sleeping enemy, except on the river side, then to attack with guns and arrows until the Comanches were reduced in number, and finally to rush them. Having decided, the Delawares began to creep upon their enemies.

In the dim atmosphere Hays could hardly see the warriors placed at intervals on either side of him, and so cautiously did each warrior crawl toward the sleeping Comanches that Jack could neither hear nor see the braves within a few feet of him. In the darkness finally one of the Indians touched him as a signal to go no farther. At dawn they would attack. Now they slept.

At the crack of daylight a Comanche brave arose. A rifle ball whizzed; the warrior fell dead. Gunfire and showers of arrows brought down startled Comanches as they sprang into action. Remembering the slain brother left on the plains, the Delaware chief signaled for a terrific onslaught by charging upon the nearest of the enemy. Hays joined in the rush with a knife in one hand and a tomahawk in the other. The Comanches rallied to defend themselves. But the advantage of surprise being with the Delawares, the Comanches ceased the hand-to-hand encounters and began to dash for the river. Fleet Delawares pursued. The crunch of the light ax into skulls or the thrust of the long knife into backs of Comanche warriors brought dying screams or gasps. Some of the swifter braves reached the stream safely. "Many of them were shot while in the water. Very few escaped." [15] And the Delawares exulted as the morning sun shone out on another autumn day.

III

CAPTAIN OF THE RANGERS

CONDITIONS along the Indian frontier of Texas at the opening
of 1839 were worse than those of the years preceding. Around
San Antonio the Comanches made raids with increasing boldness. Within a year after the Land Office had opened, there
were a hundred and forty young Anglo-Americans in San Antonio, and during that time not less than a hundred of them
"were killed in various fights with the Indians and Mexicans." [1]
Many of these "remarkable young men" [2] having arrived too
late to participate in the decisive battle of San Jacinto were
attracted to Bexar by its novelty, climate, land speculation, and
adventure.

Hays usually selected ten men to accompany him on surveying expeditions. Between trips he frequently was occupied with
the punishment of guerrillas from Mexico, who sought to prey
upon pack-mule trains or outpost towns. For paying his men
at this time, Hays depended upon surveying fees and bonuses
from those who wished their lands located, despite the danger
involved. With so little money from the government available,
Hays's surveying was often his only maintenance.

When not in the field, Hays's residence was San Antonio
where the cost of living was low, recreation was simple, and
surveying or fighting bandits and Indians provided plenty of
exciting action. One of thirty thousand white inhabitants of
Texas in 1836, he had witnessed the increase of settlers to almost
forty-five thousand by the beginning of 1839. [3] San Antonio was
the western gate to the frontier that extended to the Rio Grande.

By 1839 "Jack Hays, Ben McCulloch, Caldwell, and others
of like spirit," states Morell, "were in readiness at any hour to
engage in the most daring expeditions. . . . 1839 furnished ample

opportunities."[4] Now even the Cherokees of East Texas were becoming troublesome. Often Hays's little companies of Rangers, militia, or surveyors' helpers numbered only ten or a dozen. He was the leader of a close-knit band in a region where guerrilla warfare raged among three races.

Hays was once miles away on a surveying tour when a Comanche herald had appeared in that part of San Antonio later known as Commerce Street. On a prancing steed, he challenged the townsmen to come out to fight his band. Eleven inexperienced men followed him. Only three escaped the trap set by a hundred Comanches.

Few of Hays's platoon of Rangers in 1839 were over twenty-two years of age. There was not an ordinary figure among them; yet the most vindictive, the most dangerous one in the group had the best features, most graceful manners, and the softest voice. This man, who had been nicknamed "the Bravo," was friendly toward all. But "The man," wrote C. W. Webber, "on whom he [the Bravo] seemed to lavish most attention, and who, indeed, appeared to be regarded with particular deference by all, was a slight, raw-boned figure, with a lean Roman face, and an expression of modest simplicity. . . . and I remember feeling some surprise that so unsophisticated, easy, good-natured looking a personage should be treated with so much respect by men necessarily of hardy cast as those around. Yet this individual was the celebrated Captain . . . Hays, the leader and foremost spirit of the Rangers, a mere youth, though more distinguished for tempered skill and gallantry . . . than any man who had yet figured in the history of that frontier." [5]

Webber joined Hays's men in February. After he was received into the ranks, all stepped to a well-lighted bar. A member by the name of Fitzgerald gave the final bantering toast to the initiate as the boys adjourned for the evening: "Here's to old Kentuck! May he get the green out of his eyes, and eat his salad as soon as possible, in preparation for the close shooting and tough chewing we, the free Brotherhood of Rangers, indulge in." [6]

Those of the band who used tobacco smoked Mexican cigarettes. "And all," stated Webber, "dressed in a costume singularly composite in the Mexican and American tastes. Most of them wore the 'sombrero' . . . and the many-hued 'serape,' thrown carelessly over the characteristic suit of 'foxed' cloth, or of buckskin entire. . . . this, falling down to the waist, over the ordinary American dress, and exhibiting the gleam of pistols and knife in the belt underneath, made up a very picturesque costume."

Hays found it less difficult to teach some of his recruits indifference to weather, fatigue, and surprise than to maintain a Ranger's bearing. He sought to show that practice would improve marksmanship and to impress upon them that a fleet well-trained horse was indispensable to the following of a trail at a gallop. Sometimes he demonstrated casually with the recruit's own weapon.

At Washington-on-the-Brazos, Hays inspected the pistols of his latest recruits. He reloaded the new weapons and was standing with one of them in his hand as he talked of guns. Just then "He observed," related Webber, "a chickencock some thirty paces off in the square, which was just straightening its neck to crow. 'Boys, I'll cut that saucy fellow short,' he remarked, as he leveled and fired quickly at it. Sure enough, the half-announced clarion note of chanticleer was lost in the explosion as the bird fluttered over dead with a ball in its head."

On June 10 Hays led several citizens on a fifteen-day trip into Canyon de Uvalde in pursuit of Indians. Though the Indians hovered near the party, they would neither attack nor fight. All deserted villages found were destroyed, some stolen horses were recovered, and a few Indians were killed.[7] The citizens returned cheerful over the satisfactory results. "Very soon by consent of all he [Hays] was looked upon as the leader," wrote Mrs. M. A. Maverick in her *Memoirs*, "and his orders were obeyed and he himself loved by all."

In the late summer, Hays took the field against robbers who were harassing traders along the Nueces River, and the number of bandits in circulation was quickly reduced. Then his boys turned their attention to the Mexican border troubles.

General Antonio Canales had headed a revolt against the

Mexican government in an attempt to unite the northern states of Mexico into a separate republic. Texans were interested because the creation of a buffer state would tend to protect them from the ever-present threat of Mexico to overthrow the young Republic. Canales invited the Texans to join him, and Hays was among those who for a time aided his standard. Hays had only a small company,[8] but helped defeat the Centralists at the battle of Alcantro. When he saw that Canales was not going to take advantage of victory—was, in truth, incompetent —he returned home.

Meanwhile Texans heard that Mexico was plotting through the Comanches to incite an Indian war in Texas. People at once began to exercise greater care about their weapons. All men and women who rode horseback from Houston to San Antonio in the autumn were armed with bowie knives and pistols. Their caution was justified, for beyond the village limits eighteen San Antonians were surrounded and killed.[9]

Hays's last expedition with Colonel Karnes in 1839 was to the Pedernales. A majority of this force were from Galveston and Harris counties.[10] Near the site of Fredericksburg, Karnes's Mexican scouts became frightened, returned to camp, and refused to take the field again. Forthwith Hays selected three men and undertook the task of scouting.

Having located the Indian camp during the night, he and his men crawled slowly forward until they were close enough to the campfire to discern the figures of sleeping Indians. With his companions ready to cover his retreat if discovered, Hays crept toward the fire until he was able to count the slumbering forms; then returning to his men, he wriggled into their midst without being seen or heard.

When Hays reported to Karnes that thirty well-mounted Indians were led by one of the prominent Comanche chiefs, Isomania, Karnes promptly brought his command upon the camp; but just as the Rangers were closing in on the Indians, a horse belonging to a redskin became frightened and alarmed the sleeping band. The surprised Indians grasped their weapons, but thought more of escaping than of fighting. After the fleeing

Comanches had broken through their ring of attackers, twelve dead warriors were found.[11]

In February, 1840, Hays took a small scouting company to Laredo to investigate reports that a Mexican invasion was to be launched from there. After spying out the town, he led his men boldly through its streets. Only a few soldiers were found, and neither these nor the inhabitants were "disposed to offer resistance." The Texans drove a considerable number of horses from the city back to their encampment. But next morning Hays returned the animals, with a note to the alcalde stating that the Texans were willing to fight, but had no desire to rob. They had demonstrated their ability to retaliate with the stealing of horses, to which outrage they had often been subjected.[12]

Jack Hays was not forgotten by San Antonians while he was down on the border protecting their homes. Cornelius Van Ness wrote to President Lamar on February 15:

> Dear Sir— If you have not yet appointed a person to run the North Western line of Travis County as provided for at the late session of Congress, I beg leave to recommend to your favorable notice John C. Hays of this city. He is a gentleman of the purest character & much ability & energy. He is by profession a Surveyor, and has been employed as such in this County for the last two years, & has shown himself fully competent to any work in this line— I do not think you could select an individual who could or would accomplish the work as contemplated by the "Act" more promptly & perfectly than Mr. Hays. . . . [13]

Persistent rumors in the early part of the year that Laredo was certain to be the springboard for an invasion of San Antonio caused Hays to visit Laredo again in May. He had only thirteen men. His presence having been discovered, he watched forty-two regular cavalrymen stream from the city and move toward him. He retired slowly, selected his battleground, then advanced with one of his men for a parley. His opponents sent the alcalde forward as their spokesman. In insulting tone and condescending manner, the mayor said that, since a large force was following the regulars at hand, the Texans must surrender or be killed.

Hays, not relishing the official's tone or behavior and believing he was lying, very calmly directed his subordinate to lead-slap him from the saddle. The Mexicans charged Hays and his companion, who retreated to the supporting wings of their posted men. Then the Texans returned the charge, delivered their fire, and retreated. Since most of Hays's minutemen were inexperienced in horseback fighting, these tactics were continued by both forces for nearly an hour. In the course of the conflict Hays observed that the enemy charged, halted, dismounted rapidly and fired; then standing behind their horses until the Texans had fired, they remounted and retreated to reload and receive the Texans. He therefore ordered his platoon to reserve their loaded pistols and use only their rifles in returning the next fire. The Mexicans, according to procedure, made another charge, dismounted, and fired. Hays's men returned the fire immediately and charged, giving the Mexican cavalrymen no time for remounting. Hays killed their officer. The regulars dropped their bridle reins and fled. Galloping in front of the terrified Mexicans, Hays soon had them milling. There was no effort made to slaughter them, but Hays's boys could not resist the temptation to powder-scorch the saddle galls of the slower ones. Soon exhausted, the Mexicans raised their hands and stopped. Result: eight Mexicans lay dead and thirty-two surrendered; one Texan was wounded. Hays explained to the Mexicans that they were at liberty to leave whenever ready; he had no use for prisoners. Such generosity relieved the dispirited cavalrymen.

After other like encounters Hays's activity became so vexatious to the Mexican government that it decided to destroy him and his little band; therefore General Rafael Vasquez was dispatched with four hundred and fifty troops to liquidate the Texans. Vasquez marched to within eighty miles of San Antonio and encamped. He then dispatched a man to pose as a valley trader who wished to leave Bexar for the Rio Grande with goods, but feared being robbed. Hays began preparing an escort of forty men to accompany the merchant; whereupon a young Mexican, whom Hays had befriended, informed him that the man was a border spy. Hays requested the Mexican to go to the pretended trader and say there was nothing to fear, since the escort later would be reinforced by a hundred men from Gonzales.

The trader secretly left town to report to Vasquez. Hays with his Rangers followed him so closely, however, that they encountered Vasquez before they were prepared to meet him. In the engagement that followed, the Rangers led such a vigorous charge that Vasquez's entire force fled.

Hays dogged him almost to the Rio Grande. At intervals he could catch an occasional glimpse of Vasquez leading the retreat and watching for a flank attack from that detachment from Gonzales! When the general learned how Hays had outwitted him, he was angry and mortified. For a long time his friends made his life almost unbearable by asking if he had located the "Gonzales men."

Since this cleared the area of Mexican invaders for a while, Hays disbanded his company;[14] he participated, however, in the Battle of Plum Creek sixty miles away in August, 1840. Prior to this engagement five hundred Comanches had swept rapidly as far south as Victoria, stealing cattle, burning property, and taking captives. Thirty persons were massacred in this raid before the Indians turned back toward their villages in the mountains west of Austin.

Companies hastily assembled to intercept them. Hays[15] and others brought minutemen to throw into the fray. Major General Felix Huston of the militia took command of two hundred men and engaged the Indians twenty-seven miles southeast of Austin, at Good's Crossing on Plum Creek, in a hot battle.

One of the most venturesome chiefs rode a fine stolen horse wearing a heavily decorated bridle. A ten-foot-long red ribbon streamed from the tail of this dancing charger. The rider wore a pair of gleaming calf boots, a high-topped silk hat, and an elegant broadcloth, swallow-tailed coat, worn backwards so that the bright brass buttons gleamed along his spine. He was trouserless and carried a large opened umbrella.[16] He sang so noisily that his voice rose even above the reports of guns. The white men were so overcome with amusement at his antics that grim settlers for a short time held their fire and watched him. The fellow, an expert dodger and dextrous rider, for a while was not hit by the flying lead which eventually carried away first his umbrella and then his hat. Without these encumbrances he became more adept in using his shield and bow and arrows.

This chief and a long line of warriors charged the whites repeatedly, raining flights of arrows as they rode. The puzzled Texans could not understand why neither the chief nor his braves were being unhorsed by well-aimed shots. But Hays, who saw that the bullets glanced off the rawhide shields, ordered the pioneers to hold their fire until after the flight of arrows and then to shoot as the redskins wheeled. When the settlers poured in their lead during the next attack, the chief and several of his best braves fell. In the running fight extending over a dozen miles, nearly a hundred Indians were killed.[17] Strangely enough, no Texans were lost.

Reports of Hays's leadership and valor in the conflict reached the ears of President Lamar, who commissioned him as captain and authorized him to enlist a company of Rangers. This was his first official captaincy. He was now twenty-three.

While not employed in military duties, Hays located eighty-nine land certificates in 1840. Twenty-three of them were on the Pedernales, sixty miles from San Antonio. He missed the Council House Fight in San Antonio because he was below town on the river surveying a tract of land. [18]

IV

ENCHANTED ROCK

CAPTAIN HAYS began immediately to enlist his company of Rangers. Although the requirements appeared to be simple, comparatively few applicants could meet them. It was his caution in selecting men that enabled him to maintain "the best set of Indian fighters, taken as a whole, that Texas ever produced." [1]

A recruit had to possess good character, courage and skill in marksmanship and horsemanship, and must own a horse worth at least a hundred dollars. This last was a high standard, especially since the penalty for stealing a horse or accepting a stolen animal was death. [2] Saddles had to be the American-improved Mexican type. Each man was to carry a Mexican rawhide riata for roping and a hair rope or *cabestro* for staking his horse. [3]

A Ranger also furnished his own arms and other equipment. Weapons consisted of a rifle, one or two pistols, and a serviceable knife. Tied behind his saddle was a Mexican blanket and a small wallet which contained his ammunition, a little salt, perhaps some parched corn, and tobacco. Wild game frequently was depended upon to supplement rations. The government was supposed to furnish provisions and ammunition, but often long scouting expeditions compelled Rangers to obtain both from the routed enemy.

These Rangers wore sombreros which looked cumbersome but protected the wearers against the sun. Their long leggings of cowskin or buckskin and long boots were practical in cactus and mesquite country. The roweled spurs, which tinkled musically, could also inspire ambition in a sluggish horse. Campfire conversation frequently revealed familiarity with the works of poets, philosophers, and historians. Sam Luckey's stories always helped banish any nostalgia from which a recruit might be suffering.

Hays's campaigning was done chiefly along the southern, southwestern, and western frontier. His men moved as lightly over the prairies or through the mesquite as did the Indians or Mexicans. With a saddle for a pillow, blanket for cover, and his feet toward the fire, a Ranger camped in luxury.

When Hays's Rangers took the trail of a band of marauders, they usually followed it until they overtook the guilty and punished them. "About half of the Rangers," stated John Caperton, "were killed off every year, and their places were supplied by new men. The lives of those who went into the service were not considered good for more than a year or two." [4]

Hays always pitched camps which would enable him to observe the Indian highways to the settlements. One of his camping spots was on Rangers Creek, about three miles northwest of later Boerne. With Henry E. McCulloch as lieutenant and such men as Bigfoot Wallace, he watched in the wilds the ancient trails of the Indians.

In the fall of 1840 two hundred Comanches slipped into the settlements west of San Antonio and drove off a large number of horses and mules. A messenger raced to Hays. And although the Rangers immediately followed in pursuit, they galloped twelve miles before seeing the marauders. Hays was riding fifty yards in advance of his men when he sighted the Indians, who had stopped at a crossing on the Guadalupe River. He waited for his men to come up and then said:

"Boys, yonder are the horse thieves, and there are the stolen horses. They are ten to one against us, but we can whip them! What do you say?"

"Fight 'em!" they chorused. "You lead, and we'll be right behind you!"

"Dismount, tighten your saddle girths, and check your guns," Hays instructed.

While they were making their preparations for the fight and joking about it, the red men discovered their presence. Hays swung into his saddle, glanced at the formation of the spread A behind him, and ordered:

"Come on, boys, and shoot to kill!" And he sprinted his horse ahead.

The Rangers met a shower of arrows, aimed hastily and wildly by the long waiting line of Indians. When close, the Rangers poured on their fire. The impact of their rush carried them through the line. Indian mounts reared, sought to stampede, and painted braves struggled to re-form their semblance of line. Panic soon was imminent.

As the warriors began to tumble from their horses, their chief, wearing a gorgeous headgear and riding a decorated black horse, was everywhere. He shouted his battle cry and tried to rally his milling followers. To draw the white men's fire, he even exposed his body from behind his shield. When he fell, the Indians lost control and fled, with the pursuing Rangers dealing death and devastation on the entire band.

When Hays and his men returned to the river to round up the horses, someone recognized the fallen chief's charger as the property of a prominent San Antonio citizen. The chief's shield was taken to be deposited in the capitol.

Captain Hays was so daring and efficient in this fight that the Comanches sought to learn his name. Whereupon, he received at their hands the first of several nicknames which he was given by Indians and Mexicans—"Captain Yack." Thus he was distinguished thereafter by name as well as manner among the Indians. [5]

The Comanches established large encampments on the Nueces and on a few other western streams within incursion distance of the settlements. Hays decided to destroy these strongholds, since their location made interception of the retreating raiders difficult. He increased his force with volunteer American and Mexican citizens of Bexar and several Lipans under the command of Flacco. Then he persuaded merchants to furnish provisions on government credit.

Hays led thirty-five men westward almost to the source of the Sabinal River, where he discovered a large Indian camp. The Rangers halted near. Several hours of darkness passed while the men tested their saddles, groomed their horses, and sat on the ground or dozed as they held bridle reins, all the while wishing they could smoke. As the village slept, owls hooted and ever-present coyotes mounted nearby hills and serenaded the strangers in their midst.

Just before dawn the vigilant Rangers led their horses in a cautious advance. The first rays of the sun had not yet touched the adjacent heights when the men mounted and charged. Thundering hoofs brought naked warriors scrambling from their tepees. Some Indians were shot, a few were ridden down, and others took cover in the closest brush.

Discerning chiefs soon discovered that only a few Rangers opposed them. Routed braves were recalled and were rallied for battle. The Texans formed a square and, back to back, fought on. Rearing horses, twanging bowstrings, thrusted spears, thudding bullets, and shrill war whoops were not conducive to good pistol aim. Sheer numbers pressed in, forcing the Rangers back. When Hays noticed some brush and rocks in his path of retreat, he dismounted, placed the horses in the rear center, and encircled them with men. Ignoring their losses and confident of victory, the Comanches synchronized several charges with their war cries, which went echoing through the mountains. Rangers answered with the Texas yell.

Soon the Texans caught the rhythm of the enemy attack and retreat. When the braves faced about to retreat, the Rangers moved with them, swinging gun barrels against greased heads. After receiving hot lead at each onset and learning that their withdrawals brought knockout blows on the backs of their heads, the Comanches took cover on the nearest mountainside. From this position the entrenched Indians at last began to retreat to the headwaters of the Sabinal and thence to a mountain. Hays followed and sped their departure with searing rifle balls. Once they had scaled the mountain, the Indians scattered toward the northwest.

As Hays led his force through the wrecked encampment before heading homeward, the bodies of sixteen Indians were found: the fighting had been too desperate for the retreating warriors to recover them all. One Ranger was wounded.[6]

Soon afterward Hays followed a band of Indians all day and located them late in the afternoon camped in a cedar brake. He told his men that they might sample from their haversacks before the attack, but not to build fires because the smoke would alarm the enemy. Some Mexican volunteers who had to have their cigarettes after eating tossed a burning stub into a pile of leaves, and soon smoke was curling above the trees.

Hays was so angry that he rushed among the smokers and slashed at them with his quirt, ordering them to put out the fire. Then he led an advance toward the Indian camp, a mile distant. The signs of a hasty departure were evident.

In March of 1841 Agaton's three dozen freebooters attacked two traders who were en route southward with a long train of goods. A messenger who came to Hays reporting the ill luck of the merchants implicated Ignacio Cortez and his twenty-five brigands. The six months' enlistment period of Hays's men was now expiring. But the San Antonio citizens sent an express to Austin petitioning, on account of the activity of Agaton and Cortez, that the Rangers be kept in service to protect the trade, as well as the people. President Lamar approved the petition and directed the Secretary of War to issue an emergency order authorizing Hays to organize a company and move against the outlaws.

With a dozen men and the same number of Mexican volunteers under the command of Antonio Perez, Hays set out toward Laredo, known to be the main stronghold of the thieves. As they made camp one night, two well-mounted strangers passed. Hays knew these riders were sent by San Antonio "Tories" to apprise either the robbers or the Laredo outlaws of his approach. Ten miles north of Laredo forty men, including some regular Mexican cavalrymen, were seen streaming toward the Texans. When the force drew closer, Captain Ignacio García was recognized as the leader.

The Mexicans charged with their bugles blaring, guns firing, and their commander shouting to Hays to surrender because a large reinforcement was just behind. A few answering shots caused the Mexicans to withdraw, leaving one man dead. Dismounting his men, Hays prepared for a more determined attack. He directed his Rangers to hold their fire until within close range; then having deployed them, right and left, he led them quietly through the brush. At fifty yards from the Mexican troops the Rangers began firing while advancing. This caused the enemy to take position behind their horses before opening fire. Hot singing lead soon caused them, with the exception of García and three other men, to forget their horses and begin to run afoot. The citizen volunteers likewise ran.

In the Texan charge which followed, each Ranger selected a Mexican's horse, mounted it, and pursued the enemy. Mike Chevaille, always foremost in a fight, was leading one wing of attack when his horse stumbled and threw him in front of some of the retreating Mexicans. He arose unhurt as a half dozen of the enemy ran to intercept him. Hays spurred to his rescue, and as he passed Chevaille, he killed the leading Mexican; where-upon the others wheeled and fled. When overtaken, the Mexicans threw down their arms and begged for quarter. Twenty-five prisoners with all their equipment and twenty-eight horses were taken. Three enemy dead and three critically wounded were found on the field of battle. None of Hays's force was injured. [7] Tied to the saddles of the captured horses were tasty provisions provided by wives and sweethearts; and the hungry Rangers welcomed the unexpected treat.

Meanwhile Captain García, having spurred into Laredo, gasped out the message of disaster. Many citizens stampeded toward the interior of Mexico. The alcalde secured a white flag and rode out to meet the Texans; and begging that they spare the town, he was willing to grant any demand. Hays replied he wanted only protection for the traders. He pivoted his horse and turned toward San Antonio.

In June, 1841, Hays with twelve Rangers pursued a band of Indians who had been raiding near San Antonio. The trail led toward Uvalde Canyon, and after following the band for about seventy miles he located their main camp by buzzards he saw hovering above. He placed his men in concealment and, taking one trooper, proceeded to spy out their strength. He discovered twelve Indians leaving for a raid upon the settlements and followed until they halted to prepare venison for their expedition. He watched while his companion went back to bring up the Rangers. When his men arrived, he formed an encirclement about the marauders' camp and signaled for a charge. The Indians retreated to a thicket. As the brush was too dense to penetrate, Hays directed his Rangers to tighten the circle to prevent any escape. He with two men entered the thicket in an effort to flush the enemy into the open. Almost the first flight of arrows wounded one Ranger critically, disabled the other, and clipped Hays's finger.

To the accompaniment of war whoops Hays carried the wounded man from the thicket. On his return he brought a double-barreled shotgun. After inspecting the wound of the disabled Ranger, he stealthily approached the redskins. Only one had a rifle, but the others were armed with arrows, tomahawks, and knives. At close range, an arrow was more to be dreaded than a gun.

Realizing that they knew he was alone, Hays prepared to be flanked. He lay on his back, scattergun in hand and pistol by his side, and listened to the Indians sing to muffle the sounds of those engaged in stalking. When the stalking party was within fifteen feet, he sat up and fired at the two nearest Indians. As he dropped his shotgun and grasped his pistol, a third one fled. Hays slipped quickly from the thicket and exchanged his shotgun for a loaded rifle.

Back into the thicket, he moved toward three oak trees near a log in the center. Raising himself upon one knee, he cocked the rifle and waited. Minutes passed while the whoops and songs became louder. Then Captain Hays saw a face thrust slowly around a tree. He fired and flattened himself upon the ground as a couple of warriors from behind the other trees launched arrows. Hays reloaded, as he proposed to keep his pistol in reserve. Nine Indians were left. Whenever one exposed himself, Hays fired. At the end of three hours he had only one active opponent—the brave with a gun. And the wily Indian lay behind the log and sang his war song.

Hays remained in the underbrush, changing his position often and seeking to worry the Indian into exposing himself. Finally the captain pretended to stumble and fall. Immediately the warrior ceased singing and rose for a quick shot. Two reports rang out.[8] A bullet grazed Hays's shoulder; a rifle clattered against the log.

Taking no chances with this clever foe, Hays maneuvered until he could see behind the log. Two persons instead of one were there. He rushed them. The Indian he had shot lay desperately wounded, and at the smaller end of the log cowered a frightened squaw. When Hays brandished his gun, to his surprise the two surrendered. He had never before known a Comanche to surrender. A few minutes later his men saw their captain emerge from the thicket carrying a wounded Ranger and marching two Comanches in front of him. Indian horses were rounded up and litters were prepared for the wounded. Hays planned to return to San Antonio, get some volunteers, and resume his investigation of the large encampment.

In his report of what had happened in the thicket, Hays wrote: "The Indians had but one gun, and . . . they fought under great disadvantage but continued to struggle to the last, keeping up their warsongs until all were hushed in death. Being surrounded by horsemen, ready to cut them down if they left the thicket, and unable to use their arrows with much effect in their situation, their fate was inevitable—they saw it and met it like heroes." [9]

A few weeks later, Hays with forty men from his camp on Leon Creek, seven miles west of San Antonio, traveled up the Medina River and encamped on its bank. He planned to ride farther northward through Bandera Pass and scout the Guadalupe Valley until he reached the divide.

The Rangers were riding next morning, their advance guards out, but Hays was not requiring them to scout as far ahead as customarily. Probably because he had along several of his best men, he was less vigilant than usual. Meantime a large band of Comanches on the warpath arrived first at the pass, their sentinels espying the Rangers. The chief prepared a careful ambush within the one-hundred-yard-wide and five-hundred-yard-long pass. Its fifty to seventy-five-foot-high steep sides, were covered with bushes and boulders.

Hays and his men rode into the pass about eleven o'clock. Suddenly the war whoops of the hidden Indians resounded through the gorge. Horses tried to stampede; Rangers were knocked from their saddles. The captain had ridden into his first ambush. But his calm voice rang out: "Steady! Dismount! Tie your horses!"

Mounts were spurred to the nearest trees and halter-tied. Riders swung about with guns in hands and fanned out in a circle, their hail of shots at close range driving the charging Indians back to cover. The chief rallied his warriors and swept forward again. Hand-to-hand fights began. Ranger Sam Luckey went down shot through the body. Sergeant Kit Acklin was wounded by a bullet from the chief, but managed to drive a pistol ball into him. They clinched and fell to the ground, rolled over and over, each seeking to drive his long knife into a vital spot. Acklin made a lucky thrust and arose. He had cut the chief literally to pieces and was covered with blood.

Peter Fohr was shot through the body with an arrow, the feather being on one side and the spike on the other. Andrew Erskine, with a five-shooter in his hand, charged the Indian who had wounded him in the thigh with an arrow. The barrel of Andrew's five-shooter dropped off without his knowledge, and, in trying to shoot, Erskine almost touched the warrior. The Indian's bowstick was shot in two, but as he was unable to shoot at Andrew, he pulled an arrow and tried to stab him. At this instant, Creed Taylor shot and killed the Indian.

After an hour of this kind of fighting the Indians retreated. It was a costly victory: several troopers' horses had been killed or disabled, five Rangers were wounded seriously, and five more lay dead. The Rangers carried their dead and wounded through the south entrance to the pass and from there to San Antonio, while the Indians took theirs to the north end, where they had hidden their horses. [10]

On July 19 Hays, with a force consisting of twenty-five

Rangers, ten or fifteen men from Gonzales, and a dozen Lipans and Tonkawas, marched to the Rio Frio, where several weeks before he had overcome the twelve Comanches. Here he found signs that the Indians in the main camp had learned the fate of their detached party, murdered some prisoners, and fled.

Hays and Flacco—the latter commissioned by Sam Houston with the rank and pay of a captain—led out through the rugged country at the head of the Frio's western branch. Since the Comanches had burned the grass and shrubs behind them, thereby driving out all wild game, horses and men suffered greatly. To make their situation more acute, the extent and freshness of the trail indicated the vicinity of a large encampment. When within a few miles of the camp, the friendly Indian scouts shifted to a small trail. Hays soon discovered this when he flushed a party of Comanche hunters.

Taking twenty-five men whose horses appeared the strongest, he followed the fleeing hunters, now carrying to the main camp word of his approach. Although he rode hard in an effort to reach the Indian encampment about eight miles away, before it was deserted, he arrived just as the women and children were on the point of departure. About a hundred warriors came out to engage in a running fight. The Indians would retreat, halt and form a line, prepare guns and bows, and fire when the Texans were within range. After these maneuvers were repeated a few times, the Rangers' tired horses could not sprint close enough to give their riders a fair target.

Perceiving that some of his men had better mounts than others, Hays led these better-mounted men forward in an advance formation, hoping to come within range of the Comanches. Flacco's horse, for instance, seemed fresh, while one of the volunteers was riding an enduring animal. Hays galloped alongside and, learning that the townsman feared to let the horse have its head, suggested a temporary trade. Spurring his borrowed steed close to the enemy, the captain discharged a pistol, then tried to rejoin his men. But the horse had the bit in its teeth and bolted straight toward the middle of the line of retreating Indians. Flacco forged forward to overtake his commander. The Comanches looking over their shoulders saw two thundering horsemen coming. As Hays's mad animal carried him through the center of the line, he shot once to either side, and did not miss. This drove the horse to run faster, especially when Flacco pounded through the line just after. The two raced straight forward—the Comanches yelled and began to converge on them.

Hays, exerting his strength on one rein and spurring the horse in a large circle past the nearest flank of the Comanches, headed back to the Rangers. One well-mounted warrior attempted to block the captain's horse, but Hays shot him. Flacco still rode a few yards behind. Neither horse was totally spent when it came to the slow-galloping men. Back with the troops Flacco remarked that he would never be left behind in any charge, but Captain Jack was "bravo too much." [11]

The horses of the Rangers were done; several riders were wounded. There was no chance of overtaking the Comanches mounted on fresh ponies. Six miles of running and fighting over the rough country was sufficient for one day. Hays called a halt.

Losses of the Comanches were placed at ten, with others seriously wounded, as judged by the bloody saddles found upon the trail. The Indians were sucessful in removing their dead and wounded. In the deserted camp, Hays found signs indicating there were about two hundred Indians. They had approximately six hundred horses. The body of a Mexican prisoner, shot and lanced to death, was found hanging by his heels. [12]

Hays was next called upon to suppress horse thieves. These daring outlaws would dig through the walls of houses or spend most of a night carefully removing one side of a locked stable to get a fine Kentucky-bred horse. The Captain captured several of these felons and ordered the most notorious to be executed. Antonio Corao, for instance, who had a manifold criminal record, was taken by a detail of five men to the head of San Antonio River and was shot. [13]

In August while he was chasing Indians, the citizens of Bexar elected Hays county surveyor. Although he had not been active in politics, he was not afraid to express his opinion as to candidates or issues. Late in the same month in Austin, he foretold: "General Houston will receive four-fifths of the Bexar votes for president: the Mexicans will go for him en masse." [14]

Scouting duties permitted Hays to locate only five land certificates during the remainder of the year. His deputies were constantly engaged in surveying, and he wished that he could devote more time to it.

It was while he was combining surveying and scouting on a tributary of the Pedernales that Hays first inspected Enchanted Rock. Around the camp on the bank of nearby Crabapple Creek, the guards watched the horses and the skyline and listened. In camp all were asleep except Hays and Lieutenant Henry McCulloch, who sat watching Hays cleaning his guns. As Hays placed one of his five-shooters—new and rare weapons—in its belt scabbard, McCulloch saw him pat it gently with his hand and heard him say in a low, confiding tone: "I may not need you; but if I do, I will need you mighty bad."

Hays remarked next morning that he had heard much of Enchanted Rock. It was quite a climb to the top, but he proposed to scale it, since he would have a good view of the surrounding country. None of his companions seemed disposed to join him. As a precaution, he armed himself with his rifle, two Colts and his knife.

Hays soon arrived at the prominent landmark near the head of Pedernales River. Its north side precipitous and other sides steep, the rugged rock had many deeply worn washes extending from the top to the base. The summit appeared to be about twenty by twenty feet. The Indians believed the rock to be enchanted. Hays had climbed the sloping side, looked at its crater, studied distant landmarks, and then was descending the hillside toward camp when he saw a score of Indians advancing to intercept him. Back up the rock he scrambled. When he reached the crater, he slid down into its shallow pit and hurried to the north side, where he secreted himself between two projecting ledges under an overhanging rock. In assembling his weapons he discovered he had lost his powder horn. He could fire only eleven shots.

Hardly was he settled in his position when he saw numerous Indian heads peering above the rim of the crater. From their whoops and their calls to him, it was obvious that he had been recognized. His attackers tried ruses which would cause Hays to expose any vital part of his body as a target. They shouted "Devil Yack" and "silent white devil" and many worse names in Spanish, which they knew he understood, alternately bobbing their heads above the parapet. When the Indians made a concerted movement, Hays raised his rifle, but the red men ducked. Soon the braves sought to distract his attention by climbing upon the rock that arched above him. He accepted chances at these hastily exposed targets, and bodies thudded sickeningly near him as he emptied one revolver.

Silence reigned for a moment; then Hays prepared for a mass attack. One of the bolder warriors risked his head for a try at fame with a quick arrow shot. Hays's rifle flashed; the brave lay a corpse. At this there came a chorus of war whoops, and Hays knew they were coming into the crater after him. Rage at thoughts of past encounters and the one-man, two-hour delay of their attack had won over caution.

Most of the Indians leaped to the top of the crater and slid down into it. Hays killed one of them. He knocked over two more as they rose to their feet. As they rushed him, he dropped one and then another who fell head foremost against his shins. At the moment he was about to spring forward with his bowie knife to do what damage he could against the others, a chorus of Texas yells routed his attackers. A hundred Comanches had surrounded the base of the rock preparatory to a final assault. His men had heard his guns. [15]

As 1841 faded from the calendar, the *Telegraph* and *Texas Register* recorded:

The spy company under Captain Hays has been very efficient and has almost completely broken up the old haunts of the Comanche in the vicinity of Bexar. So great has been the protection and security resulting from the active enterprise of this excellent officer that the settlements are extending on every side around the city and the country is assuming the appearance of peace and prosperity that characterized it previous to the Revolution.

V

THE LESS SERIOUS

CAPTAIN HAYS's success was attracting more cultivated people to the town being built under the Rangers' protection. Among the Anglo-American families were those of W. I. Riddle and William B. Jacques, leading merchants; J. Moore; and the Samuel Mavericks who were deemed indispensable.[1] Often upon the Rangers' return from a long scout, these foremost citizens staged a dance in honor of Hays and his troop. Whenever distinguished guests visited the city, they were entertained with at least one ball, at which the Ranger officers were prominent figures.

Mrs. Yturri was hostess at a grand ball in honor of President Lamar and his large retinue upon the occasion of their visit to San Antonio in June, 1841. Several young bachelors assisted her husband in decorating with flowers, evergreens, and flags. The ballroom presented a "very fine appearance." But Hays and two of his friends, Mike Chevaille and John Howard, wondered what they could do about formal dress, for there was only one coat among all the Rangers. With or without coats they decided to attend.

Hays and his companions delayed their appearance until it was almost time to open the ball. Howard and Chevaille suggested that the Captain enter in full dress, greet the distinguished guests, saunter out later, and doff the coat so that each might take his turn. Hays countered with the proposition that whoever entered first should participate in the first dance. To his surprise they agreed.

Mayor and Mrs. Juan Seguin opened the ball. Soon Mesdames Maverick, Yturri, and Riddle noticed that the handsome Ranger captain was dancing only every third number. Then they saw him enter an adjoining room and discard his coat. Apprised that the limits of their wardrobe were known, the three Rangers relaxed and enjoyed the function thoroughly. The "by-play and good humor" of the two nontenants of the coat were very amusing to the ladies who were aware of the situation. [2]

Hays had little use for full dress at this time; in any case his salary would not have permitted such extravagance. Only a little over five hundred and eighty dollars a year was granted for forage for his horse and clothing and sustenance for himself. He was permitted one servant with a monthly pay of eight dollars and an annual subsistence allowance of one hundred and eight dollars. Necessity often required the purchase of such articles as ammunition and arms, and these expenses he had to bear himself.

Most of Hays's Rangers were a jolly set, appreciative of practical jokes. This was fortunate, since Hays believed that much town life was not best for those who were employed to protect the settlements. Occasionally in filling vacancies, he enlisted a man who was a good fighter, though eccentric, or one not the equal in social standards of his associates.

One of such recruits was "Alligator" Davis. Soon after Davis joined Hays's company, the Rangers were encamped on the Medina River. Floating about on the surface of a large water hole near their camp was an alligator more than six feet long. The Rangers' efforts to frighten the reptile into submerging were unsuccessful and its staring eyes irritated Davis, who growled: "I'll take the critter out and muster him as a raw recruit!"

Davis plunged into the river and clasped the alligator, trying to wrestle it to the shore. The rolling and threshing struggle of man and monster beat the water into a muddy foam. The alligator swiped Davis with its tail and knocked him backwards and under, but he came up instantly, spitting muddy water and plunging forward to gain a new hold. At last astride the beast, legs locked tight around its body, he caught a jaw with either hand. While the recruiter's companions roared with amusement and applauded his efforts, Davis forced the reptile into shallow water and toward the bank. On reaching the edge, he stumbled out to dry land and fell purposely with all his weight upon the brute which he held clinched in his arms. Though the river recruit slipped back into the water at the first opportunity, Davis had proved his mettle and had earned his accolade—the nickname "Alligator."

Hays once decided to take Alligator with him on a scout. Thirty miles from the settlements they came upon two cub bears. "Gator" conceived the idea that one of them would make a nice present for Mrs. Jacques. When they chased the bears up a tree, Davis said that if the captain would climb the tree and shake a cub down, he would catch it and carry it on his horse. Hays knew something about bears and so agreed readily.

He climbed the tree, shook a limb vigorously, and down came the cubs. Davis seized the nearer one and gave it a "bear hug" in his efforts to get its paws together. The cub clawed with all feet at once and bit vigorously at the man's face while Hays sat on a limb of the tree so convulsed with laughter that he could coach Davis only part of the time; in hearty merriment he would urge: "Hold him, "Gator" Davis! Bind his front legs first! Be calm—be kind to animals! Don't let go!" But Davis was too busy to heed the Captain's tender words of advice.

At last Hays's humor satisfied, he descended the tree and tapped the cub on the head with his pistol. While the bear was temporarily disabled, Davis tied its legs and the two fastened it back of Davis's saddle. The horse, Bally, did not fancy the presence of the bear on his back, and began to snort and prance. Whereupon Alligator Davis shouted, "Bally, you durned old fool, didn't you ever see a bear?"

On their return trip to Bexar, big, white-eyed Bally was skittish. He looked back frequently and snorted, but Alligator, quite serene and happy in anticipation of the reception of the unusual pet, ignored his horse's peevishness. On they jogged pleasantly until the little cub sampled a mouthful of Bally's rump. Now Bally wasn't carrying cubs that morning and feeding them too, so he snorted and bucked his objections. And the devilish Hays sat on his horse and encouraged: "Stay with him! Keep your feet in the stirrups! Grab the horn, Gator. Ride him, fellow! Ride him!"

At length Davis sailed twenty feet over his horse's head, as away the big brute went, bawling and bucking, with the cub bouncing and biting him. Unable to get rid of the bear, Bally quit pitching and bolted for a herd of startled wild mustangs standing on a distant hill. Although Hays spurred in pursuit he soon realized that there was nothing to do except shoot the horse if he overtook him. On toward the mustangs Bally galloped. Hays returned to comfort Davis. Scratched by the bear, bruised from being bucked off, and disconsolate at the loss of old Bally, Davis mounted behind Hays. As they rode toward San Antonio, Davis wondered: "How long you reckon that cub'll keep eatin' on him?" They never saw Bally again. [3]

In the early years of the Republic, fighting men to oppose the Comanches were much in demand. Among them were men who not only fought Indians as a business but also followed the fighting as a pastime. Such a man was old Billy Anderson, frontiersman and backwoodsman. On solitary warpaths he had been in the habit of scalping his Indians. When off duty if the occasion appealed to him as proper, he was excessively intemperate. Filled with whisky or mescal, he would entertain anybody who donated drinks of liquor with his special "snake performance."

He kept for this purpose a wiry rattler in a cage made of branches. Billy would reach into the cage, draw out the writhing, rattling snake, hold it just back of the jaws until ready, and then present the back of his left hand or the muscular portion of his left arm for the snake to strike. After the performance Billy would administer "the rattlesnake's master"—an antidote consisting of a handful of small roots. He never allowed the snake to strike him when he was sober, for, he said: " 'the rattlesnake's master' is not always sure without the whiskey." [4]

"Still," Hays observed, "Billy could participate in an Indian fight in a manner that was not to be despised." In later years he served in Ben McCulloch's company, which Hays once took on a hurried pursuit of a band of Comanches who were driving a herd of stolen horses. Hays sprang his attack at full gallop. Whooping and shouting, springing his horse from side to side, Hays leaned over its neck in order to expose less of his body. Pistol in hand, his gun arm moved in an arc and up and down, and always he was ready to fire when the long blue barrel came upon its target. This set the Indian to thrusting his shield in front of him, dodging to either side, or throwing himself alongside his mount, while he attempted to shoot arrows from under the animal's neck.

Billy was everywhere, dashing up to Indians, pointing his gun barrel toward them, yelling, but not firing. After the Indians were routed, Hays asked:

"Billy, what in the devil were you doing? Why were you capering around, aiming, screaming, and never killing your man?"

"Just bluffin', Captain. Just bluffin'," answered Billy.

"Bluffing?"

"Yes, sir. My ammunition was gone, so I just charged from one to another of the red devils, and every time they'd see my five-shooter pointed at 'em, didn't they dodge under their horses' bellies and throw up their shields? And maybe I wasn't out of that Injun's way in no time!"

When the Rangers went into San Antonio on Saturday night to enjoy a little amusement, they found there was always a special fandango which they often attended in a body. Hays occasionally accompanied them and "was seen whirling around with a fair señorita."

Admirably supple and graceful, the señoritas were towered over by the tall Anglo-Saxons whose dancing, in most instances, was clumsy by comparison. The Rangers wore wide-brimmed hats and most of the time short jackets. They had varicolored scarfs in lieu of belts. Their trousers were tucked into the tops of their high boots. Many sought to compensate by enthusiasm for their lack of grace in the dancing, with the result that the music of poor, blind Pancho, the one-man orchestra, could rarely be heard.

Rangers Ben McCulloch, Sam Walker, John McMullin and many others were remarkable men of strong character. But Simon Bateman sometimes caused the uninformed to wonder if the organization did not contain "peculiars." He was a Mississippi plantation owner who desired to live where he could own much grazing land and livestock. Once when several of his Negroes had driven some cattle into the corral for branding, a bull charged those who were on foot. Bateman laughed heartily as he watched the fierce, shaggy beast chase the men from the enclosure several times and then boasted he would prove to the herders that he was not afraid of the animal. Into the corral he went and got down on his hands and knees. The bull stopped bellowing, looked at him with a speculative eye, and became madly enraged. When the bull bellowed, Bateman bellowed; when the animal pawed and threw dirt into the air, Bateman pawed and tossed dirt; when the bull shook his head, Simon Bateman shook his likewise. If the bull feinted, Simon did the same. By moving quickly to one side Simon avoided several fierce attacks, but suddenly the bull charged and tossed Bateman over the rail fence. "Bull" Bateman, as he was called thereafter, was unable to leave his bed for months.[5]

A huge, fat Englishman named Self was encamped near San Antonio. He bragged continuously about how he would conduct himself in a fight with the Indians. Even the patient Hays became wearied from listening to the braggart, who could, to give him his due, play the violin. In a benevolent mood one day Hays invited him to bring his violin and spend several days with the Rangers. The boys enjoyed his fiddling, but detested his bragging. To forestall the worst at the hands of his men, Hays contrived a test of the Englishman's courage. Plans for the joke called for Hays and the braggart to go riding. When mock Indians, befeathered and daubed with mud, gave their war whoops and came pounding along the trail in a simulated attack, Hays became greatly alarmed. He called out to his companion, "Hear those whoops! They're almost upon us! Take your pistol and shoot at the devils!"

"Lord, Lord!" Self screeched as he turned his horse and plied his quirt. The captain rode close behind him, turning in the saddle occasionally to shoot. The fat man's big violin was in a case strapped to his back. As he rode jockey fashion to obtain more speed, the bounding animal at every leap caused the fiddle to slap the rider's obese rump. On toward protecting timber the two men raced, the whooping "braves" directly behind them. Just as the Englishman reached the woods, an "Indian" overtook and unhorsed him with a wooden lance. He climbed to his feet, started on a wobbling run, and, stumbling into a prickly pear patch, tripped and fell. Hays rode on to camp. After a long wait, as the Englishman had not appeared, the Captain became uneasy and sent a man to look for the terrific Indian fighter. The Ranger found him hiding in a thicket, hugging the ground; he would neither move nor speak when addressed—the poor fellow thought the Indians were after him again.

Hays and two other Rangers brought the bedraggled, scratched Englishman into camp and made him as comfortable as possible. When he regained the power of speech, he told how he deceived the Indians by camouflaging himself as a stump in the thicket. Shortly afterwards the man's hair began to turn white. Hays felt a twinge of remorse about the incident and at times gave him unusual consideration and support. When he saw, for instance, that the Englishman was loitering in town and indulging in prolonged drinking sprees, he always took charge. [6]

During 1840 and 1841 the Comanches suffered so many defeats and heavy losses in fighting against Hays that northern bands returned to the headwaters of the Brazos and left their southern brothers to face Captain Jack.

Whenever Hays wished to obtain information from a remote point without attracting too much attention, he traveled alone on foot. Sometimes Indians saw and recognized him. Yet they so feared "Captain Yack" that they refused to attack him. Flacco understood his captain's fearlessness and once explained it to an enemy chief.

Several Comanche chiefs were assembled on San Antonio's main plaza when Hays rode by. One, who recognized the horseman, inquired of Flacco, who was lounging near, why the Captain went alone into Comanche hunting grounds when he knew there would be no assistance if he were attacked. Flacco, gracious to the visitors in his captain's town, replied: "Me and Blue Wing," pointing to his companion, "no afraid to go to hell togedder. Captain Yack, great brave, no 'fraid to go to hell by hisself."

In February, 1842, Hays took six men to assist him in locating an ex-soldier's tract of land north of Bexar. While engaged in running a line, they were surrounded by a large band of Indians.

The red men did not attack in their usual way, but made a deliberate onset from shelter sometimes so distant that their arrows were not deadly. With his eye on his compass and a revolver in his hand, Hays continued to take his readings. The chief, nettled by the surveyor's coolness, permitted a few of the braves to creep closer. But Hays furtively observed them and when they came too near, whipped casual shots in their immediate vicinity. Although this increased their anger, it nevertheless restrained them. If several warriors moved up to attack, Hays woud lean forward for a sight through his transit and then snap his gun up to throw a bullet at the savages. If this enraged them and they revealed preparations for a rush, some of the surveyor's assistants brought their rifles into play and checked it. Meanwhile the captain carried on, and "Work was not ceased until the line was finished." [7]

Increasing duties of a more critical nature forced Hays to discontinue as district surveyor. The government directed that he attach Captain Don V. Friar's Gonzales company to his command and promised the necessary supplies and equipment to keep the Rangers in the field. [8]

In March a messenger rode into the Ranger camp on the Medina with the news that Indians had stolen some horses in the Calaveras Creek settlement and had killed several Mexicans. With a force of twenty-seven volunteers from Bexar and fifteen of his own men Hays started in pursuit. En route Flacco and a few of his warriors joined the command.

The trail led south from Calaveras Creek and then west through the sandy, brushy country.[9] Their path was easily followed in the loose soil. After the fugitives had crossed the Nueces River, the trail was so fresh that the Captain believed the Indians were not far in advance of him. Hays decided to lay a trap. He exchanged mounts with a Mexican of his group and directed him to ride until he had located the Indians, then to return as fast as possible. The Captain hoped the Mexican would be seen and pursued, and the Indians would thus be drawn into a fight. It was a Mexican region. If a lone white man were used, the device might be suspected.

Meanwhile Hays told his inexperienced volunteers that although they were following a large band of Indians and a fight was imminent, he was confident of victory. To allay the nervousness of some, he remarked quietly that at least a few of those present knew he had never been defeated by Indians. Then Flacco called the attention of all to the fact that he and his men could prepare instantly for the fight. They began tying red bandannas around their heads for the purpose of distinguishing themselves from other Indians.

About an hour later, everyone heard ahead of them the whoops of Indians and the sounds of horses sprinting. Hays recognized his Mexican and said, "Let's move up, boys. They are after our man." The spy's pursuers, seeing the Rangers, wheeled their horses and raced back to warn their companions. The Mexican reported that the Indians who had chased him constituted a sort of rear guard for the main group a mile distant. The pickets had tried to capture him, but Hays knew the speed of the horse. He had used the same animal before in a similar ruse. The Captain and the scout now re-exchanged horses and Hays led a rapid advance even before the Mexican had finished his report.

The Indians who had pursued the trooper were soon shouting to attract the attention of the main body. About a hundred warriors formed an irregular line along the slope of the chaparral-dotted ridge. The hideous Comanche war whoop was the signal for their release of arrows.

Hays shouted, "Come on, boys!" The Rangers answered with their Texas yell and spurred their horses to follow Hays and Flacco, the latter seeking to ride alongside his captain. Rifles and pistols crackled. Man engaged man, with the Comanches using lances, tomahawks, and knives and the Texans clubbing with guns and slashing with bowies. As they paired and grappled, sometimes both combatants tumbled to the ground where a last, desperate struggle occurred.

Hays and Flacco more than once saved each other's lives. The darting, dodging, revolver-shooting captain and the shrill war-whooping Lipan became the special target of the Comanches; both, however, escaped injury. Soon the Indians, having had enough of the bloody contest, retreated. A number of Rangers were wounded. The volunteers had acquitted themselves well, but the heroic fighting was done by the Rangers. [10]

A few weeks later as the enlistment period of the company expired, Hays disbanded the organization. This meant that from a military standpoint the Republic was defenseless.

Even after his Rangers had been temporarily disbanded because of the change of administrations and inefficiency occasioned by the different policies, Hays watched Mexico's military preparations through his spies. He learned that a number of San Antonio's Mexicans led by Antonio Perez had left stealthily in February, supposedly to unite with invaders. Santa Anna was again in power in Mexico when President Lamar sent out the Santa Fe expedition, which the Mexicans captured. Santa Anna resented the invasion and now sought revenge.

San Antonio was the outpost nearest Mexico. Nine-tenths of its approximately two thousand inhabitants were Mexicans.[11] Believing that danger was imminent, the Americans organized a company for its protection. Hays was unanimously elected their captain. [12]

Hays sent Mike Chevaille and James Dunn on a scout toward the Rio Grande to ascertain the strength of the invading force. [13] Meanwhile he directed his faithful Mexican servant, Antonio Coy, toward the Rio Frio on the same assignment.[14] Then he dispatched into the field Ben McCulloch and A. S. Miller, who had come from Gonzales at his request, and gave them similar instructions.

On March 4, at ten o'clock in the evening, Hays sent a courier eastward carrying his message:

Two of our spies were shot at and run in from the Medina; again this evening, near the Leona, four spies were hailed and chased but they got in safe. Our two spies McCulloch and Miller are either cut off or are behind the enemy. Nothing further from Chevaille or Dunn, who have been out ten days. We cannot give an account of their [invaders] number. We are all in the dark, and have our spies out. Tell the Colorado men to hurry as fast as possible.

PRICE ON HIS HEAD

ON MARCH 5, 1842, Hays instructed his adjutant to send the following message to the committee of vigilance at Gonzales:

The spies have just come in and report the enemy within six miles of town. . . . Communicate with the committee on the Colorado. Tell them to raise all the forces they can, and we will endeavor to sustain ourselves until they can reinforce us.

During the same evening a roll call revealed that Hays's entire force totaled one hundred and seven. He sent out scouts who returned at daylight and reported that fourteen hundred Mexicans were encamped near San Antonio.[1]

Hays placed "Keno" Ellison in charge of this detail of scouts and directed them to ride around the camp of the Mexican force. As the detail returned to town, they saw approaching a rider carrying a white flag. Two of the scouts met and blindfolded the bearer and escorted him to Hays.

The herald was Colonel J. M. Carrasco. He said that he was authorized to extend terms of surrender from General Rafael Vasquez, who had artillery, expected two thousand reinforcements, and desired peaceful possession of the city. Hays promised an answer at two o'clock in the afternoon and sent an escort to return with him.

A council of war was held with several leading citizens. They decided to parade the volunteers and have them vote whether to retreat or to fight. Their choice brought abandonment of the city.

After sending two men to apprise Vasquez of the decision, Hays formed the volunteers and their oxen-drawn piece of artillery into a column and led them in good order toward Seguin.[2] Meanwhile five hundred regulars, two hundred and fifty rancheros, and thirty Caddo Indians of Vasquez's force marched into San Antonio. They raised their flag and proposed the establishment of a Mexican form of government.

On the night of March 6, the Texans camped on the bank of the Cibolo, and Hays sent a courier to Austin with dispatches to the government. The next night's camp was opposite Seguin on the Guadalupe River. All the inhabitants of the valley had fled eastward. Here McCulloch and Miller rejoined Hays, telling him that Vasquez had remained in San Antonio only two days, then had left it in peace and retreated toward the Rio Grande.

At San Antonio again, Hays sent out spies who returned and reported that Vasquez had recrossed the Rio Grande. The Ranger captain and his citizen company assumed the task of guarding the town until the refugee inhabitants returned. There was very little business being transacted, and an air of desolation prevailed.[3] Hays understood that the demonstration staged by Vasquez was only a threat.

With the exception of Hays and his few spies at San Antonio, the frontier was left entirely unprotected.[4] The Secretary of War now directed Hays to recruit one hundred and fifty well-mounted and equipped men as spies and Rangers between San Antonio and the Rio Grande. Few could be found immediately who were "able to mount and equip themselves and willing to enter a service which promised little else than fatigue or danger as a soldier." Yet the government "could neither furnish the means to equip and mount a force nor sustain them for any length of time in the field." [5] Hays freely expended his surveying fees to provide equipment which enabled him to continue to protect the settlers from the raiders.

One recruit, who enlisted in the late summer while Hays was operating in the vicinity of San Antonio, was John Forester, of Houston. Forester later described his new associates in the field thus:

The men, in physical make-up, were as fine a body as I ever saw, but their uniforms were altogether new. . . . Most of them were dressed in skins, some wearing parts of buffalo robes, deer hides, and bear skins, and some entirely naked to the waist, but having leggings and the necessary breech clouts. All were well armed and well mounted. . . . they subsisted principally upon buffalo meat and venison, rarely ever using bread, and still more rarely ever getting coffee.

As a result of the shortcomings of the government, immigration to San Antonio was checked. Only a dozen American families returned after the Vasquez raid. Mexican Tories awaited confidently a second invasion in retaliation for the Santa Fe expedition. Hays's spies reported that trouble was coming; hence he went to the Guadalupe country[6] seeking recruits, for he had fewer than one hundred men. When he had returned to San Antonio, he sent scouts to watch the trails and to patrol the Nueces River. Tories subtly secured all the ammunition in the town. Anticipating trouble, Hays sent Nathaniel Mallon and Bigfoot Wallace to Austin for a supply of lead and powder. Meanwhile Hays decided to rid the community of the spies and criminals like Christopher Rubio, who had been in San Antonio and now was at the Mission of San Juan.

When Hays rode down to the mission and asked that the gates be swung open promptly, Rubio was seen crouching within. He sprinted away from the gate; Hays spurred along just behind him. The Mexican came to an irrigation ditch, tried to cross it, and fell in. Hays dismounted, took a long limb, and ducked the informer a few times. Then he remounted, roped the sputtering swimmer, and dragged him out. The *Ranchero,* his criminal companion, was arrested also, and both were bound and taken to San Antonio, where the people demanded that the two outlaws be executed immediately. Hays said he intended to turn them over to the citizens of Seguin, where they had perpetrated numerous crimes. Some still insisted on their having custody of the prisoners, but as Hays was firm, the disturbance was quieted.

Hays permitted the impression to get around that he intended to send a large guard in charge of the brigands. Accordingly, late in the afternoon he placed the felons in the center of his escort and led the mounted column from town. After dark, when out on the Seguin road several miles, Rangers Lee and Askew were given charge of the culprits, and the convoy rode on. The two Rangers and their prisoners set out across the prairie, while the escort continued along the road for a few miles farther and then returned to the city.

Mexican bandits had become so troublesome that Hays decided to make a scout in retaliation. Just as the Rangers were starting, Flacco volunteered his services for the trip. Hays was glad to have him along, as he considered the Indian superior to either a Mexican or an American ᴜᴊ a scout. After a few days the Captain announced a stop for a midday meal and the grazing of the horses, though it was not yet noon. John McMullin, who was the latest recruit, watched Flacco leaning against a tree. With arms folded the chief looked slowly around him, an almost imperceptible smile hovering on his lips. McMullin invited him to have something to eat with his mess.

"No," answered the chief as he drew himself erect. "No, warriors never eat much on warpath. Too much eat—too much eat," and he shook his head. "Captain Hays great chief, but American eat too much on warpath," the Lipan concluded.

The party forded a river and rode slowly along the valley beyond with advance guards on either flank and one in the front. Flacco vanished on an unassigned bit of scouting. When they approached a cedar-covered peak lying to their left, Hays ascended it to have a look while the men rode on. On the summit of an opposite ridge he discerned a horseman wearing a Mexican sombrero. The silent figure gazed intently at the Rangers moving up the valley. Hays judged that the man was a sentinel, probably one of several occupying posts leading toward Bexar and watching for Rangers. So he descended the knoll on its opposite side, intercepted his men, and explained the plan of action.

Hays and two men would flank the lookout. When sufficiently near, they would shout as a signal to their associates, charge the picket, and, having enclosed him on both sides, frighten him into leading them to his camp. Soon the three flankers could see the Mexican riding parallel to and slightly behind the Rangers he was watching. Whereupon Hays shouted, and the fellow looked over his shoulder to find three gringos charging him. As he lashed his horse into a run straight along the ridge, the Rangers pretended to quirt and spur desperately. Hays's object was to allow the picket to think he could escape by racing for his camp. The Captain's maneuver succeeded, as the fugitive suddenly jumped his horse down the ridge and struck across the plain, quartering a little toward the three pursuers.

"Go to the top of the ridge and signal the boys, Fitz!" Hays sang out. "He's making for his camp!"

Now Hays, Fitz, and Al, the third Ranger, gave their mounts the reins. They must not permit him to race into camp in time to give the alarm. Behind the three came Flacco, overtaking them with a tremendous burst of speed. Hays faced about and held up both hands with palms out in a command for silence as their horses skimmed along the thick grass. Beyond their quarry, woods began to be distinct. Spurs, quirts, ends of long bridle reins were applied by every rider in an effort to get a final spurt of speed.

Buzzards, perched upon a tree just outside the edge of the brush, marked the location sought. Hays saw the scavengers take flight and, throwing his rifle to his shoulder, knocked the picket from his laboring pony. The captain shoved his rifle back into its scabbard, jerked off his hat and placed it under his seat, and pulled a revolver just as the four Rangers swept over the body. Through the outer brush and trees they crashed into an open space surrounded by dense thickets. Here nearly three score men, with surprise and fear registered on their faces, were springing from the ground or running on hands and feet, rolling, plunging, and crawling to escape the charging hoofs. Only a few turned to toss a frenzied shot now and then at the dismounting horsemen.

The popping of pistols, the darting figures of Hays and his men, the clubbing of guns, thrusting of knives, clash of bodies in combat, screams for mercy, the scattering through the brush on foot after individual opponents—all constituted a frightful scene. Several scalps swung from Flacco's waistbelt. The men, as a whole, were sweaty, dusty, and bloody. The victory was definite; still Hays was disappointed. If any known brigand leader had been in charge of the band, he had escaped. As the Rangers rode back into the valley, they met a messenger who pressed Hays to return to San Antonio immediately.

On September 10 two of Hays's Mexican spies told him that a large Mexican force would reach San Antonio during the night or early next morning. He forthwith called a meeting of the people and asked for information from anyone present. Two Mexican citizens volunteered that Mexican people had been notified to evacuate the town by noon.

Believing that they were to be confronted only by plunderers, the Americans voted to defend the city. Numerous Mexicans decided to remain and assist them. These Mexicans under Salvador Flores and the Americans led by C. Johnson asked Hays to take command.[7] A check revealed that eighty-odd Americans and about one hundred Mexicans were armed and willing to resist the robbers. They agreed that if the approaching group were regular troops, resistance would not be feasible.

A letter which Hays wrote to the Secretary of War on September 12 from Seguin affords a succinct but clear explanation of his activities during the 10 and 11th.

. . . I immediately made the best arrangements of the citizens, and started with five other persons to spy out their approach and number, but was not able to find them on any public road, though during the night I discovered that they came down through the mountains to the city. On the morning, or rather some time before day, I attempted to enter the town but found it surrounded and impossible. What followed is communicated by the prisoners that surrendered. The Mexican army is . . . commanded by General [Adrian] Woll. . . .I stayed around town all day of the 11th, and have left spies behind. If I can, I will try and watch their approach to this river.[8]

While Hays was watching San Antonio, he sent out a message to the citizens of Texas. The latter half read:

. . . They [Mexicans] attacked the place on the 11th, the citizens made a slight resistance, until finding the army to be too strong for them, surrendered, fifty-three in number. I examined the camp the night they entered town and found it to contain 1300 men, mostly regulars, and two pieces of artillery. . . . I shall continue to watch their movements and would like a few well-mounted men to join me as quickly as possible for the purpose of spying.[9]

Americans in San Antonio had been skeptical;[10] false alarms had come to them often. That attitude together with Hays's inadequate force had enabled Woll to descend on San Antonio.[11] Hays captured a Mexican spy who said that reinforcements were coming to aid Woll, but Hays did not believe they were near. He thought new men should assemble at Seguin to repel any scouting parties which might be sent out.

Hays encamped on the Cibolo, but when reinforcements began to come in, he took a couple of men and returned to the outskirts of San Antonio. In response to his request Matthew Caldwell, in command by casual agreement of the assembling settlers, sent ten volunteers. Hays was by that time camped on the Salado. The settlers elected Caldwell commander of the volunteers. Hays, though on the Salado, was elected unanimously to command all scouts.[12]

When the detail from Caldwell's army approached Hays's vicinity, they signaled their presence by keen whistles, which Hays answered promptly. He divided the dozen men into three groups and instructed one to guard the camp, another to scout east of the town, and the third with himself as leader was to ride entirely around San Antonio to ascertain whether reinforcements were coming. As Hays approached the rear of the city, the Mexicans discovered him and sent out a large force of cavalry which drove him back. He saw no reinforcements.

By the 14th Hays's letter, a note from the prisoners under Woll, and a translation of that general's proclamation had reached La Grange. Woll's proclamation to his soldiers stated: "The second campaign against Texas has been opened."

Hays meanwhile made another effort to scout the enemy's rear. They drove him away, but he captured some of the horses which they had out grazing under a small guard. Just as he reached camp, forty Mexican cavalrymen appeared in pursuit. Hays told his dozen scouts to break camp, mount, and follow him. Out on the prairie, he wheeled his little force and charged the Mexicans, but as they could not face his pistols, they spurred wildly toward town. Hays let them go.

Hays had no provisions, no time for hunting game, and no means of securing fish. Fortunately Henry McCulloch and thirteen men from the Guadalupe rode into camp, five miles from San Antonio, with fresh beef hanging on their saddles. Soon broiled meat so encouraged the men that they insisted on organizing a company by combining their forces with those of McCulloch. Hays was elected leader, and McCulloch his lieutenant.[13]

Next day Hays instructed Preacher Z. N. Morrell and three others to scout in front of the city. If they were seen, as he fully expected, they were to stage a demonstration while he and three companions made a third attempt at riding around the city. He succeeded and captured a Mexican spy.

Caldwell's entire force totaled two hundred and twenty-five, while Woll had picked up three hundred Indians and Mexicans. Caldwell marched his army to within a mile of Hays and encamped. A council of war held at midnight decided that it would hardly be "prudent to attack the enemy within his fortifications."[14]

Who was to choose the battleground? Well, the councilors agreed that Captain Hays knew the topography. So he selected a brushy, level ground skirting the Salado on the west, which had a bank on one side that could serve as a breastwork. The odds of eight to one looked less formidable after Hays drew a rough diagram in the sand near the campfire. But who was to decoy the enemy to the selected battlefield? Why, of course Captain Hays and his company of scouts would do that! Out of more than two hundred horses, only thirty-eight could be found whose riders believed they could make the trip to town and have enough strength remaining to gallop back.

Next morning before sunrise Hays led his troop of thirty-eight to within one mile of town. He explained that he was going to make a feint to draw the enemy out. Those not with him should rest their horses to be ready for any emergency. Then he gestured to McCulloch and six men, and off they rode toward the Alamo. Hays and his friends approached the fort on the east and began to whistle, shout, and gesture challenge to the enemy to come out and fight. Instead of forty or fifty cavalrymen coming out, six hundred poured from the gates of the Alamo.[15] Feigning alarm, Hays led his squad in a gallop toward the waiting detachment, soon calling out to them to join him. In the hot rush Hays and his scouts were still in advance at the end of four miles and had reached the prairie two miles from the waiting Texans. McCulloch was in charge of a rear guard, and the Mexicans were firing so heavily at him that he pressed close upon the ranks of those he was protecting. The horse of Captain A. H. Jones began to fall behind. Hays noticed this and "threw the whole company behind him [Jones] and regulated its speed to the ability of Jones's horse to keep ahead. From there to camp the skirmish was brisk, our men being compelled repeatedly to wheel and fire, to save Jones, a man highly esteemed by all his comrades." [16]

The well-mounted Mexicans sought to cut Hays off from camp. He forded the Salado half a mile below camp with the enemy very close. As he wheeled and led his company dashing through Caldwell's camp, where the men were engaged in cooking and eating—they had not expected Hays to carry out his orders so promptly—the Mexicans "passed obliquely across the valley to a ridge some three hundred yards east."[17]

In camp, Hays formed his company, still mounted, in line for a hasty inspection. He dismissed them with instructions to cool off and water their horses, check their guns, and be ready for action within a half hour.

Morrell wrote: "Captain Hays, our intrepid leader, measured five feet ten inches, weighing 160 pounds. His black eyes[18] flashing decision of character from beneath a full forehead, . . . [he] was soon mounted on his dark bay war horse and on the warpath. Under our chosen leader, we sallied out and skirmished two hours or more with the enemy at long range, killing a number of Mexicans and getting two of our men severely wounded. In a short time the enemy retired out of range, and we fell back to the main command." Yet Hays had been constantly in the saddle "day and night for eight days and scarcely slept at all during that time." [19]

About two o'clock Woll arrived with the remainder of his command. He distributed on the prairie and ridge four hundred infantry, his artillery, forty Cherokees, a hundred San Antonio Mexican volunteers, and his cavalry. Grapeshot smashed into the trees above the heads of the Texans. Glistening ornaments, sabers, lances, and bayonets flashed in the sun's rays. Noticing that some of the enemy were attempting a flanking operation, Hays checked it by selecting ten men armed with double-barreled shotguns loaded with heavy slugs. They took care of the ambitious Mexicans.

Meanwhile the little army of volunteers formed in position as planned and held their fire until the enemy were within thirty feet. General Woll, observing from the hill on which he had placed his cannon, could see his men falling, but could not see the Texans. He speedily ordered his bugler to sound the retreat. The Texans had their answer as to Hays's judgment in selecting a battlefield.

Among those who fell within twenty paces of the settlers' line were Vicente Córdova and eleven of his Cherokees. One of the Indians wounded two or three of the Texans. He lay in the grass off to the right of the line and was a dangerous threat to the inexperienced men who did not know how to fight him. After conferring, Hays crawled in one direction and McCulloch in another. In minutes they were within sixty feet of the Indian. When aware that the Indian had seen them, both fired. The Cherokee sprang erect—dead before he could point his rifle.[20]

Woll reassembled his forces at sundown, marched into San Antonio, conducted funerals, and prepared to retreat. Caldwell lost one man killed and three wounded.

Hays and his company followed Woll's army and watched their movements. On September 20, when Hays notified Caldwell that Woll had just evacuated San Antonio, Caldwell started in pursuit. Woll camped on the Medina River about twenty-five miles from San Antonio. Hays and his men stuck close to the Mexican camp, acting as advance guard.

Hays and McCulloch discussed the possibility of entering Woll's camp to determine the number of men in his command. McCulloch reminded Hays that it was a tremendous risk, because Woll had placed a price on the Captain's head, but Hays thought there was a chance of their overhearing something of the enemy's plans. Both men understood Spanish, often had dressed like the Mexicans, and knew something of their peculiarities from living a half dozen years in the same town with them. In preparation for the hazardous mission, the two put on sombreros, serapes, and Mexican spurs; they then criticized each other's appearance. Satisfied, they selected a courageous volunteer to go along to hold their horses ready for mounting quickly if they had to run. They rode near the camp, dismounted, and, lighting their Mexican cigarettes, stalked casually into the camp. Since they were not challenged, they decided that pickets had been placed only on the road, which they had avoided when approaching.

As they sauntered among the Mexicans, they saw that some were asleep, others were sitting around smoking and talking, but none noticed the disguised gringos. Having gained the needed information, the two Texans strolled away. But on coming from the camp they saw an outpost guard, who also saw them. He had been stationed since they had entered the camp. Hays refused to run—perhaps Caldwell would like to quiz a prisoner. So when the guard challenged, "Who goes there?," Hays replied, "Texans, damn you!"

McCulloch warned: "Take care, Jack, or that fellow will shoot you."

Hays responded, "He won't shoot. I judge by his voice that he is scared. Hold your gun on him. I'll take him."

McCulloch pointed his revolver at the Mexican while Hays disarmed him. Then he tied his arms, gagged him, and pushed him along in front of them. When they came to their horses, they made the prisoner mount behind the trooper.[21]

Hays and McCulloch took their captive to Caldwell. It was learned that Woll had about three hundred fewer men than formerly. James S. Mayfield had joined the Texans with a hundred volunteers from Bastrop County, and a similar number were on their way from La Grange. Hays urged that they attack the next day. The retreating force was disheartened and should be struck before reaching the Hondo. But when told by the officers of the new troops and a few of the old that the men did not care to go on a reckless expedition, Hays dropped the matter. Next day Hays again urged an attack before the Mexicans crossed the Hondo. Again, his suggestion was declined. Finally numerous citizens said frankly that they did not wish to face cannon. Hays averred that he would capture the artillery first.

Hays's scouts, who were along both sides of the road and in advance of Caldwell's main force, overtook Woll's rear guard at the Hondo. Hays sent a courier to notify Caldwell, a mile to the rear, that Woll was crossing the river.

As Hays and several of his men sat their horses and listened to Woll's men crossing the rocky bed of the Hondo, they were startled by a rifle shot. The ball struck "Storyteller" Luckey, a large, handsome man, who was riding by Hays's side on a fine horse. Hays called Morrell to go to Luckey's aid, while he, followed by several horsemen, spurred toward a puff of smoke. They caught a glimpse of a Cherokee gliding swiftly into the brush.

All believed that the Cherokee had mistaken Luckey for Hays.[22] Woll had made it clear to every man in his force and to all allied sympathizers, that he was offering five hundred dollars to the person who would kill or capture Hays.

After Caldwell's army had crossed the Hondo, they saw that Woll was ready for battle. The Texans formed a line; Woll's cannon blocked their advance. Here properly aimed grapeshot could mow men down like a scythe against grass. Seeing that the soldiers continued to stare at this artillery four hundred yards in front of them, Hays told the officers he could take the cannon if furnished a hundred men.

Mayfield, who had been recently elected major, made an eloquent appeal for fifty volunteers to join Hays's party in the charge. Not a man responded. Then Caldwell asked Morrell to address the men. The minister got results. Caldwell promised to support the charge.[23]

Hays and his company sat calmly listening and watching. But when the number of men asked for were provided, he told them to follow his example, how and when to shoot, and reminded them that Mayfield's and John Moore's men were to sustain their charge. For several seconds Hays sat his horse in front of his line of men in a final hurried inspection. His reddish-brown hair glistened in the rays of the descending sun; and those immediately confronting him saw the color of his eyes changing with his moods. No longer hazel, they seemed to blaze —were now indescribable. The few Rangers present knew, as General Ed. Burleson used to say, "When Jack Hays's eyes begin to darken with a flash in them like lightning out of a black southwest cloud, it's a good time to let him alone."

Just then the sun touched the horizon, and Hays pivoted his horse while his "shrill, clear voice . . . sounded. Away went the company up a gradual ascent," recorded Morrell. They swept across the quarter mile of prairie, their yells and pounding hoofs deafening their watching comrades. "In a moment," said Morrell, "the cannon roared, but according to Mexican custom overshot us. The Texan yell followed the cannon thunder and so excited the Mexican infantry, placed in position to pour a fire down our line, that they overshot us; and by the time the artillery hurled its canister the second time, shotguns and pistols were freely used by the Texans."

A hundred yards in front of the cannon, Hays's horse had bounded sharply to the right, and the Captain knew that the animal had been hit. Forty yards from their objective, Nick Wren's horse was killed and had thrown his rider; Bigfoot Wallace's mule brayed every jump, only yards behind the leading horses; Kit Acklin leaned from his horse as he came to the cannon and killed a gunner by shooting through the wheels. Past the cannon they poured, killing every man around it, and riding down some scattering infantry to clear a spot around

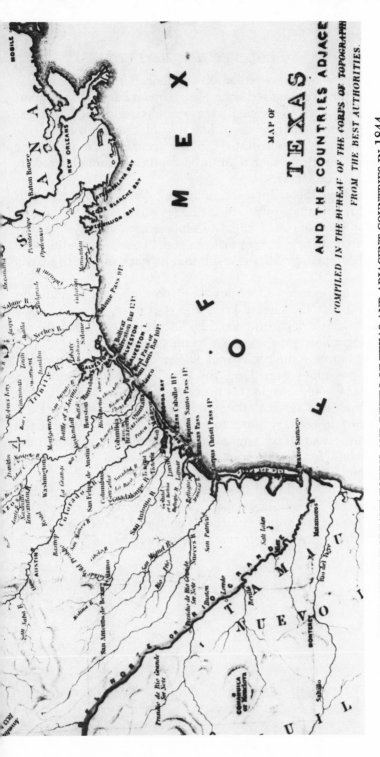

THE MORE IMPORTANT TOWNS AND RIVERS OF TEXAS AND ADJACENT COUNTRIES IN 1844

After a map of Texas by the War Department of the U. S. in 1844

them. But when Hays pulled up and looked about him, he saw none of the two hundred volunteers who had agreed to support the attack. Five of his men were wounded, and one horse was killed. A cannon from the other side of the creek and some musketry now concentrated on his troopers. Prudently, he decided to retire rather than to be captured or annihilated by the enemy on all sides.

Hays kept the cannon ten minutes.[24] Caldwell stated in his official report that "owing to the boggy situation of the ground and the tired horses, I failed to support him."[25] Hays was not aware that the officers back on the Texan line were disputing who should command, with the result that no force moved to sustain him.

Hays again assumed an advanced position, and at midnight reported that the uneasy Woll was retreating. Soon the noise of the enemy's departure could be heard. But the Texans' commanding officer gave no orders to pursue.

Next morning the regimental officers held a council in which the overcautious gained control. Mayfield enumerated all the reasons he could imagine for turning back to San Antonio. Morrell, Hays, and several others protested this decision. Nor did Hays and his company fail to express their displeasure at the order to retreat. Hays sent a detail to watch Woll's departure. The volunteers drifted back to San Antonio in small parties, Hays and his command coming in last.[26]

Hays's spies followed the Mexican army thirty miles west of the Nueces. The able and gallant Colonel Carrasco declared that if the Texans had supported Hays's charge at the Hondo, Woll's army would have been driven from the field.[27]

VII

DOWN MIER WAY

By late September, 1842, twelve hundred Texans had assembled in San Antonio. Edward Burleson stood in a window of the Alamo and delivered to them an oration, concluding with the suggestion that they return home, make preparations for participation in a military expedition, and reassemble in San Antonio on October 25.[1]

When Hays returned to San Antonio from observation of Woll's retreat, he found a letter from President Houston written on September 14 addressed to "Major" Hays. The government had promoted him before it had learned of his services against Woll. This letter read, in part:

> You will receive dispatches from the War Department which will relate to your duties on the frontier. Feeling for you as I do a paternal anxiety, arising from an uninterrupted friendship with your gallant father, I write to you unofficially; but will advise you, and if you can, if you will, estimate it in a twofold view.
>
> . . . You are situated so that you can determine what course will be proper and safe to pursue. I have thought that advantage might result to us if trade were opened to San Antonio and to such other points as would be safe. . . . how it would be proper to attempt the re-establishment of trade will be for you to determine. You are on the frontier and I will allow you to decide. It does seem to me that the inhabitants of the Rio Grande would find it to their interests to open the trade with Texas and cease all annoyance to our citizens. . . . Can our people be restrained; and if so, by what means can it be achieved?[2]

Houston supplemented this letter next day with a second missive, in which he expressed his desire for peaceful relations in foreign affairs. He asked Hays to send him constant information, as he could not hear what was happening at Bexar. The dispatches accompanying the letters authorized Hays to declare martial law in Bexar County and ordered him to take command.[3]

When Houston heard of the meeting at the Alamo, he directed Brigadier General Alexander Somervell to assume command. At the same time two regiments of militia were ordered to report to Somervell, and he was instructed to concentrate these troops east of the Cibolo. Houston knew that Texas could not finance a formidable force for the invasion of Mexico, yet he gave tacit consent to the popular demand. He was undoubtedly skeptical about the success of the project.[4] But if he could not have the full cooperation of the people in maintaining a defensive policy toward Mexico,[5] then perhaps he could minimize the probable results.

Houston's orders to Somervell indicate that Somervell was supposed to understand the president was adhering to his policy as far as was practicable:

. . . You will proceed to the most eligible point on the South Western frontier of Texas, and concentrate with the force now under your command, all troops who may submit to your orders, and if you can advance with a prospect of success into the enemy's territory, you will do forthwith. . . . Our greatest reliance will be upon light troops, and the celerity of our movements. Hence the necessity of discipline and subordination. You will therefore receive no troops into service, but such as will be subordinate to your orders and the rules of war. . . .

You may rely upon the gallant Hays and his companions; and I desire that you should obtain his services and cooperation. . . . Insubordination and a disregard of command will bring ruin and disgrace upon our arms.[6]

In the meantime Major Hays was discharging the duties of his new position. Then Somervell selected San Antonio as the point of rendezvous for the expedition to the Rio Grande. When he arrived, Hays resigned his authority to him and shortly thereafter furloughed his men. He reported his action to Secretary Hamilton.[7]

Hamilton and Houston were disappointed in Somervell. Hamilton wrote to him a severe criticism for failure to observe orders and disrupting a part of the government's work. Hamilton's letter approved of Hays's conduct:

> ... This was proper in him [Hays], though it was not expected at the time the orders were issued to him that you would organize your command, under any circumstances, west of the Cibolo, and that his [Hays's] command would operate almost exclusively west of San Antonio. This step was deemed essential to the safety of the citizens and their property, and it was desired that Major Hays should remain permanently at Post San Antonio, and retain the separate and independent command, unless you might find it necessary to occupy the Post with your troops, in which event he would of course be subject to your orders.
>
> If the expedition moves forward, Major Hays will report to you and act under your orders. Should you, however, relinquish the design of crossing the Rio Grande, he has been instructed to execute the orders forthwith upon the disbandment of your force.

Hays was not associated with the organization of Somervell's army. He did feel responsible, however, for the condition of his Rangers and used some of his own funds to supplement the government's inadequate appropriation. He expected to use the services of his company of spies again when they were needed.

On November 12, Hays wrote G. W. Hill, Secretary of War and Marine:

> ... I was compelled to incur a debt [for company expenses] of some $400 in par funds for which amount I became personally responsible, having full confidence that as soon as circumstances would admit of it, it would be furnished for the payment of the same. ...
>
> I also have the pleasure to report that the western settlements have, for several months past, enjoyed ... almost an entire immunity from the incursions of the Indians. The only source from which danger is now apprehended is the robbing parties of Mexicans (which may be expected to increase since the disbandment of the ranging companies) that have, until recently, been employed by the Mexican government upon the frontier, which were composed chiefly of men destitute of principle and without the resources to enable them to obtain an honest livelihood. Many, it is thought,

will be ready to engage in any enterprise, however disreputable, or hazardous, that may promise to afford them the means of subsistence.

There are now . . . many Mexicans who depend wholly for their subsistence upon robberies. . . . If a small force could be kept up of well
mounted men, sufficient to keep them in check, which might be done at
small expense to the government . . .

At the same time I would suggest, that the officer in command should
receive from your Department particular instruction as to the manner in
which those who were formerly Citizens of the Republic and joined the
enemy should be treated on their return, some of whom are now in San
Antonio and no doubt will be ready to do the country what injury the
advantage of living among us may give them.[8]

President Houston commented on Hays's letter in his message to the Eighth Congress: "For the past two years the officer
[Hays] acting on the southwestern frontier has rendered the
most important services to the country and even more than
could have been expected from the limited means appropriated
to sustain him."

Somervell's dilatoriness and failure to report relative to his
progress brought a severe censure from the War Department.
He was reminded that he knew it was difficult to organize troops
at San Antonio, as no supplies were available there, and the place
was conducive to the operations of spies. His troops, volunteers
and militiamen, numbered about seven hundred and fifty.

Hays was placed in command of a battalion of scouts composed of members of his recently furloughed spy company and
Captain Samuel Bogart's Washington County company of sixty
men. Hays's men elected Henry McCulloch first lieutenant, Eph-
raim M. McLean second, and James W. ("Old Smoky") Henderson first sergeant. Flacco and Luis, an Apache from New Mexico
who had been smuggled out of a Mexican prison by the Santa
Fe prisoners, were also attached to his company.[9] The battalion's
strength eventually numbered one hundred and twenty.[10]

When the order to march was given on November 22, Hays's
battalion led. At the rear of the column were two hundred pack

mules and five hundred beeves. After they had crossed the Medina and had reached a stream called the Tascosa, Hays notified Somervell that he, with McCulloch, Flacco, and a few others, was going down the Presidio de Rio Grande road to a certain stream to scout ahead. Somervell later ordered a "left oblique" for the Laredo road, apparently hoping to reduce the time.[11]

Soon the troops came to a sandy post-oak country, where all horses and other animals bogged down to their bellies. Most of two days was consumed in making five miles. When they reached the Laredo road, few had much regard left for Somervell.[12] Five miles along the road the army camped for the night.

Hays exerted himself to see that no prowling bands of Indians or Mexican bandits made a sudden attack upon any part of the formation. With McCulloch, Flacco, and two other Lipans, Major Hays was ever in front of the troops or on one or both points of their advance. Those who kept journals recorded frequently that when the main body encamped, there was "Hays's company in our front," or "The next morning we again moved on, and at noon came to where Hays had encamped the night before."[13]

Hays led his advance scouts on to the Nueces River. For only a moment he hesitated at the half mile of flooded bottom and the swampy approach to the river. Horses frequently floundered in mud almost to their bellies only to plunge free and sink into holes of water that set them to swimming. At the channel Hays and his companions halted to rest their horses. The waters before them whirled, eddied, and rushed swiftly. Hays set the example by dismounting, undressing, and tying his clothes in a bundle and suspending it between his shoulder blades from a loop around his neck. Then making a necklace of his belt and revolvers and holding his rifle in his right hand, he remounted and spurred his horse into the river, aiming in a quartering direction at the opposite bank. Man and beast were buffeted by the cold, swirling current, but clothing and guns remained comparatively dry. Safely across, Hays decided to pause in order to be of possible assistance to his company.

His command soon forded the stream. While directing the men in making a comfortable camp, he sent a messenger to notify Somervell regarding the swollen river and to suggest the construction of a brush bridge to facilitate crossing. These details attended to, the Major and four companions rode off toward Laredo in search of information.

Bogart's company used a raft and ropes to assist in their fording of the river, and when they came within a few hundred yards of Hays's camp, they too encamped. Both units worked together to construct, as Hays had suggested, a crude bridge for the remainder of the army. Hardly more time was consumed in crossing the main body of the troops than Bogart's company alone had taken. As the hours passed, Somervell awaited word from Hays before continuing to advance. Late in the afternoon of the second day, the general, becoming tired of inaction, instructed Bogart to march on until he should meet or be contacted by Hays. Bogart moved forward about four miles. It was now December 5.

At daylight next morning Flacco arrived in Bogart's camp bearing a message to Somervell. Hays and his four companions had reached the outskirts of Laredo. While scouting the town, they had captured two spies. The Indians had severely wounded one of the Mexicans in capturing him, but Hays had lassoed the man who sought to outrun him on horseback. Unfortunately, just after he had made his cast, Hays's horse had lamed itself. Therefore instead of riding all the way back to the army, he had camped with his three remaining men and two prisoners, about twenty miles beyond the Nueces. No Mexican force of any size was at Laredo or near there.

Hays's company marched toward his place of encampment. Bogart's company followed. The main force, however, was delayed by a night stampede of its animals.[14] When the rain ceased, Somervell's army built fires and thawed out. Hays and his little party, serving as the eyes of the expedition, dared not risk a fire. They hovered with their prisoners behind their horses and took the rainy blast—shivering in their lightweight clothing, since they would have been in Laredo but for Somervell's inefficiency. Hays united with his company thirty-five miles away from Laredo.[15]

One night the wounded Mexican made his escape and, it was supposed, fled to Laredo. Hays had the guard put under arrest.[16] Then with Ben McCulloch as his only companion, he set out for Laredo, hoping to intercept the escapee. In the vicinity of town, he met his resident spies and ascertained that the escaped prisoner had arrived, spread the news of Somervell's approach, and informed the Mexican garrison across the river. The Texan force halted two miles from Laredo while Hays's scouts checked the town to learn whether the Rio Grande was fordable. Just before day the troops surrounded the town, and Hays's men, scouting along the river bank, discovered the Mexican force had retreated from the post across the river.

Hays led his battalion into the town and had a detail hoist the Texas flag on one of the main steeples. Laredo was on the Texas side of the Rio Grande, but had harbored guerrillas and quartered Mexican soldiers so long that it was generally thought of as being pro-Mexican. Fifteen minutes later Somervell appeared and ordered a parade. With Somervell and Hays leading, a very good appearance was presented, and every man enjoyed being a part of that mounted formation.

Citizens lined the streets, greeting the horsemen by doffing their sombreros and exclaiming in Spanish, "Good morning, gentlemen! We are friends of the Americans." It sounded good, and the salutations were well delivered, since they had been used often before. Somervell halted the parade a mile and a half above town. The day was December 8. The hungry men had been traveling for more than two weeks. Some of them had lost their blankets and expected Somervell to make the alcalde supply their necessities. The general did make a requisition, but did not secure enough food for one day's supply. Besides, the men had thought they were going to be led across the river at once. Instead, late in the afternoon, Somervell countermarched the force and encamped four or five miles below town. The commander was taking up the line of march for home. A large majority of his army were so dissatisfied with this move that two days later he permitted his officers to change his determination.[17]

On December 11 the general paraded his little army and addressed the men. He stated that those who desired to do so could return home without dishonor. Under this permission two hundred soldiers and their officers turned back. The remaining five hundred encamped opposite Carrizo, six miles from Guerrero.

Hays found two large flatboats on the river and by making two trips transported his battalion across. Seven hundred rancheros appeared and were distributed on the rear hills by General Antonio Canales. Hays formed his men and moved toward the enemy, which aggressive movement gave the signal for their hurried disappearance.[18]

Hays and his company dined on mutton that night. It was abundant in the abandoned village of Carrizo, which they occupied. The alcalde of Guerrero appeared at the camp with a French interpreter. He begged that the Texans would not camp in his town, but promised to furnish clothing and food if it were desired. When this message was translated to Somervell, he granted the request.

On the 15th, the Texans moved to a hillside near Guerrero and made camp. Somervell demanded of the alcalde a hundred horses and requested Hays to remain with his own company to secure them. The alcalde declared to Hays that upon the approach of the invading force all the horses had been driven from the village to the interior.

Meanwhile Somervell had recrossed to the Texas side of the river; the alcalde's statement had made him furious. He ordered Hays to return to Guerrero with his command the next day and demand five thousand dollars of the alcalde for not meeting his requisition. Hays also was to state that if the alcalde declined, Somervell was going to turn five hundred men loose to sack the town.

Hays delivered the message, adding that while he was there to collect the money under orders, he would be glad to exchange lead if they cared to resist. Hays was aware that he was taking considerable chance, since the town contained several thousand inhabitants who could, by fighting from ambush, make his departure a critical problem. There was the additional hazard, too, that hundreds of Mexican soldiers had been brought into the place during the night.

The alcalde manifested great distress at the news. He scurried about in an effort to raise the money, but obtained less than four hundred dollars, which he brought to Hays, but Hays refused to receive anything less than the whole amount. The alcalde besought its acceptance, but Hays told him that he could tell his story to General Somervell.

When Hays recrossed the river, the alcalde went along and and tendered his collected funds to Somervell. The general heard his declarations and summarily dismissed him. He had decided that sacking the town probably would fail to yield five thousand dollars. If he had not already done so, Somervell now made the decision that he could not "advance with a prospect of success into the enemy's territory." On December 19 he issued a general order directing that the army return to Gonzales. About three hundred of the men refused to obey.

Hays said good-by to Luis, who was rejoining his tribe, and suggested to Flacco that he leave with Somervell for the interior. To Flacco, Hays's suggestion was equivalent to an order.

As many of his command lacked horses and others rode animals which were lame or weak from crossing the Atascosa bogs, the General granted permission for any who desired fresh mounts to confiscate horses from an old rancho near the Rio Grande, since the herds were a source of supply for bandits. In keeping with the admonition to take as many as they could find, Flacco obtained a drove of forty animals.

Among those of the "Three Hundred" who averred they had not come to view the Rio Grande and then go home were some courageous men who desired the issue settled. Yet too many of them persisted in responding to reveille by turning over and snoring, or tossing off a blanket, springing erect, flapping arms, and crowing like a saucy rooster. Not a few gobbled like turkey cocks, whooped like owls, or brayed like jackasses. Noncommissioned officers were forced to plead: "Do get up! Tumble out boys! Turn out, for God's sake! On your feet—immediately, if not sooner!" [19] These men who announced their desire to stay on the Rio Grande elected Williams S. Fisher to lead them to Mier.

Some members of the new organization had, at one time or another, served under Hays. A few of them were now in his company and were his old friends; he would allow each man to decide for himself. Samuel Walker and Bigfoot Wallace urged the Major to assist the new enterprise. Although Hays and a large majority of his company refused to affiliate with the Fisher organization,[20] he promised to remain with them a few days and perform voluntary scouting services.

Next day, December 20, saw the Fisher group seize several boats below Guerrero. After Hays and his company were transported across the Rio Grande, the three hundred men climbed into the boats, and Thomas Jefferson Green hoisted a red flag over the leading boat in which he was riding. At a given signal, the boats were headed down the river, the men's horses were driven parallel to them on the Texas bank, and Hays led his company along the Mexican side of the river to guard against an attack. The plan of approach brought the expedition down the river to Mier at the end of three days. A landing was made opposite the town, and the men encamped to spend the night and await a report from the scouts.

Hays entered the desolate adobe town with his company and soon learned that no soldiers were there. He dispatched a courier notifying Fisher of his findings and of his intention to remain in town for the night. As Hays felt four days of assistance for the sake of friendship was all he could spare, he explained to Fisher that, under his orders from the Department of War, he was obligated to resume his independent command at San Antonio. He furthermore became doubly bound to recommence his work under his new commission and instructions when Somervell ordered a return of all forces. He advised Fisher to abandon his plan, because he had learned in Mier that a large force was being assembled to oppose the Texans.[21]

Hays's knowledge of the Mexicans' plans caused him to warn his friends, but several of them, including Walker and Wallace, decided to remain with Fisher instead of returning with him to the settlements. Within a few days Bigfoot Wallace wished that he had heeded Hays's departing words; he had gained increased "respect for his old commander . . . Jack Hays," [22] who presaged the tragic ending of their expedition.

Hays and his companions set forth for San Antonio during the predawn hours of December 24. When they came to within a few miles of the city, Hays was horrified to see the corpse of Flacco. The chief, Hays learned, had been assisted in driving his horses[23] by two Mexicans and a Lipan, who was an elderly deaf mute. While they were encamped near San Antonio, the two Mexicans herding the horses murdered Flacco and his companion and drove the animals away to sell. Major Hays and his Rangers so cherished Flacco's memory that they determined to protect his tribe as long as those Indians remained in the vicinity. And it was not until after Hays had left Texas that the Lipans, who came to believe that the Anglo-Texans were Flacco's murderers, began to prey openly upon Texans.

When Hays arrived in San Antonio early in January, he wished to inaugurate his new program at once. He visited the Secretary of War and explained the need of revised legislation which would enable him to provide immediately some sort of protection for the frontier. Congress was in session, and the act of January 16, 1843, enabled the Secretary of War to authorize Hays to raise the requisite number for a small company.[24] Within a few weeks Hays had enlisted twenty men and was ready for duty.

VIII

NO NEUTRAL GROUND

MAJOR HAYS'S first movement was against the noted bandit Agaton, in April, 1843. With fifteen men and provisions for thirty days, he followed down the Nueces, shifted to the Rio Grande, and descended to a point opposite Matamoros, but did not encounter Agaton. Fortunately he captured two Frenchmen, who had made illegal entry into Texas, from whom he learned that only four hundred soldiers were garrisoned at Matamoros.[1] The platoon also recovered a drove of horses and mules from local Mexicans who had taken them from settlers.

Spies among the irreconcilables in San Antonio noted Hays's departure and reported the news to Agaton, who gathered a hundred of his bandits and rode to intercept the returning Rangers. They found the Texans camped on the Nueces, asleep and exhausted from their long excursion. The recaptured *caballada* grazed some distance from camp. Agaton surrounded the Rangers; then in the darkness the outlaws huddled in the river bottom and held a lengthy discussion about killing "Devil Jack." As they were never able to muster the courage to attack, they compromised by driving the livestock away. Next morning Hays discovered that the herd was missing. Signs told the story. As there was little use to follow on jaded horses, he led his men on to San Antonio and prepared for another incursion into the land of the bandits. [2]

The Republic all the while was seeking to win the services of the United States as a mediator with Mexico and was attempting to make treaties with Indians. "You might as well attempt to exterminate the crows as to kill them all off," wrote Isaac Van Zandt to Secretary of State Anson Jones.[3] Incursions, whether retaliatory or otherwise, were delaying this assistance from the United States. President Houston moved to end these activities by placing under military law the territory between the Frio and Nueces rivers and the Rio Grande. All armed parties except that of Hays were ordered to disperse, and Hays was instructed to deal with any persons found there not bearing the authority of the government of Texas. [4]

To execute Houston's orders, Hays went scouting west of the Nueces. He had not found Agaton, for the bandit lived in such terror of him that whenever a San Antonio henchman galloped up and started his report by saying "Devil——," Agaton bounded toward his horse for a getaway, leaving the word "Jack" still hovering in the air. A noticeable revival of trade always followed a Hays tour through lawless territory.

On June 15 while negotiations were pending, Houston proclaimed a continuation of the armistice with Mexico. In spite of the proclamation, spies from below the border persisted in their activities. Hays arrested three, tried them by martial law, and ordered them shot.[5] Despite Houston's evident sincerity, Hays learned that General Woll was fattening horses at Guerrero and having boats constructed at Presidio to transport soldiers along the lower Nueces. Moreover, in utter disregard of former commitments, Mexico announced she was not surrendering her jurisdiction below the Nueces, and President Santa Anna decreed that foreigners who invaded Mexico should be executed. This announcement, which came while the Comanches were negotiating a treaty of peace with Mexico, was immediately followed by increased Indian depredations. A farmer was killed in his field almost within the shadow of the Alamo. With thirty men Hays, who in mid-July had moved his camp to Leon Creek west of San Antonio to escape the spies ever among the Mexicans in town, followed the Indian trail for a hundred and twenty miles, but failed to overtake the redskins. [6]

During Hays's absence, spies of Manuel Perez, understudy of Agaton, raced to report that Hays was away. Perez soon reached the Medina River with a hundred men. He was going to exact vengeance upon the few Anglo-Americans in San Antonio.

Hays and his men returned to sun-baked San Antonio on a hot August afternoon. Though the Major sat erect in the saddle, his horse showed it had suffered from the recent pursuit far beyond the settlements. Some of the rangers were obviously tired, and for once they appeared to be dispirited.

Hardly had Hays given the order to dismount before a townsman apprised him of the plans of Perez. Ignoring the summer's blistering atmosphere, he hurriedly visited several houses along the street. While his Rangers quenched their thirst at a bar, the Major was everywhere, making the essential but simple preparations to meet the approaching lawless callers. There was no time to make the round-trip ride to camp and recruit horses and men.

Some of Hays's men were sick at the time and others were tired from the two hundred and fifty mile ride, but mention of a prospective encounter with the robber chieftain worked a marvelous recovery. Hays led out fifteen Rangers to attack Perez. A sentinel reported the approach of the Rangers, and the Mexicans fired at them. Hays gestured to his men to fan out to position. Kentucky rifles cracked, and Perez fled down the stream. Behind him pressed the wary Hays. As his men fell around him, the running fight became a losing game for the bandit. Gringos shot through the head! In an effort to save his band, Perez set the grass on fire. Hays then waved his men into places for the attack which he hoped was coming. Within a few minutes he discovered that the Mexicans had little appetite for more Ranger bullets. The smoke screen was to conceal Perez's riders before they spurred into a run toward points south.

On September 26 commissioners from Texas and Mexico met at Sabinas and discussed an armistice to succeed the inadequate truce of June. Already Secretary of State Anson Jones had written the British chargè d'affaires in Texas, through whom negotiations were being carried on, that if Mexico wished to remove obstacles to existing difficulties, she should release all captive Texans. Mexico replied that if Texas would deliver Mexican prisoners to General Woll, Santa Anna would release all Texans held. Jones rejoined that Texas held no Mexicans. To conciliate Mexico, however, Houston invited any Mexicans in Texas who desired to return home to report to Hays at San

Antonio, where they would be provisioned and escorted free of charge to the Rio Grande. [7]

On the Rio Frio in early November, Hays with a few men attacked a small party of Mexican outlaws. One was captured and another was knocked from his saddle by a rifle ball. The wounded man, recognized as Leandro Garza, traitor and noted spy, dived into the timber and escaped.[8] Hays also found some Mexican regulars on the Nueces. They promised to restore any stolen property which they recovered, told him of the San Antonio spies, and pledged aid in suppressing the bandits between the Nueces and the Rio Grande. Hays was aware of the continuing activities of Antonio Perez and Leandro Garza, though he had reduced their operations to a minimum. Perez longed to plead for forgiveness as a traitor. The Rangers chased him so much that he had become lean and aged. It was on this scout that Hays learned Agaton had been killed by a party of traders.

As the governmental appropriation was exhausted, Hays furloughed his company until funds were available or an emergency should arise. The report of the Secretary of War on November 25 to President Houston stated:

. . . since the first of March last his [Hays's] command has been in active service up to the 12th of November inst. . . .

This force, though small, has been active, vigilant, and efficient. . . .

The ranging companies of the enemy on and near the Rio Grande have been disbanded and the principal portion of their regular troops withdrawn to the interior.[9]

Hays gloomily foresaw a revival of the Indian incursions and a resumption of the troubles with Mexico and decided to discuss the situation with President Houston. It was Thanksgiving, and en route to the capital he visited in Seguin, where friends argued that his business could better be attended to after Christmas.

While a guest of several leading families, Hays renewed acquaintanceship with Judge Jeremiah H. Calvert's attractive daughters, whom he first met in San Antonio through the courtesy of Mesdames Elliot and Riddle. The Calverts were newcomers to Texas from Florence, Alabama. One of the sisters, Susan, a young, slender girl of medium height and with dark hair and brown eyes, attracted him at once. She had the charming individuality and graciousness of the Southern woman. The Major's stay dated the beginning of their courtship.

While Hays was still in Seguin, Congress passed a joint resolution compensating him and his men, including any liabilities created for their support while protecting the southwestern frontier during 1843. It authorized the payment of the money directly to Hays, who was to render his account of disbursements to the proper department. [10]

As he set out on horseback for the capital, New Year's Day saw Hays joined by Captain G. T. Howard, the Honorable F. Paschal, Congressman W. G. Cooke, and Captain J. Antonio Menchaca, of San Antonio. The party arrived on the afternoon of the 4th and was invited to call upon the president.

Probability of trouble with Santa Anna and the possibility of Mexico's agents inciting the Indians against Texas were considered. Hays informed Houston that representatives of four companies of Cherokees from the United States had visited Woll at San Fernando to tender their services against Texas. The Major thought that Manuel Flores, agent among the Indians in Arkansas, had instigated this action. Hays then suggested plans which he believed would enable him to give more adequate protection to the southwestern frontier. The president assured him that next day he would send a special message to Congress urging protection of the frontier and would use his efforts to secure the needed legislation.

Houston told Hays that a part of the armament of the Texas navy consisted of new Colt five-shooters and advised him to obtain the guns for arming a force which the Congress undoubtedly would authorize him to enlist. Since 1839, when the revolvers first appeared in Texas, Hays had known the value of these weapons.[11] He, Sam Walker, and a few others secured one or two. Still very scarce, they brought exorbitant prices, when one could be found for sale, and were almost unknown among the inhabitants generally.

Bigfoot Wallace said that S. M. Swenson, prosperous Texan visiting New York, bought four Colts and gave them to Hays because "he was a great friend;thought he [Hays] was the only fighter God ever made." Hays's first revolver may have been obtained through David K. Torrey, prominent trader of Waco. Certainly Torrey later wrote Hays from New York about a "beautiful pattern of belt pistol with all his [Colt's] improvements—do you want a pair? . . . don't fail to write Sam Colt." Once Colt presented Hays with a pair of "elaborately engraved and superbly finished" revolvers.

Hays, accepting Houston's suggestion, procured an order from the Secretary of War and started to Galveston the next morning. He got the Colts and their accessories, including the extra cylinder and bullet molds.

While returning to San Antonio, he discovered between La Grange and Gonzales a small band of Mexican outlaws. Several friends now were traveling with him, and he asked one of them to guard his pack mule, upon which he had loaded the revolvers. Then they attacked the marauders, who headed for the swamps of the nearby river bottom and escaped. One of their horses fell into Hays's hands. [12]

Hays's departure from San Antonio had been noticed by spies from lawless and disloyal elements, who had learned of his plan to visit the capital. No sooner was he reported to have reached Seguin than messengers notified those who had not dared to appear when he was at Bexar. The town suddenly filled with robbers, who staged a Tory meeting on the main plaza. But one day no swaggering bandits or traitors dominated the stores; no reckless, wild horsemen were seen in San Antonio's streets. A little later Hays and some friends rode in from Gonzales. The outlaws had gone; San Antonians resumed their normal activities; and serenity reigned, for Hays was at home.

He listened to the reports of the indignant citizens and called together his disbanded company of fifteen men. Hays equipped each with two of the new Colts with an extra cylinder for both. All had a rifle or a double-barreled shotgun, one or two pistols if desired, a knife, and a hatchet. During the last of the month

Hays led his company northward over the routes he formerly had followed and found Indians. This time he discovered none. After three weeks of riding, he turned back toward home.

When they came to Sisters Creek, two miles above where it it empties into the Guadalupe, a scout discovered a bee tree. San Antonio was fifty miles away, and as men and horses had earned a rest, Hays permitted Kit Acklin and John Coleman to rob the bee tree. Thirty feet above the ground, the men paused occasionally as they chopped. After a time Coleman glanced back over their trail and gasped with astonishment: twenty-five Indians were sitting quietly on horseback three hundred yards away watching the bee robbers.

"Indians!" Coleman yelled, pointing and beginning to descend. Acklin was stepping on his friend's fingers in his haste to get to his horse. Hays and the others were tightening girths and examining their guns preparatory to mounting. Soon all were climbing the slope which they had descended.

The Comanches, legs crossed in front of them, still sat on their horses. There was one sure way to ascertain whether the calm impudence was designed. "Come on, boys!" Hays shouted, sending his horse into a run. Since the Indians never changed their positions, Hays became more wary as he charged. Suddenly within sixty yards from the line of warriors Hays halted his men as he plowed his mount's forefeet through the sod. Behind the row of braves, just appearing over the opposite side of the hill, were two other lines of warriors. Hays motioned his boys to some timber off to one side. Each man held a revolver in his hand. When the Rangers wheeled for the timber, the first row of braves charged, their war whoops ringing across the prairie to terrify the white men. With Hays in the rear and his guns silent, his men rode swiftly without panic. The last two lines of warriors dashed rapidly off the hill and fanned far to both sides.

As the Texans came within fifty yards of the timber, a shower of arrows and shrill whoops met them from an unseen group within. Hays spurred through the center of his racing line, crashed hard into the brush, and fired. An Indian sprang erect and fell, with the horse's shoulder striking the corpse. Indians

[96]

scampered to get away from the horses and the spitting guns. No attempt was made to follow them as they rushed twenty strong for their mounts behind the thicket. Hays and his men wheeled, dismounted, and gave their horses' reins—five animals to a man to hold.

The three parties of Indians united and charged the thicket. When Hays shouted "Now!" bullets thudded into warriors and their gaily decorated horses. The line of riders divided, thundered by on each side of the thicket, and circled to safety. Beyond rifle range the chiefs re-formed their men. When the long line trotted forward, the rifles of the palefaces began to speak. Because this had been expected there was no confusion. The red men were galloping now, and as chiefs shrilled their war cries, braves rode recklessly at the grove. The line parted, and horsemen raced in a semicircle to unite for a charge before the white men could reload.

With deadly lances poised in their hands, back they came whooping and shooting arrows and rifles. But right in the faces of their paralyzing war horses the white men rose and stood with a smoking stick thundering from both hands. Braves and horses went down hard, dying as they fell and rolled. The charging line halved at the thicket, and the survivors galloped on. Here and there warriors swooped up behind their shields as many wounded and dead as possible. Then the chiefs led a slow withdrawal to a prairie height for council. Watching their gestures, Hays saw that they were whipped. He decided to take the initiative and inflict more punishment.

When the Rangers charged, the Comanches showered them with arrows. Three men were hit and reeled in their saddles; whereupon a companion caught each man to prevent him from falling. In the terrific attack, Hays and nine comrades pierced the line of warriors, then broke back through the line. Braves tumbled to the ground. Their wounded horses screamed, reared, and stampeded, but the Comanches continued to fight. Hays motioned to the three Rangers who were supporting their friends to lead a retreat, while he and the others hurriedly spread out to protect them. The Indians followed, keeping as much as possible behind their shields, shooting their arrows, and riding zigzag to avoid the white men's aim.

When near the timber, Sam Walker shot an Indian who was trying to get close enough to thrust him with his spear. In the encounter, Walker's back was turned a second, and another warrior drove a lance through him. John Carlin saw the brave make his thrust and shot him through the head just as another Ranger spurred forward, jerked the lance out, and assisted Walker to the thicket. Seconds later, Ad Gillespie stopped an arrow and fell from his horse at the edge of the grove.

The Comanche war chief galloped forward to stab his lance through Gillespie, but as the chief poised, Ad sent a bullet through the red man's brain. Two dismounted Rangers dashed to Gillespie and pulled him into the brush. Indians galloped toward the three, but Hays and the others drove them back. Warriors crowded forward in an attempt to rescue their chief's body. The odds were seven to one in a desperate conflict over the corpse. Other Indians galloped up and joined in the struggle. There was danger of the Rangers' being surrounded and overcome by sheer numbers.

Hays ordered his men to leave the body and retire into the thicket, where the five wounded Rangers lay. Firing as he moved backward behind his men, the Major watched the braves pick up their chief's body, place it in front of a mounted Indian, circle their horses about the fallen leader, and gallop off. Three Rangers sat down within the thicket and pulled arrows from each other's bodies.

As the Indians moved rapidly away, chanting loud lamentations, Hays remounted. "Follow me!" he shouted, and seven men streamed out behind him across the prairie. When within range Hays began firing. The Comanches fought back only halfheartedly as the Rangers unhorsed a number of them. In trying to carry away their dead and wounded, they could neither travel fast nor offer other than a haphazard rear-guard resistance. The Rangers followed them until darkness began to make targets uncertain.

Back at the thicket, the eight Rangers were found to be seriously injured. At least half of the red men must have been killed. On his return to San Antonio, Walker for several months was a slow convalescent. Hays unhesitatingly gave the revolvers the credit for their survival.

While Hays was on this scout, Congress authorized him to "raise a company of mounted gunmen to act as Rangers," [13] consisting of forty privates, one lieutenant, and a commander. The unit was to be organized by February 1, or as soon thereafter as practicable. [14] Congress also passed an act declaring martial law along that portion of the frontier and gave Hays absolute command. This legislation gave him the first real chance to establish law and order for which he had toiled for years.

Hays worked to remedy the evils which had come to ill-fated Bexar. Since the "Runaway of 1842" ranches employed few hands, farmers produced only for their own use, and merchants kept very small stocks of goods. [15] Recently some Texans had begun to steal cattle. Once Hays took a few men, pursued a band, and recovered a herd of two thousand. [16]

Hays re-enlisted his fifteen men and began to contact those who had served with him before. A few were in such serious financial straits that they could not report properly equipped; so he assisted them. It was not easy to obtain the select body of troopers he sought. On the frontier such young men did not live long. When Hays entered the Republic, he was a quiet lad traveling with ninety men. Now, seven years later, he was one of five or six of the ninety who were still alive. [17]

On March 15 Hays reported his company ready for duty. They were, perhaps, "the most happy, jovial, and hearty set of men in all Texas." [18]

When a band of Comanches appeared in San Antonio seeking a peace treaty, Hays encouraged their overture by suggesting a rodeo which would be enjoyed by all in the vicinity. The chiefs agreed that this was a fine idea.

Fifty Comanche warriors, as many Mexican rancheros, and Hays's Rangers were to participate. Hays was to be master of ceremonies, assisted by a Mexican ranchero and Chief Buffalo Hump.

Local families and visitors from other settlements thronged the principal street en route to the field, a prairie one half mile west of the plaza. Showy *caballeros,* mounted on prancing steeds with heavily decorated riding gear, cantered through the mass. Rangers were dressed in slouched hats, buckskin hunting jackets, and long leggings. [19]

At the arena the Comanche warriors occupied one side. They were dressed in their gaudiest paints, feathers, and furs, and sat their horses looking proudly toward the crowd. Immediately opposite them were the Rangers and rancheros.

Prizes were handsomely mounted pistols and bowie knives. The judges awarded the first prize for horsemanship to John McMullin, a Ranger; the second to Long Quiet, a Comanche brave; the third to a ranchman-trader, H. L. Kinney; and the fourth to Señor Don Rafael, a ranchero from the Rio Grande. The judges also gave presents of various kinds to all the Comanches, and the contest was ended. Of the "riding match" one onlooker wrote: "I had seen what I had thought to be many astonishing performances in the ring but none of them could compare with those I witnessed that day on the prairie near San Antonio. The Comanches were famous riders and so were the Mexican rancheros, and some of Hays's Rangers were fully equal, if not superior, to them." [20]

Some of the competitors and spectators attempted vainly to persuade the master of ceremonies and his assistants to perform some riding feats. A contemporary wrote: "As a horseman . . . he [Hays] was equal to the best trained circusmen, being able to ride at full speed and pick up a half dollar from the ground with his hand. No Comanche could surpass him in throwing his body from one side of his horse to the other, and thus dodging Indian arrows and sometimes bullets." [21]

Buffalo Hump waxed expansive following the distribution of the presents among his braves. Just before the Rangers and the Comanches left for their camps, he even inquired concerning Hays's matrimonial plans. He advised the Ranger leader to get married and have many papooses to carry on "Devil Yack's" name. He suggested that when the first-born arrived, it should be called Buffalo Hump, Jr., and insisted he be notified of the happy event. Hays indulgently nodded his agreement.

A few days later some traders bought six thousand dollars worth of goods in San Antonio, but were afraid to leave, believing that Manuel Leal would rob them just after they forded the Nueces. Leal was one of the chieftains who had terrorized San Antonio during Hays's absence near the close of 1843. [22] After Hays's return to the city in January, this bandit had operated west of the Nueces. He had been under the impression Hays would consider that area a sort of "neutral ground."

When the traders appealed to him, Hays took a detachment of his company and started for the Nueces. He scouted the vicinity of the ford carefully and captured nine of Leal's gang, but the chieftain was not with his men. He brought the prisoners to Bexar, where they were held for trial before the district court.[23]

Hays again sought to circumvent Mexican spies by establishing his camp on the Medina, several miles above later Castroville.[24] Leal and his maurauders seldom rode far from the Rio Grande now that Hays was on the lookout for them. There would be no "neutral ground" as long as the government left him in charge of a military force.

FAME

Bɛxᴀʀ and farther west witnessed Comanche raids again in April, 1844. Hays started on a scout into the maze of Indian trails with fifteen men who, with one or two exceptions, had served in his old company. An Irishman called Paddy was one of the new recruits.

On the second day's ride down the Nueces Canyon one of the force discovered a bee tree. Honey was ever a welcome addition to their plain and scant provisions, and it was now about noon. Hays halted the platoon, but warned the men to put a stake rope on each horse and remove only the bridles. Noah Cherry climbed the bee tree and began chopping into a hollow about fifteen feet from the ground. The other men rested on the grass and occasionally tendered witty advice to Cherry on how to get the honey quickly. While pausing for a moment, Cherry's roving eye became fixed and his features hardened as he gave a low whistle and exclaimed, "Je-ru-sa-lem! Captain, here comes a thousand Indians!" Hays bounded to his feet, fatigue and worry banished. He wasted no words or steps as he directed: "Come down from there quickly! Men, bridle your horses and take up your ropes! Be ready for them! Be ready for them!" [1]

Hays, first as usual to have his horse ready, sighted the Comanches rushing headlong down the canyon on the Rangers' trail. There were more than two hundred in the party. The Rangers, standing coolly by their horses, wondered how long it would take the red men to detect their presence. At length an Indian signaled the discovery.

A war chief's gobbled whoop and a chorus of battle cries set the air in the canyon dancing with echoes. With poised spears and shrill yells the charging Comanches sought to terrify the scouts into panicky retreat. Several of the most eager men began to raise their rifles, but Hays cautioned: "Let them come closer! Stand your ground and aim carefully! We can whip them!"

The Indians were almost upon them when Hays's shot signaled the moment for defense. Rifles cracked, revolvers roared, and a wide gap suddenly appeared in the foremost Indian rank. As horses went down, riders were thrown over their heads, spears flew wildly through the air, and men and animals piled up, blocking those behind them. Around their wounded and dying, warriors, relentlessly swinging bows and launching arrows, kneed their horses past the Rangers. Just as the last brave raced by, Hays spurred his nervous horse toward them and shouted, "After them! Crowd them! Don't let them turn back!" Revolver bullets knocked red men from their mounts. The attack from the rear surprised and stampeded them. Chiefs tried vainly to rally the terrified braves. The fighting was at close quarters—so close that the revolver explosions often burned the red men's bare posteriors.

Finally, terrified ponies, yelling Rangers, popping revolvers, and screams from powder-burned braves precipitated a panic. Warriors threw their spears away, whipped and kicked their horses for more speed, dropped their bows and lost their quivers in a mad effort to escape. Occasionally an Indian rode down the canyon screaming into his horse's ears to urge him forward, while he held his shield against his buttocks with his left hand, and stabbed backwards desperately with the spear in his right to thwart another attempt to powder-burn him.

The Comanches were too much occupied with trying to get away to ask for quarter. Kit Acklin saw a warrior riding a blue mule and sought to capture the animal. The poor mule was so frightened that he outran Acklin's horse.

When Hays at last halted the pursuit, he had escaped any loss of life, though some of his men were wounded. While the Rangers were turning their attention to sampling their neglected honey and getting a few moments of rest, Paddy remembered that he had seen a wounded Indian crawl into a thicket. He declared that he was going to finish him. Hays warned, "If there is an Indian in there, you had better let him alone. If you go in where he is, he will surely kill you before you even see him."

Paddy hesitated only for a few seconds and then loudly avowed that he was not afraid of a crippled Injun. Hays offered no further warning as the Irishman walked boldly into the thicket. Within a few minutes a sharp cry of pain was heard. Four of the Rangers dismounted, took their distance, and with revolvers in hand walked cautiously into the brush. A small bush quivered, and they fired simultaneously at the ground under it. A wildcatlike squall followed. The four resumed their walk and came upon an Indian in death agony. There, almost covered with leaves, lay the brave flat upon the ground. Paddy was fifteen feet away with an arrow through his heart, the tip protruding from his back. The warrior's leg had been broken during the beginning of the fight. Four fresh bullet holes showed in his body.

Paddy's corpse was taken to the bee tree and buried. As all had lost appetite for honey, they set about preparing to return to their camp near San Antonio, some pausing long enough to gather a few pieces of the Indians' scattered equipment as souvenirs of the battle.

The most dependable account of the losses sustained by the red men came from the war chief who had commanded. In San Antonio later, he was talking with Bob, a friendly Delaware. When the fight on the Nueces was mentioned, the Comanche inquired concerning the identity of the white commander there. Bob told him that "Devil Yack" led the Rangers. The Comanche shook his head slowly, saying: "I never want to fight him again. Every one of his men had as many shots as I have fingers on my two hands. I lost half of my warriors in the battle, and many others died along the route when returning to my country on Devil's River."[2]

After his return Hays made a trip to interview President Houston.[3] John W. Lockhart, a veteran of the Texas Revolution who was staying at the hotel where Hays registered, wrote:

After he had registered . . . I looked over the book to see who the stranger was. Imagine my astonishment at seeing the name of John C. Hays. I thought my eyes had deceived me. Could that small, boyish-looking youngster, with not a particle of beard on his face, be the veritable Jack Hays, the celebrated Indian fighter, the man whose praise was sung by all Texans? It could not be, I thought, but I soon found out that he was the "Captain Jack."

As soon as he registered he left the hotel to transact his business . . . and as soon as he had finished his business, he was off. Many men who visited the seat of Government with such a reputation as Hays had, would have stayed a month, if for no other purpose than to be lionized. . . .[4]

During May the Indians began to harass the settlements again. Hays led fourteen men from his camp near San Antonio to ascertain "what tribe of Indians were committing so many depredations."[5] On June 8 they encamped on Walker's Creek, four miles east of the Pinto Trace,[6] at a point about equidistant from Austin, Gonzales, and San Antonio. Pickets discovered ten Indians following the Rangers' trail. When the two parties discovered each other, the Indians rode into some brush nearby, which was heavily laced with timber.

Hays instantly ordered his men to saddle and prepare for a fight. "For I," he wrote, "could have no doubt that their intentions were hostile. After being mounted, I proceeded slowly toward them."[7] Four made their appearance, pretended to see the white men for the first time, and, feigning alarm, raced away. When the Indians perceived their ruse was not successful, all emerged from the timber, formed a battle line, and sat watching the Rangers ride deliberately toward them. Though he could see that he was outnumbered at least five to one, Hays decided to attack.

Behind the Indians was a dry-bottomed ravine, which ran along the base of a high hill. From base to rim, the front of the height was covered with a heavy growth of timber, underbrush, and rocks. As Hays led his Rangers forward at a slow trot, the Indians crossed the ravine and ascended the face of the steep peak. Reaching its summit, they dismounted and formed a line along the crown. The Comanches from this superior position began to taunt the Rangers with gestures and insulting epithets in Spanish. When they thought they could be heard, they urged, "Charge! Charge!" As Hays and his men continued their measured advance, this overt disregard of the Indians' most studied affronts angered their head chief, a large man. He called for his horse and mounted in front of his force of braves and Mexican allies. His powerful mustang's rich bay sides shone in the sunlight like burnished metal. He caracoled up and down the line of men, rode as far in front of them as possible, then turning his rear to the Rangers made frequent indecent gestures, shouting all the while daringly, "Come on! Come on!"

Seeing that some of the Rangers were on the verge of losing their tempers, Hays cupped his hands and deridingly shouted back to the chief, Yellow Wolf: "Yellow Dog, son of a dog-mother, the Comanche's liver is white!" This so infuriated the chief that his violent gestures in reply almost caused him to fall from his horse.[8] In seeking to get the white men to scale the hill, despite their prepared stand, the Indians redoubled their insults, yelling and screeching until the noise reverberated from the hillside.

Reaching the ravine, Hays rode down into its bed, then spurred stealthily unperceived along its course around the brow of the hill, his men following in close formation. Once in the rear of the Indians, the mounted troops climbed the bank leading to the prairie behind the red men and charged the still screeching line. The Rangers caught them as each brave stared down into the ravine and knelt with guns and arrows fixed for deadly aim. Suddenly hoofs thundered behind them. Every warrior ran toward his horse. Hardly had they succeeded in mounting before the Rangers drove through them in a V-shaped charge.

The Comanches wheeled on either flank and counter-charged in a semicircular formation, trying to drive the white men over the face of the hill. When the Texans did not yield, they converted the semicircle into a circle and tried to ride through their surrounded prey. But Hays met these tactics by also forming a circle and, back to back, the Rangers employed their rifles. At last Hays shouted, "Throw down your rifles!"

The Rangers dropped the discharged weapons behind them. As most of the twenty bullets had been effective, the attack momentarily broke.

When the Comanches galloped forward in a second onslaught, the Rangers used their belt pistols. Arrows, spears, and shields were pitted at close range against five-shooters. Almost every trooper was grazed by spears or arrows; Gillespie and Walker had been lanced through and through. Now only the voice of the chief was heard among the Indians. The warriors fought doggedly. Twenty-one of them were killed within fifteen minutes, and many others were wounded. The chief led a retreat; the Rangers pressed them closely in the running fight. During the course of two miles the chief rallied his braves for three different onslaughts upon their pursuers, and each time he lost warriors. Hays had his men fighting in relays. Several would spurt ahead, fire their revolvers, and check their horses while the others charged, fired, and paused.

Hays was careful to have men with loaded guns always ready to receive the oncoming Indians. Usually the Rangers met the attacks with a countercharge. Still, Hays's numbers were reduced at last by his men having to drop behind because of loss of blood.

Only about thirty-five warriors were able to obey their chief's orders as he zigzagged amidst them, preparing for the last rally. Hays looked over his own force and observed that only a few had any loads. Suddenly he halted his men and asked, "Anybody got a loaded gun?"

Gillespie, wounded and weaving in his saddle, replied, "Jack, I reserved my rifle."

"Dismount and shoot that damned chief!" ordered the Major.

Already advancing at the head of his braves and preparing to signal a charge, the chief, with shield in front of his chest, faced Gillespie who was only thirty yards away. Gillespie shot him through the head. Before the valorous Indian fell, his horse had sprung forward several bounds.

When the war chief tumbled from his horse, the Indians fled. The Rangers pursued and killed a few, as the terrified braves forgot to place their shields behind their backs. With the extra cylinders almost emptied and their horses practically exhausted, Hays stopped pursuit. The running fight had covered nearly three miles and lasted about an hour. Hays reported to the Secretary of War: "Whenever pressed severely, the Indians were making the most desperate charges and efforts to defeat me. Had it not been for the five-shooting pistols, I doubt what the consequences would have been."

Peter Fohr was killed, and four other Rangers were wounded. The Rangers found twenty-three dead Indians, and at least thirty were seriously wounded.[9]

The Houston *Morning Star's* story of the fight was written on June 23. An extract from a paragraph reads:

Thus ended a fight unparalleled in this country for the gallantry displayed on both sides, its close and deadly struggle, and the triumphant success of the gallant partisan captain of the West. . . . I scarcely know which to admire most, the skill and courage of the officer who commanded on that occasion, or his modesty. . . . 'Concealing his own deeds, he did ample justice to his comrades, and . . . *blushed* to find himself *famous.*' As a brave man, he was before celebrated; as a skillful and able officer, he now holds that rank to which he was justly entitled, and well does he deserve the admiration of his countrymen.

In this encounter not over one hundred and fifty shots were fired.[10] Thus, because the new guns were so effective in this fight, soon the Colts being manufactured bore an engraving which represented this engagement.

Hays took his wounded men to San Antonio and placed them under the care of Mrs. Jacques. Then he left Lieutenant Ben McCulloch in charge of the Ranger camp and patrol duties while he hurried to the capital with his spies' reports that Woll was preparing to recommence hostilities. In Washington-on-the-Brazos, newspaper reporters attempted to interview Hays, and persons there sought to stage entertainments in his honor. Remembering his wounded Rangers and the threats leveled at the frontier, he declined all honors, expedited his business, and set out for San Antonio.

Upon his arrival Hays's first act was to visit his wounded men. When he found them improving rapidly, he rode out to the Ranger camp. There he learned that the Indians and bandits appeared to be inspired to renewed activity. During Houston's second administration, Corpus Christi and San Antonio alone remained as settlements west of the San Antonio River. Only Hays and his forty Rangers stood between numerous bands of Indians and Mexicans bent on further recession of the frontier. If San Antonio were abandoned, then the Guadalupe settlements would be exposed. One small company of Rangers to patrol and defend several hundred miles of frontier, while the Comanches and Apaches could place between sixteen hundred and two thousand warriors in the field! [11]

President Houston and Hays had read General Woll's manifesto, isssued on June 20, in which communications with Texas were declared at an end and war was recommended.[12] On July 21 Hays wrote from "Headquarters, Southwestern Command" at Bexar to G. W. Hill, Secretary of War and Marine:

About ten days ago, a spy in my employ . . . informed me that preparations were in progress to mount . . . a force of six hundred men, to be divided into three divisions — one of which was to proceed with rapid marches to this place, and enter the town, if practicable; if repulsed, to retreat. Immediately on their return, another division would advance with the same instructions; . . . and keep up a constant annoyance on this portion of the frontier. Two days ago he returned, confirming his previous statement; . . .

Hill, immediately after discussing the matter with Houston, dispatched a copy of Hays's letter to Secretary of State Anson Jones.[13] Jones said that Mexico intended, at least, to "renew a system of predatory warfare against Texas" and had been "induced to her course by the negotiations pending between Texas and the United States." Hays's report soon reached Washington, D. C.[14]

Having decided to make a personal investigation, Hays took fifteen men, traveled down the western bank of the Nueces, and extended his scout to the lower Rio Grande. While returning, he visited Captain P. H. Bell,[15] who had been with him for years around Bexar and was stationed with a few Rangers at Corpus Christi. There he heard of a large band of Comanches who were raiding below the city.

At the Agua Dulce, Hays overtook the seventy-five Comanches and led an immediate attack. The Indians fought bravely, but did not like their introduction to the five-shooters. After having thirty of their warriors killed and numerous others wounded, the red men gave up the fight. Several wounded Rangers were taken to Corpus Christi for surgical attention; Hays and the remainder of his platoon returned to San Antonio.

Hays learned that Henri de Castro, who had contracted with Houston to settle a colony west of the Medina River, now sought an escort for his advance unit of French-German colonists. Most of them spoke no English, which was excuse enough to tempt Buffalo Hump's braves to scalp them, for "They must not be 'Captain Yack's' people," Buffalo Hump contended.

On July 21, Hays wrote to Secretary of State Jones:

... I will do everything in my power to enable him to effect his object ... as soon as possible.

The small force that I have under my command will not be sufficient to afford the colonists much protection in their new settlement. I think, however, if my force were increased to 15 or 20 in addition to my present numbers, they could proceed to the lands and commence their operations in safety.[16]

Castro noted in his diary on August 25 that the Indians had killed and mutilated one of his immigrants. Next day the Comanches borrowed eleven of Henri's mules. Continuing their efforts as a reception committee, the Indians surprised four volunteer scouts in swimming and almost killed two of them.[17]

When Castro set out for the country west of the Medina with his colonists, Hays supplied a part of the guard and five days later he and Mike Chevaille personally conducted Bishop

Odin to the site of Castroville. But in a fortnight Castro wrote Houston again, requesting Rangers for protection. Secretary of War Hill answered:

> . . . The company of Hays was raised as a corps of observation upon the movements of the enemy, and, in case of emergency, to give whatever protection it might to the frontier inhabitants against marauding parties, both of Mexicans and Indians . . . . Corpus Christi, San Antonio, and other remote points have at different times, and sometimes at the same moment, claimed the services of the company for their exclusive protection.
> . . . Its range will include and cover your settlement, and of course give to it equal protection with the rest. . . .

Yet Castro chronicled: ". . . Major Hays and his noble companions . . . were equal to any emergency, but such a company, can, in my opinion, only be compared to the old musketeers . . . of France." [18]

Numerous immigrants had landed on the Texas coast around Easter, 1844, expecting to be assisted by Castro in making their way to his colony. Unfamiliar with the geography and the language, and destitute of transportation, money, and food, soon they were huddling along the sands of the shore, hunting dazedly for cactus to eat. News of their plight reached Hays. Working with Johann Rahm, one of his men, the Major expanded his credit sufficiently to have the settlers brought by wagons to San Antonio. Because of his aid to these and other European colonists, Hays later received a fine inscribed rifle in token of appreciation from Prince Solms of the Society for the Protection of German Immigrants in Texas.

Prince Karl, of Solms-Braunfels, found the Rangers dependable and Hays accommodating in discussing land and in escorting him to a colonization site. "Major Hays," wrote Prince Solms, "is an honorable and trustworthy man, and perhaps the only one from whom accurate information of the mountainous regions can be obtained."

By dividing his men into platoons, Hays was able to protect more of the frontier. He would ride out with one, and upon returning to his headquarters camp, would lead another scout with the rested group. "Hays was gifted with such an iron constitution," chronicled J. W. Wilbarger, a witness, "that he was enabled to undergo hardships and exposure . . . which would have placed the majority of men completely *hors de combat.* I have frequently seen him sitting by his camp fire at night in some exposed locality, when the rain was falling in torrents or a cold norther, sleet, or snow whistling about his ears, apparently as unconscious of all discomfort as if he had been seated in some cozy room of a first-class hotel; and this, perhaps when he had eaten for supper a handful of pecans or a piece of hardtack." [19]

Mexico, seeing that the adherents of James K. Polk for President were in the majority, renewed the armistice. Hays was enabled to police the frontier more effectually, since patrols toward the lower Rio Grande indicated no immediate danger from there. This was fortunate because Congress had failed to appropriate sufficient money for defraying expenses over a considerable period of time. Hays used his own credit to keep the company in the field for a while longer. Finally, with apprehensions, he furloughed his men.

Robbers soon learned that the Rangers were inactive and promptly began to prey upon the citizens of Bexar and to steal horses from the Guadalupe settlements. Mexican sympathizers, angered by the prospect of the annexation of Texas, again became insulting to the Anglo-Americans in San Antonio, and Indians raided the horses of settlers near Seguin. [20]

The settlements sent spokesmen to the capital, and the government asked Hays to resume his work. Soon the outlaws were scampering into hiding, insolent Mexican Tories were becoming courteous citizens, and disorder was being suppressed. Still the restless Comanches were again threatening because the government's policy of shifting the Indian country boundary line was about to interfere with their buffalo hunting.

President Anson Jones believed that the Rangers had been overworked in attempting to defend such an extensive frontier; therefore, since the people requested it, Jones recommended and Congress passed legislation providing for expansion of

Hays's Rangers. Congress also adopted a joint resolution for the settlement of the accounts Hays made on behalf of his men. The repair of firearms and the shoeing of his troops' horses in 1844 had cost Hays four hundred and five dollars. [21]

On February 12 new recruits were all mustered in for six months' service.[22] The lieutenants were men who had served under Hays. He was authorized to combine at will any or all the four other county stations of Rangers with his own company.

At this juncture Hays received reports that several hundred Indians were assembling on the Rio Grande, probably to attack the Mexican frontier villages.[23] The Indian chief Santa Anna, in command of fifty Comanches, had passed near Corpus Christi early in March. Hays made an immediate scout to that town, where he concluded definitely that the Comanches again were hostile.[24] But the Comanches themselves now pretended that they desired a permanent peace and asked permission to purchase in frontier towns ammunition with which to carry on war against Mexico.[25] Tribes in the Indian Territory were taking so many of the buffaloes that the Comanches complained they were compelled to supplement their resources by encroaching upon Mexican settlements.[26]

After discussing the Republic's policy with Secretary of War Cooke, Hays talked with Buffalo Hump and other chiefs and tried to show them that in the long run war against either Mexico or Texas could bring only disaster to the Comanches. [27]

Meanwhile, in mid-May, Hays's spies along the Rio Grande reported that reinforcements had arrived for the Mexican troops on the river. They declared soldiers were encamped on the Nueces near the mouth of the Rio Frio. Hays decided to drive back any Mexican force he found east of the Rio Grande, and wrote the government accordingly.

There was good reason to believe that President Anson Jones, who had been inaugurated in December, 1844, preferred independence to annexation.[28] His attitude caused Hays to work vigorously to promote annexation. Hays expected a battle on the Rio Grande, and C. A. Wickliffe, confidential agent of the United States in Texas to counteract the efforts of France and England, wrote President Polk that he was going to urge Hays to drive the Mexicans from the region west of the Nueces. [29]

President Jones proclaimed in June, 1845, a cessation of all hostilities between Texas and Mexico, pending a treaty of peace. When the Texas Congress approved of annexation, President Polk instructed General Zachary Taylor to concentrate his command at Corpus Christi.

Perhaps these proceedings stimulated several visits of Comanche and allied chiefs to San Antonio. They palavered much about peace. Chief Santa Anna was one of the brazen visitors who called upon Hays and made overtures. Hays asked him to return, but conferred with Secretary Cooke before holding a talk with the influential war chief. [30]

A few weeks later Buffalo Hump put considerable strain on the pacific policy of the Republic, which had signed a treaty of peace with the southern Comanches in October, 1844. This chief told Indian Agent Benjamin Sloat that he was going to lead a war party to the Mexican border. He maintained Hays would join him as he went by San Antonio. Sloat attempted to explain that Hays would not accompany him, but Buffalo Hump was so insistent that Sloat had to go along himself. This the wily chief had foreseen would provide him with an official companion past the settlements. Near San Antonio the Indians encamped, and Buffalo Hump went with Sloat to talk to Hays, who was unsuccessful in persuading the leader to forego the trip. The crafty chief laughed to himself as he rode boldly forth toward the Rio Grande at the head of over seven hundred warriors,[31] certain that Hays would not attack him.

X

WHITE DEVIL!

AFTER Texas had approved the annexation terms, the constant vigilance of Hays's Rangers alone stood between the capture or possible death of those men engaged in making the state constitution in Austin.[1] Comanches recently had killed settlers near town. On the San Pedro, in August, 1845, a band of one hundred and fifty Comanches killed one Mexican trader and captured five. Hays, by treating with them, was able to secure the freedom of the prisoners and the release of most of their livestock. The chief argued that since Mexicans west of the Rio Grande were at war with Texans, he, as a Texan, had a right to kill Mexicans. Hays communicated the facts to the Secretary of War for a decision. [2]

Hays learned also about this time that the Comanches and Kickapoos were at war. Although the Kickapoos had firearms, most of the Comanches lacked guns; peace with the white men would enable the Comanches to buy them. Peace would also prevent Hays from killing Comanches as they hunted down the Kickapoos.[3] The sudden friendliness of the Comanches became now understandable.

Thinking that the United States government soon would assume the responsibility of defending Texas, the Texas government directed Hays to disband his Rangers. But the Republic's officials then realized that weeks would elapse before Congress approved the constitution of Texas and sent it to the President's desk; hence within a few days after Hays had released his force, Secretary Cooke asked him to organize and command a new battalion of Rangers. Hays recommended three old comrades as captains and set them to work enlisting their men. Though captains were permitted to enroll their companies first, Hays's own headquarters company quota of thirty men began to fill rapidly.

While Texans were enlisting, President Jones graciously invited General Taylor's suggestions concerning the defense of the frontier. Taylor recommended that Rangers continue to do the work.[4] He wrote the adjutant general at Washington on September 1 : "The commander of the rangers at San Antonio, Major Hays, has reputation as a partisan, and to him I have especially intrusted the duty of keeping me advised of any movements on the Rio Grande in the neighborhood of Laredo." [5]

A correspondent of the New Orleans *Picayune*, attached to Taylor's army at Corpus Christi, wrote his editors:

Hays takes my eye. He is . . . not over 27 or 30, very youthful in appearance, modest and retiring in his manner; but it is said he has the courage of the lion, and he has complete control over the Lipans. . . . Castro [chief] told him if he wanted the Lipans to go against the Mexicans or Comanches, he should have all the warriors. Hays has constant communication with the Mexican borders.

It is Hays's opinion that if we remain here, the Mexicans will not come to attack us, but if we go to the Rio Grande we shall get a fight. . . . Hays says whenever he wants to know anything about Mexico, he tells one or two of his trusty fellows to "go bring him in a Mexican." He says he has hooked several out of Laredo and other towns on the borders.[6]

As October ended, Hays led Ben McCulloch's ten recruits from Gonzales on an expedition to Laredo. He found the people there were anxious to acknowledge the authority of Texas. They expressed the hope that Major Hays would concentrate many Rangers there.[7] As for the renewed Indian forays, the New Orleans *Picayune* averred: "Give him [Hays] the men and means and in six months we should hear no more of Indian depredations." [8]

President Jones confirmed Major Hays's rank as leader of the battalion of Rangers in mid-December. Authorized to increase his force to sixty-five men, Hays incorporated Ben McCulloch's and R. A. Gillespie's men and retained the services and association of these officers.

To observe movements along the upper portion of the lower Rio Grande, Hays scouted southward and encamped opposite

Presidio de Rio Grande. He sent a detail across to inquire about purchasing beef, but practically every male fled in dismay at once. There was no one with whom business could be transacted. While a messenger was sent back to notify Hays that there would be some delay, some of the señoritas consented to stage a fandango. Hays instructed the messenger to return to the village and say that he would remain only a couple of days in camp. The supplies must be brought during this period. Men could go to the fandango if they desired, just so they were back on time with the provisions. The messenger, accompanied by additional Rangers, recrossed the stream and waltzed to the notes of a bugle, while a boy was sent to deliver the emphasized request for purchase of food. In the afternoon of the second day the Rangers returned with their orders liberally filled. They believed there were Mexican armed forces in the vicinity, yet none had appeared. [9]

During the last of the holidays Hays visited Austin in company with Secretary Cooke. They called upon President Jones and conferred regarding border defense. Hays stayed in the capital long enough to witness a parade of United States dragoons and to attend the New Year's Eve cotillion. [10]

Hays now maintained his headquarters in San Antonio because he was also district surveyor, but he continued close contact with the Ranger camp on the Medina River. The Rangers now lived in tents the year round and changed their camps from time to time. Occasional visits to town still were permitted the men, but only a portion of them were in town or in camp at a time. Scouting expeditions in alternate thirds or fourths of battalion strength provided rest and work in better balance.

Dr. Ferdinand Roemer of Germany visited San Antonio on February 10, 1846, and there met Hays at a fandango. Roemer chronicled: ... "Discipline ... is replaced by absolute loyalty to their leader [Hays], who set an example for all in enduring personal privations and exertions.... I was surprised to find the outward appearance of the man so little in keeping with his mode of life and the qualities attributed to him. Instead of a fierce, martial, powerful figure, I saw before me a young slender-built man whose smooth, beardless face as well as the black dresscoat which he wore, betrayed in no wise his military occupation and inclination. In the piercing eye alone the careful observer might discover traces of his hidden energy." [11]

By an act of Congress on December 22, 1845, the Rio Grande had been declared the western boundary of Texas. In the meantime a Mexican army was concentrated at Matamoros. General Taylor was instructed to take position on the Rio Grande in anticipation of the announcement of President Jones of Texas on February 19, 1846, that "the Republic of Texas is no more."

When news came to San Antonio that Taylor was preparing to move his army, Hays visited him and offered to place his Rangers under the general's orders to serve as scouts. Taylor declined, saying that his dragoons could do his scouting. After a short experience Taylor changed his mind and called for two companies of Texas mounted men to relieve his cavalry of the difficult task of keeping open his line of communication, and later, when the Mexicans captured sixty of his dragoons who were trying to scout, he asked the governor of Texas for two mounted regiments. [12]

While Hays was at Corpus Christi, his men heard that six hundred Indians had raided the settlements southwest of San Antonio and were retiring northward with their booty. On the day that the Major returned to his command, a detail of Rangers discovered the marauders had passed a well-known landmark two days before. At dawn Hays rode from camp on the Medina with forty of his best-mounted troopers. The course was northerly toward Bandera Pass, and from there to Enchanted Rock, eighty miles to the north, which they sighted late in the afternoon. A few miles south of this peak, the Rangers picked up the fresh trail of the raiders. Beyond Enchanted Rock the Indians appeared to be bound for a small lake at the base of Paint Rock, a favorite haunt of the Comanches. Hays abandoned the trail for a more direct route to the watering place, hoping to arrive there before the Indians. Not until after midnight did he allow the men and horses a short rest. Then the detachment

rode almost continuously throughout the next day, arriving at
Paint Rock about one o'clock in the morning.

Moonlight revealed the lake to be a hundred yards wide and
three hundred yards long, east and west. At the west end, Paint
Rock could be seen towering precipitously a hundred feet from
the water. On the north shore of the lake, mid-distance from its
ends, was a grove of willow trees with thick undergrowth.
Satisfying himself that he was ahead of the Indians, Hays stationed his men in this flimsy but concealing shelter. As the lake
behind could be crossed only by swimming, rowing, or floating
on timber, the Major posted pickets and ordered the remainder
of the men to sleep.

At early dawn guards announced the approach of the Indians.
In a few minutes every man was in position. The Indians, well
within their own country, rode unsuspectingly and listlessly in
disorder almost to the willow grove. Hays thereupon shouted,
"Now!"

Only a few warriors were knocked from their horses, as it was
too hazy for good shooting. The foremost Indians, wheeling
their ponies, retreated and waited beyond range for the scattered column of warriors to gallop up. Daylight permitted the
chiefs to examine the trail, and all the Comanches became
exuberant over the odds of fifteen to one.

Just before sunrise the Rangers watched the war chief prepare
for his onslaught. The Comanches obviously were proud of their
horsemanship "not equalled by any other Indians on the con-
tinent." [13] They were well mounted and armed with effective
short bows, quivers containing about fifty bone and flint arrows,
fourteen-foot spears that were deadly at close fighting, and some
rifles. Each brave carried a shield that only a bullet which struck
at right angles could penetrate. Until Hays secured revolvers
for his men, the Indians were better equipped for warfare in
their country than were the Rangers.[14]

Northeast of the Rangers' thicket the Indians formed the line
of attack. Hays passed the order to the men: "Pick a warrior
facing you and aim carefully!" The first rays of sun gleamed
brilliantly on the hundreds of ponies, shields, and painted bodies

of the Indians. It was a terrifying scene, particularly to a sixteen-year-old Ranger, who affected indifference but could not hide his nervousness. Two men who flanked his position began to talk for his benefit:

"Injuns look too pretty to shoot."

"Yes," came the reply, "it's a pity to spill blood on that ocher."

"Look at the flashy chief. Somebody will hate to have to kill him," was the rejoinder.

The sun eased above the horizon, the chief gave his war whoop, and six hundred war horses sprang toward the thicket. F. W. Harrison, the boy Ranger, said afterward: "I saw the long line of painted savages coming and felt the hair rise on my head, and it seemed to me that all the devils from the lower regions had been turned loose upon us; but I braced myself and the panicky feeling passed away." [15] The Rangers lay still until the Comanches were within fifty yards, then poured a volleying gunfire on the attackers that knocked many from their horses. The chargers faltered and the chief swung west, leading a frontal line that wavered in wild confusion. Each brave sought to fire one or more arrows at the little grove as he galloped by. Warriors on the right wing suffered most, since they had to pass all the Rangers. Riderless ponies followed the mounted horses toward the rock or turned and galloped wildly across the prairie. Here and there a wounded warrior began crawling in an effort to get beyond rifle range. The Texans reloaded and waited.

Near the rock the war chief signaled a second charge— this time the braves racing with the sun in their faces, hoping thereby to cut into the thicket. Hays understood the maneuver and shifted his position slightly, still concentrating their fire at close range. Again the Indians swung into a half circle and rode past the grove. This cost the Indians many horses but few men, for every brave had a loop of hair rope braided into his war horse's mane, and swinging by this, with one heel on the horse's back, was able to screen himself behind his racing mount.

After a council at the northeast end of the lake, the chief determined on a lance charge. War bonnets fluttered in the breeze, war cries filled the air, and excited horses speedily brought riders so close to the timber that the Rangers could see their features. As the Indian line swept forward, revolver explosions burst in horses' faces, and long spears dropped from dying hands. Survivors who were able spurred away toward the rock. All day the conflict went on. At nightfall the Indians withdrew beyond rifle range and camped on the prairie. A few braves attempted to get to water at the lake, but most of them rode in detachments to the nearest water about twenty-five miles away. They had no thought of leaving in a body or permitting the Rangers to escape.

Hays posted a heavy guard and changed it often so that all the men might secure some rest. They could water their horses and obtain water for themselves under cover of darkness. Occasionally throughout the night the guard fired upon parties of stealthy figures who were attempting to remove their dead; no chances could be taken. Every time a gun blasted, the Rangers were awakened; none obtained too much sleep.

Daylight saw the chief divide his warriors into three and four groups and send them at the thicket in rapid successive waves. At times the charges came so fast that Hays's men emptied their guns and scarcely had time to reload. The fourth wave of attack, composed of a hundred braves, once followed so closely the three preceding ones that a few warriors crashed into the border of the thicket. Only the final shots from several revolvers prevented them from spearing some Rangers.

The Indians also attacked from the south side of the lake and from the top of Paint Rock, which could be ascended only from its western side. Arrows launched from the rock proved ineffective, as the whites remained close to the ground. The rifles of the Rangers toppled several from the rock into the lake. At dusk the Indians ceased their onslaughts, again camped beyond range, and again rode to and from their distant supply of water.

On the second day of fighting when the Indians became certain that "Devil Yack" was in command of the white men, some of the warriors expended much breath in shouting taunts at the "Silent White Devil!" Apparently the spirits of their departed brothers were calling upon them to exact vengeance of "Big Brave." [16]

Hays and Gillespie did much of the guard duty that night, as they had done the night before. They urged their men to secure as much sleep as possible to be ready for anticipated determined attacks. Ammunition was nearing exhaustion, and there was always the possibility that the Indians would send a courier to bring reinforcements.

Next morning the Indians staged their first rush earlier than usual. The war chief was everywhere, inspiring his men. His war dress was "a long buckskin garment with a heavy fringe on which were many silver ornaments, and it also bore many paintings." [17] His headdress was the horns of a buffalo. A heavy tuft of buffalo hair attached to the horns covered his face. He carried a long shield that protected his body entirely.

All attacks now were launched from the north side, the chief sending simultaneous waves of men from several angles. Never before had the Rangers been so hard-pressed in meeting this type of attack, which forced them to divide their fire. Frequently the Indians thrust within forty yards. More than one rifleman tried for the chief, but his rawhide shield afforded excellent protection, and he handled it dexterously. About ten o'clock the chief formed his men beyond range and harangued them. The breeze brought occasionally to the Rangers an emphatic tone as the leader rode slowly along his line of mounted warriors.

Their horses were rested. With the chief in front, the entire band then charged desperately. On they came, apparently set for a suicidal attempt, with whoops echoing and lances poised.

"Heap Injuns!" laughed Mike Chevaille.

"Fighters, too," said Gillespie.

Several yards in advance of his line of warriors the chief thundered straight at the heart of the grove. Hays knelt with cocked rifle and watched him through the sights. Negligently the chief looked backward to shout something to his men. As he swung his body half around, his shield, carried in front of him, moved also, leaving his side exposed. Hays squeezed the trigger. The chief fell heavily, then tumbled over on his back.

Warriors near skidded their bounding ponies to a stop and whirled back toward their dead leader. As they grouped about his body, the Rangers poured in such a withering fire that the Indians retreated. Hays knew they would re-form, charge, and pick up the body at almost any cost. He gestured to a Ranger, who, leaping to his horse and spurring out to the body, put his lasso around the chief's neck and galloped back with the corpse dragging. All this was done so rapidly and with so much effrontery that the warriors were unable to stop him, but recovering from their astonishment they charged like hornets. A burst of gunfire brought them up short. One more fast retreat and another halfhearted rush, then the whole band abruptly left the field. Traveling rapidly in a northwesterly direction, they soon disappeared.

For several minutes Hays kept his men at their positions. Though the sudden retreat was according to custom, it might be a ruse. When he led his force out of the little grove to follow the Indians, he was astonished to find that they had fled so hurriedly they had neglected to notify six wranglers grazing about fifty head of ponies. Hays directed the men in surrounding and killing these horse-thieves. The settlers' horses were driven back to the lake and watered. As Hays's men had little provisions left, and hardly any ammunition, he ordered a prompt departure.

In looking over the field, the Rangers chose a few souvenirs for themselves. The chief's decorations and war gear were collected to be sent to the capital. Their count showed over one hundred dead Indians. Others were probably carried off by their fellows, and some likely died from wounds. The Rangers had a horse killed by one of the thousands of arrows.[18] Emory Gibbons had received an arrow wound in the forearm. This conflict marked the last major encounter in which Hays was involved with the Indians in Texas, since their worst depredations were over in the territory that he was guarding.[19]

Often frontiersmen were thoughtlessly hopeful of not being molested. For instance, one morning before sunrise a boy galloped his horse into the Ranger camp and gasped out a story of an Indian attack upon a family several miles away.

Within a few minutes Hays led his spurring men toward the place. "Two children were lying dead, their skulls crushed in with murderous tomahawks. The father was near with two ugly gunshot wounds in his body. A seventeen-year-old girl had been carried away captive, and the mother seemed bereft of reason." [20] She staggered with unseeing eyes, back and forth across the yard from one body to the other, sobbing and frequently screaming. When Hays attempted to speak to her, she responded only by imploring him to rescue her daughter. So he left two Rangers to bury the children and to try to comfort the frenzied mother, while he led his men in pursuit of the Indians.

After trailing the redskins at a gallop for an hour, his advance scouts sighted the Indian camp near the Llano River. The Indians had sent out a strong hunting party and were preparing for its return. While Hays was studying the camp two hundred yards distant, some dogs chased a rabbit near the force who were sitting their horses in anticipation of the order to attack. The dogs quit the rabbit's trail and turned back toward the red men's camp. It was obvious that the Indians would take alarm.

"Now, boys," Hays said, "some of us must spill a little blood; but keep perfectly cool. Show your usual pluck, and I do not fear the result." [21] Facing the camp and swinging his right hand in which he held a revolver in a gesture of direction, he shouted, "Come on!" His eager horse bounded into the short run.

The first sounds of thundering hoofs sent the Comanches scampering for weapons they seemed unable to find. Those who secured arms could not shoot accurately. Some ran to their horses, mounted, and flailed them into a run toward the river. Many Indians used trees and logs as screens from behind which they fired as they retreated. Hays and his Rangers rode straight through their camp, shooting right and left as they flushed the warriors. Those who retreated in an orderly manner converted the panic into a short but sharp running fight. A warrior ambushed a Ranger, but a charge drove the sharpshooter from cover and killed him.

The remaining Indians were driven into the stream. As it was shallow, they forded it with ease and fled from the sight of the Rangers, who stopped at the bank. In checking losses, Hays found two of his number dead and five wounded; the Indians had lost five. Not a Ranger had seen the girl. This fact created more excitement among them than the most hotly contested part of the conflict.

"Boys," said Hays, "we will find that girl or remain on the warpath until we die of old age."

After searching around the camp, they discovered her dying among some trees just outside the open battleground. The Comanches had murdered her when they could not take her along with them.

Hays asked for suggestions as to where to bury her. Some of the men were crying; others walked a few paces apart, and, with heads bared, stood staring out over the countryside. Finally, "It was decided to . . . bury her on the loftiest peak of the precipice, where . . . the gurgling waters of the Llano . . . far below, could chant her requiem through all coming time." [22] The burial over, Hays swung into his saddle and gave the familiar gesture for column formation. The usually jovial Rangers fell into line silently.

ROAD TO MONTERREY

WHEN Hays arrived at camp with his detachment of Rangers on March 18, 1846, following the fight at Paint Rock, the term of enlistment of his men was expiring. Next day both companies disbanded. Though Gillespie organized a company from the discharged men for a three months' period, Hays returned to his headquarters at San Antonio.

Here he learned that General Taylor's army was advancing to the Rio Grande, for not until the United States saw that war was inevitable was Taylor ordered to move below the Nueces.[1] His new position opposite Matamoros became excuse for an incident on the part of Mexico.

Already General Mariano Arista, in command at Matamoros, had instructions to attack the Americans. On April 24 he sent General A. Torrejón across the Rio Grande with sixteen hundred troops and announced that hostilities had begun. Next day members of this force killed or wounded and captured Captain S. B. Thornton's reconnoitering detachment of sixty dragoons. Taylor reported that hostilities "may now be considered as commenced." [2] He called upon the governor of Texas for four regiments—two to serve as infantry, and two to be mounted.

As Hays's veteran Rangers and many of their friends had urged him to organize a regiment if war were declared, even before Taylor's appeal, he decided to go to Austin to discuss the matter with Governor J. P. Henderson. Henderson approved. Hays, in company with Sam Walker, then rode from Austin to Washington-on-the-Brazos with the idea of contacting former Rangers, whom he preferred as recruits.

The people of Brenham welcomed the two Rangers with appropriate festivities. They were escorted to a beautiful grove where John Wilkins, Sr., made an address in which the Major's career was lauded and his project was approved. After the program there was a barbecue, and in the evening, a gay ball.

Next morning Hays and Walker rode eastward, visiting a few towns, and began to hear reports of intentions of the Mexicans to sever Taylor's line of communications. Hays decided to hurry back to San Antonio, and Walker rode to offer his services to Taylor.

While inspecting a company of Rangers in San Antonio, Hays learned that Susan Calvert was also there, visiting her cousin Elizabeth, Mrs. W. I. Riddle. Straight to Mrs. Riddle's home a-courting he went. Susan had grown with the passing days. She was at the winsome age of seventeen, pretty, charming, and gracious. Her father was a descendant of the Maryland Calverts of Lord Baltimore lineage; her mother was the former Priscilla Smithers of Virginia. In the Calvert family were six children— James, Samuel, Katherine, Susan, Bettie, and Mattie—who with their parents and their few slaves had migrated to Texas in 1842. These people reminded Hays of his mother and father and the gentle Little Cedar Lick folk.

Hays was known as a bashful man when he was being complimented, but his bashfulness was not such that he ever appeared awkward or timid. The sunny days of early spring now gave an excuse to transfer his wooing from the parlor to the outdoors where only one pair of ears could hear the sallies of the ardent leader of light cavalry as he wooed the lovely Susan.

Mrs. Riddle, inspired by the prospect of having the young officer in the family, gave a farewell ball for the Rangers. Already the Major had declared his intentions and, likely assisted by the historic surroundings, the moonlight, and the soft notes of Elizabeth Riddle's piano, was successful in persuading Susan to become his bride. But his stay in gay San Antonio came abruptly to an end; military duties demanded his return to Austin. He was inspecting a company of Rangers when the legislature granted the governor leave to command troops to be mustered by Federal order.

While the governor recruited his infantry, Hays resigned his position as commander of frontier defense and labored at assembling light cavalry. He chose mostly Westerners who were experienced Indian and Mexican fighters and others who were attracted undoubtedly by the prospect of adventure under his leadership.³ He refused applicants who shrank from privations, shivered when drenched with deluging rains, or shook with chattering teeth from sleeping under a dripping sky in a pool of water fanned by an icy norther. Grumblers about mud, sand, ice, or rocks were likewise rejected. Denial was also given anyone who blanched at accounts of tarantulas in his blankets—if he had blankets— or flinched at red ants, centipedes, or scorpions in his clothes or at a rattler coiled to sleep on his chest. Ability to swim skillfully, ride a bucking horse, wield a knife, and throw off fevers was taken for granted.

Louis Haller clerked in a store in San Antonio in 1846. He bought a good horse, a brace of pistols, a long knife, and rode out to the camp of the Rangers to enlist. The first man he met near the tents was currying a horse. Louis asked him if he could see Major Hays. The Ranger walked over to a tent and called out, "Another one, Jack!" When Hays, who was in conference with one of his captains, appeared, he was fully armed. Haller said, "Major, I'd like to join your Rangers."

Hays looked Louis straight in the eye for a moment, said nothing, then walked slowly around rider and mount. "Come with me!" he invited. Followed by Haller on horseback, he walked rapidly a hundred yards beyond the camp, and pointing toward two trees about three hundred yards away, said: "Jump your horse into a run, pull your pistols as you go, and put a ball into the first tree as you pass it. Circle your running horse beyond the second tree, and shoot into its trunk as you come back."

The Major watched Haller spur his horse into full speed and then draw both pistols—one with each hand—from his belt. As the dry turf was thick, the running horse made little noise. When Haller reached the first tree, he fired the pistol in his right hand. Hays watched the dust fly from the grass beyond the tree as the bullet struck. Narrowly circling his horse, Haller charged back toward the last tree, thrusting his empty pistol into his belt and shifting the gun from his left hand to his right. Even with the tree, Haller fired, and Hays saw a twig fall from another tree several yards away. Louis raced past Hays, pulled up his horse and rode slowly back to the Major and dismounted.

Hays said kindly, "You ride fairly well, but you can't shoot."

"I could do better with that fine rifle of yours, Major," Haller explained.

"Would you like to shoot it?" asked Hays.

"I sure would!" answered Haller.

"Try for those trees again," suggested Hays. Haller aimed deliberately and thudded a bullet into each tree.

"You're a good enough standing shot," said Hays. "Your horse is all right. And I think you're a brave man. Still . . ."

As Major Hays's voice halted, he faced about and motioned toward the tents. With silence between them and Haller leading his horse by the reins, they walked slowly to the camp. Hays silently shook hands with Louis, who climbed on his horse and headed back toward San Antonio. A few weeks later when Hays and his men rode eastward to join other recruits for his regiment, Haller was not along.

Some of Hays's former Rangers traveled three or four hundred miles to meet him at the rendezvous selected for organization and there again signed for service with him. Hays was elected colonel without opposition; Samuel H. Walker, lieutenant colonel; and Michael H. Chevaille, major.[4] The unit was officially designated as the First Regiment Texas Mounted Volunteers, but was known popularly as Hays's Texas Rangers.

Hays's regiment reported to Taylor by companies or as individuals. Walker had already reported, and Ben McCulloch arrived three weeks later. Gillespie's company was marching from San Antonio and was not expected until July. Hays permitted McCulloch's and Gillespie's companies to be assigned to detached service with the understanding that they would rejoin him later. Several days were spent at Corpus Christi and Point Isabel in securing equipment,[5] including the army-size Colt revolvers with extra cylinders for each man. Wagons and camp equipage were also issued, but the men refused army uniforms. In late July, they marched to Fort Brown and from there moved to Matamoros and encamped nearby on August 2.[6] Meanwhile, Hays had received his commission as colonel.

When Hays learned that tents could be secured at Burrita, he sent a detail for them, because he did not know how long he might be camped near Matamoros.[7] Previously no tents had been available, but the Rangers had not complained.

In Matamoros Hays's men had a brief respite from drill. Some attended the theater, where the volunteers stared at them standing quietly in the lobby before going to their seats. Holding rifles, carrying holstered revolvers, with pistols and knives in their belts, and some also wearing swords, the Rangers attracted curious attention.[8] In turn, the Texans directed their glances at the regulars who wore enough color to provoke speculation among the frontiersmen about how the hues would appear through a rifle sight. Frequently they mused upon the drunken volunteers who had succumbed to pulque before earning the right to a celebration.

Hays was charged with "the communication of the policy of the Government, the ascertainment of the operations of the army of the enemy, as well as the feeling of the people, and the cutting off, capturing, or destroying all armed parties."[9] His orders instructed him to march immediately to San Fernando, one hundred and thirty miles southwest of Matamoros, and then in a circuitous course to join the main army which would be en route to Monterrey.

A few volunteers from the Louisiana area were added last to Hays's command. F. A. Lumsden of the *Picayune*, with Hays, wrote from Matamoros on August 5: "Gen. Taylor, it seems, intends giving the Rangers a chance on their own hook to get into a scrape and then get out of it as best they may. The regiment, I learn, is about 700 strong."[10] Taylor knew there were two routes to Monterrey: one by the Rio Grande and the San Juan; the other by way of Linares, which was the route of the retreating Mexicans. The China or "Linares route was impracticable, lacking in subsistence and water . . . impracticable in either wet weather or in drought."[11] "Old Rough and Ready" must be sure that the enemy did not lurk around China!

General King said: "He [Hays] and his officers and men were not only the eyes and ears of General Taylor's army, but its right and left arms as well." [12] This scouting march alone that Hays now was to do could have been considered a task for a second army. Taylor, trying to move his army, urgently needed mules. Hays's reputation plus his proximity saved the general from a predicament. As Henry Whiting, assistant quartermaster general, wrote from Matamoros: ". . . the mules can be had only of the Mexicans. I have . . . called on the alcaldes to assist us. . . . This call might have been ineffectual, had not a Texan mounted regiment (Colonel Hays's) been moving into the quarter whence we expect these mules. . . . In two or three weeks I hope . . . to restore our means of transportation . . . on which so much depends." [13] Texas Rangers were indeed effective mule buyers, though the quartermasters paid for them and received the general's plaudits.

Messengers from the municipal authorities came to Hays's column when it was six miles from San Fernando. They declared there would be no opposition to his entrance, but begged that he would spare the property of the citizens. Hays, replying that he would talk to the alcalde, detained the couriers because he proposed to camp near town and did not care to have the strength of his force known. He then instructed the officer of the guard to throw a picket line in the direction of the town. Just before dawn an armed rider moved between two pickets and rode toward the Colonel's tent. As guards attempted to seize him, he spurred away. One of the guards fired a shot at the horse and another at the rider. The horse fell dead; hoofbeats were heard drumming away into the darkness. If the unknown horsemen were spies, "they didn't catch Hays's men napping— nor will they be apt to," reported Lumsden.[14]

Early next morning the order was given to break camp. An advance guard was sent through the streets while the Colonel led the main column beyond the outskirts and gave instructions for encampment. Troops had left the preceding afternoon.

In the interview with the alcalde, after delivering a proclamation from General Taylor, Hays said he had come to make war only against soldiers. This announced policy of occupation tremendously relieved the numerous onlookers. It was evident that the populace had feared the worst from "Captain Jack." Most of the doors of the business houses had been secured, business had been suspended, and the few people visible were peeping out through the barred windows of their homes.[15] Faces registered an admixture of fear and hatred. Hays's kindness gained at least temporary rewards, for several of the men and officers were invited to billet in pleasant aristocratic Mexican homes and the alcalde dispatched a few servants to assist at the officers' mess in camp.

After three days, the regiment resumed its detour in search for the enemy. This so-called "route to China" wound along the very edges of yawning precipices. Often chaparral and prickly pear narrowed the trail until the men could barely squeeze through in single file, while overhead thorns and inter-woven brambles forced them to stoop to retain their hats. Occasionally Hays would hear that troops were at a place nearby, but only children, women, and a few old men ever were to be seen. A great portion of the one hundred and fifty mile march from San Fernando to China was through such an arid region that a few of the animals became exhausted and had to be left. China, located midway on one of the two roads from Camargo to Monterrey, had a population of two thousand people, only a few of whom emerged to be seen on balconies or upon housetops when Hays arrived. Encampment was made because Hays wished to establish communication with Taylor before rejoining him. Already the first units of Taylor's advancing army were at Cerralvo, northwest of China across the San Juan Valley. Hays thought as the enemy was concentrating at Monterrey, that battle would not be offered north of that city.

While the troops were bivouacked one night, a horse thief crawled up to where the animals were picketed and stole three good horses. Hays decided to make an example of him. He was captured, tried, and shot after he had confessed.

Hays instructed Walker to rest the force two days and then

to make camp upon the San Juan River while he himself took twenty men and descended the river to Camargo to report to Taylor. Taylor was tremendously interested in Hays's report and began to accelerate the movement of his army. He requested the Colonel to urge those whose enlistment was expiring to remain in service, since he had only a few companies of regular cavalry. Hays reassured him that his command was ready for further orders and knew the enemy was at Monterrey.

Among Ben McCulloch's men at Camargo who had never seen the commander of their regiment was Samuel C. Reid, who had resigned as adjutant of a Louisiana regiment to enlist as a private in McCulloch's company. Reid recorded a description of Hays as he saw him on August 26:

We had heard so much of Colonel Hays that we were anxious to be introduced to the commander of our regiment. The quarters of Lieutenant Forbes Britton, commissary of subsistence, was at that time the general rendezvous of all officers. . . . We saw a group of gentlemen sitting around, among whom were Gen. Lamar, Gov. Henderson. . . . we tried to single out the celebrated partisan chief, and were much surprised when we were presented to a delicate looking young man, of about five feet eight inches in stature, and was told that he was our colonel.

He was dressed very plainly, and wore a thin jacket, with the usual Texan hat, broad-brimmed with a round top, and loose open collar, with a black handkerchief tied negligently around his neck. He had dark brown hair, a large and brilliant hazel eye, which is restless in conversation and speaks a language of its own not to be mistaken, and very prominent and heavy arched eyebrows. His broad deep forehead is well developed; he has a Roman nose, with a finely curved nostril; a large mouth, with the corners tending downwards; a short upper lip, while the under one projects slightly, indicative of great firmness and determination. He is naturally of a fair complexion, but from long exposure on the frontier, has become dark and weather-beaten. He has rather a thoughtful and careworn expression; from the constant exercise of his faculties and his long acquaintance with dangers and difficulties; the responsibilities of a commander, have given an habitual frown when his features are in repose. He wears no whiskers, which gives him a still more youthful appearance . . . his manners are bland and very prepossessing, from his extreme modesty. . . .

. . . So great is his reputation among the Mexicans that he is everywhere

[133]

known as "Captain Jack." Notwithstanding his rigid discipline, for his word is law among his men, he is a bland and pleasant companion when off duty, and the men familiarly call him "Jack," though there is that about the man which prevents one from taking the slightest liberty with him.[16]

Hays was directed to rejoin Taylor at Marin on September 17 after scouting from China to the west of Cadereyta, and then south of Monterrey. This was the southern route from Camargo to Monterrey, but there was little water on it. After passing through Cadereyta, Hays would complete a semicircular movement by marching near to Monterrey and thence to Marin. Hays's maneuver not only required him to prevent the enemy from making an attack from the south upon Taylor's rear but also assigned him to a position in front of the slower moving army.[17]

Hays marched his command from a crossing on the San Juan and swung along east parallel to that stream. When he had only two days in which to complete a march of one hundred miles, some of the men wondered why he led them only thirty miles the first day and encamped several miles below Cadereyta. Even Adjutant Harper speculated upon the reasons for leaving seventy miles to be covered the last day. Harper, proud of their position nearest Monterrey but worried at the thought of losing it, fretted. Not only did Hays lead the regiment to keep its date, but he also had an extra hour's report to give General Taylor.

Next morning further orders placed Hays's Rangers in advance of all forces.[18] The companies of Gillespie and McCulloch were reattached to Hays's regiment, which rode the length of the army during the day in a screen for the flank nearest the enemy.[19] Encampment was made seven miles from Monterrey.

At sunrise General Taylor, accompanied by members of his staff, marched with the mounted troops. Gillespie's company, followed by the remainder of Hays's Rangers, led the entire column. Hays's regiment rode to within about three-fourths of a mile of Monterrey by approximately nine o'clock.

Taylor and his companions assembled at the head of the column. The steeple of the cathedral could be seen in the lovely valley which surrounded it. Silent chaparral, fields of corn, sugar cane, and fruit trees added to the sense of repose. While all were admiring the beautiful setting, a bugle blared in the town and a regiment of Mexican lancers rode out.

Hays ordered his men to form sections of five and prepare to charge. The bugler signaled the advance; the Rangers moved toward the lancers at a brisk trot. The lancers suddenly wheeled and retreated, placing them too far to be charged. Hays, suspecting a ruse to entice him within cannon shot, halted his force. At this instant a cannon boomed and a ball fell in front of them. A second one whistled over their heads, and spent balls struck near.[20] Round shot and shells belched rapidly from the black fort or citadel. Hays ordered the Rangers to fall back out of range, and Taylor and his staff already were countermarching.

General Taylor now directed that the army encamp in a large grove of trees at Santo Domingo, about two miles from Monterrey. The troops called this beautiful camping ground Walnut Springs. Under various pretenses many men later walked or rode to the hill midway between Walnut Springs and Monterrey. Some of them strolled far down the height in their eagerness to "see that as yet unseen biped, a Mexican soldier." [21] Among the onlookers were numerous Rangers on their fleet horses. Without orders and organization, these Rangers began to scour the plain. They obviously were challenging the fire of the black fort, which at intervals threw a shot at them without doing any injury. "Like boys at play . . . these fearless horsemen, in a spirit of boastful rivalry, vied with each other in approaching the very edge of danger. Riding singly and rapidly, they swept around the plain under the walls, each one in a wider and more perilous circle than his predecessor . . . the Mexicans might as well have attempted to bring skimming swallows down as those racing daredevils." [22]

Monterrey was built upon a plain on the northern side of the San Juan River. East and west the town was a mile long and north and south, a half mile wide. Hedging the city on the south and east was the Santa Catarina River. Streets were regular, and the buildings were of hewn stone. Spurs of the Sierra Madre Mountains crept in close to the city and limited the plain, which opened to the north, whence the army had approached. The main road from the Rio Grande to Mexico City passed through the southern portion of the town and thence to Saltillo. General Ampudia now had more than 7,300 men and officers in the place.

Less than a mile from the main plaza and to the right of the road from Monterrey to Saltillo was Independence Hill, halfway to the top of which was a redoubt called La Libertad. Back of and above this battery was a large stone building, the Bishop's Palace. About three hundred yards beyond the Palace, which stood midway up the ridge, the height gave way to a sharp peak. Fort Independence, a sandbag redoubt, crowned the summit which bristled with artillery and infantry. Six hundred yards south, across the Saltillo highway and Santa Catarina River, was Federation Ridge. To the east was Fort El Soldado, defended by two nine-pounders. It was all too evident that "the troops selected to storm them were generally regarded as *enfants perdus.*" [23]

A network of such strong defense had not been anticipated. If the troops should penetrate the city, it would be a bloody and likely losing conflict. They would find every street barricaded and every low, flat roof transformed by sandbags into ramparts from which Mexican infantry could rain down destruction on the attacking Americans. General Taylor could muster only a total of 6,230 troops, less than half of whom were regulars. He had no battering train and not enough field artillery. He had completely underestimated the Mexican opposition.[24]

XII

SLIPPERY STREETS

SHORTLY after noon next day, Sunday, the twentieth of
September, 1846, Hays led "by fives" two hundred and fifty
picked men across the Marin road to some chaparral. General
W. J. Worth's Division, totaling two thousand, followed Hays.
Worth, who had requested that Hays's force be added, was
ordered to turn Independence Hill, occupy the Saltillo highway,
cut off supplies and reinforcements, and, if practicable, secure
the defenses in the western area of the city.[1] With Hays riding
at the head of the column, the division moved down the Marin
road and then off to the right. To many thoughtful men among
the remainder of the army it seemed the height of rashness to
do a flank march with the enemy watching, and pass by the
defenses at that entrenched army's feet.

Hays led the column north of the citadel in a wide detour to
the right in such a direction that Worth would be able to attack
the opposite side of the town. "A Mexican prisoner, with a
hempen cravat around his neck, was led by the Texans as a
guide." [2] Through the cornfields, where the fine tassels brushed
the full beards and handlebar mustaches of the Rangers, and into
the chaparral, the Colonel slowly advanced.

When Hays rounded a spur of a hill to his right, he brought
his men close to the redoubt on the toe of Independence Hill.
Now on the Topo Road, they could see troops hurrying along
the ridge from the Bishop's Palace to the redoubt, the point
nearest the road. The Colonel halted his command and sent
some pickets forward while he and Captain McCulloch climbed
the hill to reconnoiter. A few minutes later they were joined
by Worth and members of his staff. They saw American troops
at the opposite end of the town being displayed as a menace,
for Taylor had observed the Mexican reinforcements hastening
toward Independence Hill.

[137]

After the officers had descended, Hays selected a second detachment of scouts and rode on with General Worth and Colonel P. F. Smith. The battalion was to follow slowly and be ready for any emergency! Upon a trail leading to the Saltillo road Hays combined the two scouting forces, consisting of thirty-five men. Near the highway they were fired upon by a split ambush while the battery of Independence Hill added a deluge of shells which fell short. Then a cavalry detachment approached. Seeing that he was heavily outnumbered and in danger of being cut off from his main column, Hays ordered a retreat.

This brought Mexican lancers forward rapidly. One of Hays's men had his horse killed under him, but the rider struck the ground on his feet and stood over its body firing deliberately at the charging horsemen. Lieutenant John McMullin, seeing the boy's predicament, raced back in the face of almost sure death and swung the valiant Ranger up behind him while the lead was whistling close.[3] After Hays had escorted the general to the column, he led his Rangers in a charge which scattered the lancers, and then they poured such a strong fire into the other two forces that they retreated. Not a Texan was wounded. As it was sunset Hays bivouacked in a corral adjacent to the San Jeronimo rancho. Before they could post guards or had unsaddled, a burst of fire came from the enemy, hidden on a hill to the right.[4] Hays placed a portion of his men behind a fence, and then led three companies in a slashing revolver charge. One dead Mexican was found, and several who were seen to fall could not be located in the increasing darkness. A Ranger was wounded, and several horses were injured.

Hays's men had no food, coats, or blankets, and now the rain began to pour heavily. When General Taylor had been asked on the twentieth about rations, he had merely replied that "they'll find something over there." A few Rangers foraged some pigs and chickens, but when fires were lighted to barbecue the meat, cannon on the hill opened fire, and the coals had to be extinguished. Some unshelled corn was found, and the Rangers munched that. As the Texans slept on the saturated ground, hungry, wet, and cold, they awoke at the slightest noise and grasped their rifles.[5]

Worth, who had halted for the night just beyond range of the battery of Independence Hill, sent a note to Taylor suggesting a strong diversion against the eastern end of the city to divert the attention of the enemy. This note arrived early in the morning of Monday, the twenty-first, and was in accord with Taylor's intentions.

Before dawn of the same morning, Hays and his Rangers were in the saddle. With many nodding as they rode, the force moved toward the Saltillo road. If the enemy were up and about in an effort to attack Worth's camp to the rear, this advance would reveal it. Behind them came Captain C. F. Smith's light infantry. They had ridden over a mile and were half that distance ahead of Smith's infantry when the Colonel halted them near the Saltillo road. He had decided to wait for daylight. The column moved to one side of the road, and the men dismounted. Some sat and instantly were asleep; others groomed their horses or checked their equipment. Dawn appeared and with it a regiment of lancers, the two forces discovering each other simultaneously.

The Mexican colonel halted his men and began to form them into line. Each cavalryman had a pennon waving from his lance. "They were good horsemen, mounted on lively steeds, and made the most beautiful spectacle," wrote Sergeant Buck Barry, "of mounted men I ever expect to see."[6] Over two hundred yards away, their well-executed movement and equipment created very little noise. The silence was so noticeable that the Rangers could hear their companions' hurried saddling. Hays saw that some of his boys were barely awake and others were occupied with tightening girths. He coolly told one of the captains to get the men ready, then rode slowly toward the lancers.

Hays had a saber in his hand. When he had covered almost half the distance, he bowed to the Mexican officer and in Spanish challenged him to a duel midway between the opposing forces. The Mexican colonel doffed his headgear, bowed his acceptance and then began divesting his horse of encumbrances. The Rangers stared at Hays; they knew he was not skilled with the saber. They noticed he wore six-shooters and was warming up his horse by reining him in tiny circles as he rode back half the distance to his men. He had lost his hat the night before and was wearing a bandanna for a headdress.

The lancer colonel began brandishing a saber. Seeing that his antagonist was ready, Hays walked his mount toward him. The Mexican's horse "seemed to dance rather than prance" as his gallant master rode to meet the Ranger. Parched grass almost muffled the hoofbeats. When the two officers were about forty yards apart, the lancer, standing in his stirrups and with his long saber in rest, charged. Hays suddenly swayed to the right and, dropping the saber, snatched a revolver as he swung far over and fired under his horse's neck. The heavy ball knocked the lancer from his saddle, and he struck the ground—dead. His saber clattered. Hays reined his running horse in a quarter-circle and spurred back toward his men, shouting as he came: "Dismount! Get behind your horses!" And as his horse bore him through the line, he yelled, "Here they come, boys! Give 'em hell!" [7]

"They charged us," wrote Sergeant Barry, "like mad hornets. The Colonel's . . . order saved us much blood. By the time, and even before all were dismounted, they were among us. They fought through our line, formed in our rear and charged through the line again, formed in our front and charged through our line a third time. I have never called a Mexican a coward since.

"They left many of their dead among us. We had only one man killed, but many wounded. They would have ruined us if we had not dismounted. We killed about eighty, but we should have done better, as we only had to shoot them down but a few feet from behind our horses. We had shot our muzzle-loading guns empty, and they had charged us so fast that we had no time to load again." [8] Sergeant Barry could have added that many of the Rangers lacked Colt's revolvers because not enough of them were available. Hays's report only said, ". . . we discovered the enemy's advance, which we drove back to their main body." [9]

Hays learned the enemy was advancing to prevent the Americans from securing the Saltillo road. He dismounted five companies and directed Acklin's men to hide in a cornfield on the left, while the other four were posted in gullies or behind a fence. Every fifth man was ordered to the rear with the horses. McCulloch's company was to move to the right, and feign a retreat if attacked. The fifteen hundred Mexicans did not seem to comprehend this movement. Their two regiments of cavalry charged McCulloch furiously. He retired as planned. After firing their escopetas, the Mexicans raced past Hays's ambush with their lances leveled at the apparently yielding men of McCulloch; [10] whereupon Green's company opened fire. From a distance of ten to twenty yards, the other companies poured in their lead.

McCulloch's men counterattacked and numerous desperate fights between individuals occurred. Jim Freaner, a recent recruit and formerly of the New Orleans *Delta*, was unhorsed by a lancer. He rose from the ground with revolver in hand and shot his foe out of the saddle; then he seized the reins of the fallen man's horse, mounted, and sought another opponent. After the battle, "Mr. Freaner of the *Delta*" was dubbed "Mustang" by his companions.[11] With five companies dismounted and McCulloch's in the saddle, Hays's men advanced upon the wavering enemy. As they retreated toward the Saltillo road, McCulloch pursued them.

Hays lost one man and had seven wounded. The enemy loss in killed and wounded was approximately one hundred. Worth was about half a mile behind and coming up fast when the encounter ended. The general was "much pleased with the skill displayed by the Rangers in this engagement, and pronounced it a beautiful maneuver." [12]

Now reports of artillery and musketry in the lower parts of the city indicated Taylor was attacking there, the Tenería redoubt and the northerly side of town east of the bridge being his first objective. Hundreds of Brigadier Generals D. E. Twigg's regulars and J. A. Quitman's volunteers hurled themselves against the city throughout the day. Other units joined them, and all suffered heavy losses. But day's end saw the Americans retreat from all of Monterrey except the Tenería redoubt and a few adjacent buildings. Heavy rain plus the guns of El Diablo made garrisoning the Tenería a disagreeable night's task.

Meanwhile, Worth ordered the occupation of the Saltillo road and posted artillery at its junction with the Topo road. A large force of Mexican infantry was stationed at the foot of Independence Hill. The Rangers had hitched their horses during this movement of the American infantry and artillery and were waiting for the next assignment.

When Hays's remaining companies had arrived, he deployed the regiment to the right as skirmishers and led them in single file through a cornfield for three hundred yards. When he came to the fence along the roadside, he placed them behind it. Hardly were they settled when a couple of concealed heavy guns on Federation Hill, which lay across the Saltillo road and to their right, opened fire upon them with roundshot. The Colonel ordered one of the younger boys to climb a tree and observe the movement of the Mexican infantry. As the enemy batteries began knocking limbs from the trees, the boy waited for only a few minutes before asking if he should descend from his perch.

"No, sir," answered Hays, "wait for orders." A few minutes later the regiment was moved to a new position. Off the regiment started; then someone reminded the Colonel that the boy in the tree was being left. Hays so regretted his inadvertence that he ran back to the tree and called, "Where are the Mexicans now?"

"Going back up the hill," answered the boy.

"Well, then, hadn't you better come down?" asked Hays.

"I don't know," the Ranger replied. "I am waiting for orders."

"Then I order you down," Hays said. And the observer, who by now recognized his commander, scrambled down hastily.[13]

Worth was out of communication with the main army seven miles away and was being shelled when in range of Mexican troops. There was always the possibility, too, that the enemy would advance up the Saltillo road and reinforcements would arrive from the south to catch him between their lines. This situation impelled him to attack at once. But he held a council to determine whether to risk the heavy losses involved by attacking Federation Hill, crowned by a fort and a redoubt which were the keys to unlock Monterrey. Could it be stormed successfully? When Hays was asked for his opinion, he answered: "It can be done. In my opinion, the Western Regiment can take it." [14] After the Colonel's quiet assurance, the others readily agreed that the assault should be made.

General Worth's plans called for the storming of the redoubt and the capturing of Fort Soldado on the opposite end of the same ridge. He placed Captain C. F. Smith in charge of two hundred men, then conferred with Hays, who ordered Chevaille to take three hundred men and act in conjunction with Smith.[15]

After Chevaille's force had crossed the river and engaged the enemy, Worth decided to take no risk of failure; therefore he requested Hays to lead in person a detachment to support the capture of the hill. The Colonel selected one hundred men and led them in single file through the cane and cornfields. When their advance was discovered, the artillery from Federation Hill opened fire with grape and roundshot. The Rangers slid down the rocky banks, plunged into the swift river, and began slipping and stumbling on the loose stones as they crossed. The Santa Catarina's current swept some from their feet. The enemy got the range, and bullets and grapeshot boiled the water, wetting the troops on heads and shoulders. Hays led his Rangers up the bank and into the chaparral in a hurried scramble to join Smith. Here they stopped for a moment to regain their wind and let some of the water drain from their clothing and shoes. Four hundred feet high, the peak just ahead looked impregnable. The forces now divided and struck from two sides. Despite the grapeshot which whined and shrieked above their heads, Hays led his men in an oblique movement and staged a surprise assault. Down the peak Mexicans fled as Gillespie's men scrambled over the top of Fort Soldado. Seconds later Hays and his reinforcements toppled over the wall of the fort and began firing at the falling, sliding enemy.

One of the men from the Fifth Infantry exclaimed to some

of the Rangers, "Well, boys, we almost beat you!" and he pulled a piece of chalk from his pocket and wrote on one of the cannon, "Texas Rangers and Fifth Infantry." Others staged a flag-raising exercise. Hays's losses were two killed and nine wounded.[16] The Texans declared that a Mexican always shut his eyes before he pulled the trigger. In no other manner could the incredibly small loss of the Rangers be explained.

Hays retired with his troops to the junction of the Topo and Saltillo roads and directed them to water and feed their horses. The men had not eaten in thirty-six hours; now some withheld an ear of corn from the horses to feed themselves. Then they lay down on the ground to sleep. It was about six o'clock.

At the request of Worth—who had sent a courier to Taylor —Hays, Colonel Duncan, and Captain Sanders made a reconnaissance of Independence Hill. They studied that part of the hill north of the Bishop's Palace.[17] Having secured Federation Hill, it was now imperative that Independence Hill must also be taken.

A violent storm and the closing in of darkness halted operations. But the general had plans for the night. He assigned Colonel Childs and Hays to lead a storming party up Independence Hill. Hays detached two hundred and fifty men from seven companies of his regiment and directed Walker to see that they were ready. The combined forces, numbering four hundred and sixty-five men, were to move at three o'clock in the morning.

Fatigue won over hunger and the torrential rain which swept gravel against some of the Rangers, who had not slept for three nights and had been riding and fighting almost continuously for nearly three days. When a stone rolled against a man, he would sit up, holding to his rifle, and doze again. A little food, a coat, or a blanket would have helped these shirtsleeved Rangers. Hays was not sleeping. He was up touching certain men on the shoulder, assembling them for conference. There was work he sought to do before he had to leave for Independence Hill. Only side arms were to be worn. It was a secret mission—secret now and later.

After midnight Hays led these men in Indian file from the camp. With the swirling water and darkness all about them, it was easy to get through his own pickets. Across the boggy corn-fields and toward Independence Hill, the little column moved. At the base of the hill, Hays reached back and checked the man behind him. The Colonel went down on his hands and knees in the mire while they waited for enemy pickets to be changed. After learning where two or three guards were stationed, they relaxed. Now they had only to wait until the new sentries became a little drowsy.

Hays walked forward very slowly, passed between two of the pickets, and led his file around behind one of them. The sentinel did not challenge. He was seized, prodded tenderly by a bowie knife held against his back, and was made to lead the Rangers to the next guard. In this manner the squad captured all the pickets near the base of that portion of Independence Hill which was to be scaled. The party hurried to camp with its prisoners. The Colonel was on schedule.

At three o'clock the sergeants awakened the storming force. The wind was still howling; it had turned cold and was raining. The order was: "No noise. Move forward!" In two columns the men filed from the camp, General Worth standing at the head of the columns uncovered until the last man had passed.

General Ampudia considered the peak to be unassailable, except on the eastern side, where it sloped toward the Bishop's Palace. Hays's report stated: "We reached the foot of the hill . . . undiscovered . . . the command was divided. Col. Childs and myself taking the right, Col. Walker and Maj. Vinton taking the left. . . . In this order we ascended the hill."

The almost vertical peak was believed to be eight hundred feet high.[18] As columns moved slowly, the soldiers climbed guardedly; overturned stones frequently went rolling down the mountain in silence, their noise deadened by the storm. Each time this happened the men paused, expecting some watchful sentinel to challenge or to roll large stones at them. Projecting crags were less difficult to ascend than the perpendicular ledges of rock. Fissures in these enabled the men to gain footholds.

Men shoved and dragged each other up the bluffs and pulled themselves upward by branches.

When dawn flashed, they were within one hundred yards of the redoubt on the crest. They were creeping for shelter to some large rocks, among which were clefts, when suddenly there was a report and bullets whistled over their heads, chipped the rocks, and cut their clothing. Not an answering shot was fired, as the men continued their advance among the large rocks.

During those last long yards from the summit, as the Rangers fanned out to right and left, Hays's voice rang out, "Give them hell!" The command was followed by the infantry's "Fire!" Muskets crashed and rifles cracked, but the Americans stood on the sandbags of the redoubt! Hays scrambled upon the wall, a pistol in one hand, a revolver in the other. Captain Gillespie stood upon the sandbags, in the act of jumping within, and staggered awkwardly from the thud of a bullet. Herman Thomas, a lad from Baltimore, fell at the base of the wall. But the men sprang over, grappling, stabbing, and smashing. Enemy survivors went leaping down the slant to the Bishop's Palace. As Hays put it: "They fled with great precipitation to the Castle."

The regulars grouped together, amid hearty cheers, and unfurled the Stars and Stripes to the morning breeze. The Rangers stood silent. Gillespie and Thomas had fought their last battles. Gillespie—educated, gallant, close friend of Hays—had pretended to be only slightly wounded and had waved his men on into the struggle when several sought to help him.

There was still much to be accomplished. Lieutenant Roland of Duncan's battery was bringing a disassembled howitzer from the main camp. The enemy had retreated with a piece of artillery and two six-pounders, which now laid a heavy fire upon the Americans from the Bishop's Palace.

As a precautionary measure, Hays's Rangers, Vinton's Company of "red-legged infantry," and Lieutenant James Longstreet's company of Eighth Infantry moved nearer the Palace and discouraged the enemy by picking off any who exposed themselves. Scott's company from the Fifth Infantry and Blanchard's Volunteers joined them later.

Hays wearied of the feints, sharpshooting duels, and cannonading between the strongholds. A participant in the battle wrote:

> Captain Vinton came over, and I heard Colonel Hays advise him of a plan to try and draw the Mexicans out of the Palace, and it was at once approved of. . . . Part of the force [Hays's] were to be concealed on the right of the ridge, and the balance [under Walker] were to take position on the left side . . . all to be hidden over the steep sides of the ridge. . . . the Mexicans could be seen forming by battalions in front of the Palace. . . .
> Captain Blanchard's company now advanced and fired. When the enemy advanced they [Blanchard's] retreated hastily back to our line, as had been arranged. The lancers rode boldly up the slope, followed by their infantry, eager to make an easy conquest. When they were close on to us, . . . Vinton's men and Blanchard's company formed a line across the ridge, and the two flanking parties [Hays's and Walker's] closed the gap completely across the ridge [behind the advancing enemy].[19]

At this juncture, the American infantry in front began firing, and the Rangers too commenced a deadly cross fire which decimated the lancers so fast that they raced back toward the Palace, and the infantry broke and ran in massed confusion. The enemy was, as Hays reported, "so vigorously pursued by our men that they were unable to regain the Castle and continued this retreat to the town, leaving us in possession of the works with four pieces of artillery and a large quantity of ammunition."

Inside the Palace the defenders began throwing down their arms and rushing about, "leaping from the windows and running from the rear of the Palace down the hill toward the city." [20] Many never reached their destination.

Taylor's men had cheered the sight of Worth's capture of Independence Hill on Tuesday, the twenty-second, and were greatly encouraged in the afternoon by seeing the American flag over the Bishop's Palace. But the day passed without any operations at the eastern end of the city to assist Worth. Taylor did not give Worth any new orders or arrange concerted action with him, though he knew Worth's division had completed all the work assigned it.

About four o'clock, with the infantry and artillery in charge of the Bishop's Palace, Hays took most of his Rangers back to the junction of the Saltillo and Topo roads. Their horses had been watered and fed by their comrades, but the men had only corn to eat: there was dry corn on the cob and, to the delight of many, green corn in the fields nearby. Some, however, could eat very little of the corn.

Many of the Rangers now had a captured serape in which to roll up for sleeping. A cold rain fell during the night, but those who had fought in the daytime did not heed it. As the boys rolled into their serapes, they began humming, "Cry, Vengeance for Texas—and God speed the right!"

All talked of what the morrow would bring. One of Hays's captains uttered a brief prayer on the matter: "O Lord, we are about to join battle with vast superior numbers of the enemy, and, Heavenly Father, we would mightily like for you to be on our side and help us; but if you can't do it, for Christ's sake don't go over to the Mexicans, but just lie low and keep dark, and you will see one of the d——est fights you ever saw in all your born days." [21]

Soon after daylight next morning, Wednesday, the 23rd, Hays took two companies and joined Major Brown in an excursion toward Santa Catarina Creek. There was a bridge on the Saltillo road some three miles to the south, over which the enemy might attempt to bring in supplies. Hays had waited several hours when a courier from Worth requested him to dismount his regiment to fight with the attacking force. "On the afternoon of the 23rd," wrote Hays in his report, "when Gen. Worth led his division from the Bishop's Palace into the city, I proceeded under his orders with my entire command (save about sixty men who were engaged in scouting and other special duties) consisting of about 400 men to the church where he had established his batteries. There[I] divided my command, Lt. Col. Walker, commanding the left wing, proceeded toward the enemy's batteries by Iturbide Street." [22]

Before noon, Worth had heard the roar of battle from Taylor's end of the town and judged that it meant a serious attack. The

sound Worth heard was made by Quitman's volunteers and
Colonel G. T. Wood's regiment of East Texas mounted volunteers, now dismounted, entering the city by advancing from
house to house until they reached a street only one square in
the rear of the main plaza. Yet Taylor withdrew Quitman's and
Wood's men to the outer works, stating they had been on duty
the previous night, and that he wished to plan a concerted attack with Worth.

Hays commanded Worth's right-hand column that proceeded down the Calle de Monterrey, the other main street of
the town, which became the Saltillo road beyond the city limits.
A glance at them justified the lines of the poet C. S. Hoffman:

> We were not many, we who stood
> Before the iron sleet that day;
> Yet many a gallant spirit would
> Give half his years if but he could
> Have been with us at Monterey.

In addition to the Texans, a part of the Seventh and Eighth
Infantry, the artillery battalion, and field batteries came into
the attack. [23]

While Hays was advancing near the river side of the city,
Walker and Childs were marching parallel, but Hays's street
soon bore to the right before entering the main plaza, while
Walker's ran straight and was heavily barricaded. Walker also
had to move between two rows of housetops that were manned
by defenders. Hays discovered that as he had fewer housetop fighters to oppose, he could be of great assistance to Walker
by picking off sharpshooters commanding his street.

Hays divided his men into a half dozen groups: one file he
placed against the buildings on both sides of his street; two files
were to work parallel to each other on the housetops on either
side; the two remaining detachments he ordered to proceed
through the open yards. This enabled him to combat street
barricades, fortified buildings and housetops, and to maintain
direct, cross, and sharpshooter fire. When men advanced, they
rushed, taking advantage of cover as much as possible.

At times the Hays battalion found holes in high yard walls cut there by the enemy to enable him to retreat. Often men moving along the right side of the street came to a defended building, where they were fired upon through loopholes in a strong door. They would halt and dive into a building next door, while their comrades across the street peppered the front door when a rifle barrel protruded. While restrained, they put their crowbar detail to breaking a hole through the wall between the buildings. Then they would take a six-inch shell with a three-second fuse, light it and drop it through the aperture, throwing themselves flat as they did so.[24] After the explosion had enlarged the opening, the men crawled through and "mopped up" inside. But sometimes it was "nothing strange for the muzzles of the Texans' and Mexicans' guns to clash together, both intending to shoot through the hole at the same time."[25]

Often the Rangers were in the lower story of a building while the enemy was in possession of the upper story and the roof. These defenders could usually be handled by an accurate pattern of cross fire from the roofs, or a combination of fire by those on the roof and the Rangers on the opposite side of the street below. If a street barricade proved a problem against the combined attack of the men on the street, in the yards, and on the roofs, then the house-to-house-through-the-walls method finally enabled the last group to gain a flank position. This failing, the other advancing column on the street parallel was signaled to bypass the barricade and then fire upon its rear.

"When the report of a Texas rifle was heard," wrote Sergeant Barry, "it was safe to bet a bullet had been bloodied." [26] A defender fought stubbornly and bravely, but if he showed a hand at a loophole, he became a cripple. Some of the Rangers watched the embrasures; when these darkened against the clear sky, rifles cracked, and light filled the embrasures again. If a Mexican raised his head above a parapet, a rifle ball pierced it. The well-aimed rifles finally drained the enemy's spirit of resistance.[27] By sundown Walker's men were within one block of the principal plaza. Hays's column occupied a like position on its street.

At twilight Hays received an order from Worth to return to camp to care for his horses. Hays left some men to assist in holding the gains of the afternoon and retired with the remainder of the column. On the way back to camp they took with them several head of cattle and sheep which they had captured after entering the city. No longer on the firing line the men were now thinking of eating. Walker also dispatched a detail to care for the horses—horses were all-important on the road to Mexico City.

Hays hurried a detail to Walnut Springs for the pack mules and cooking utensils. By the time this equipment had arrived, butchering had been done and fires were ready for cooking. Walker's men came up and ate. For most of the Rangers this was the second meal in four days; they had missed the last ten. Those still on the firing line did not eat until the next day. The Rangers now anticipated sleep, but the Colonel sent nearly all of them out on picket duty; the Saltillo road must not be open. [28]

Hays led one detachment of Rangers to the Santa Catarina. From this post he sent pickets down the road. After a couple of hours they rode in and reported the approach of fifty horsemen. It was decided to give them a check. Some men were placed behind a fence and others lay down in the road. When the enemy came within close range, Hays gave the signal to fire. While the Mexicans retreated, the Rangers mounted and followed carefully, finally firing a volley of shots at them. Five pack mules loaded with hard bread, several wounded, and five dead were found.

At midnight this detachment was relieved and returned to camp. But at three o'clock in the morning, they were awakened and were led into town to resume their places on the housetops. Some new positions were seized by quick rushes at an hour before dawn. Daylight witnessed the opening of concentrated firing by the Rangers and the infantry. A cannon at a street barricade of the enemy was fired one time, and seconds later not a man was alive to serve it.

By ten o'clock on Thursday, the 24th, the Rangers were in

position to prevent Mexican heads from bobbing above parapets of sandbags. The principal plaza and the streets leading to it, the cathedral, and the main highway were under their rifles. The enemy was trapped; American troops operating on the eastern side of the city now could be seen and heard. Suddenly the order came to cease fire.

Hays sat with his men from ten until five o'clock in the broiling sun, only eighty yards from the cathedral and within a few hours of securing an unconditional surrender. When Taylor agreed on an armistice and gave liberal terms of surrender to the city, Hays led his angry and disappointed Rangers back to camp. For the first night since the 19th all the men had a blanket for a bed. They were grateful for a night's sleep and for their tobacco chewing friends who dressed their wounds with fresh chews. [29] Next day Hays's regiment returned to their old camp site near the junction of the Topo and Saltillo roads. Taylor's loss in killed and wounded was approximately eight hundred, while Worth's, whose men advanced according to orders—nonhaphazardly—was about seventy.

General Worth issued an order on September 28 in which he said: "The General feels assured that every individual in the command unites with him in admiration of the distinguished gallantry of Colonel Hays and his noble band of volunteers. Hereafter they and we are brothers, and we can desire no better security of success than by their association." [30]

One day while awaiting the discharge of his Rangers from the army, Hays called at the home of Señor Don José Maria Gajar. A wealthy, intelligent Spaniard who had been ill-treated by Ampudia's forced "loans," Gajar had watched a column of the Rangers come down the street. "As they came near," Gajar said, "my heart almost failed me; for the Texans, with their coarse hickory shirts, and trousers confined by a leather strap to their hips, their slouched hats, and their sweat and powder-begrimed faces, certainly presented a most brigandish appearance! They came along, yelling like Indians, and discharging rifles at the Mexicans on the housetops. . . ." [31]

During the attack Gajar had kept open house. The men

showed their appreciation by not taking any of his valuable silverware and other articles that would have made prized souvenirs. Hays's call was a gracious acknowledgment of his generous gesture. [32]

Taylor began mustering out the Rangers on the last day of September. Food was scarce and inaction was at hand; some had already overstayed their period of enlistment, and the general knew where they were if he needed them again. He thanked Hays and the other officers personally and in his correspondence. [33]

Years after the temper of war had cooled, one veteran wrote: "I was with the regulars but . . . Had it not been for their [Hays's, McCulloch's] unerring rifles there is no doubt we would have been whipped at Monterey."[34] Chroniclers referred to Hays's column "charging on the guns which swept the slippery streets of Monterey," but the Colonel said "they were damn poor shots or not a mother's son of us could have got there."[35] Yet in November the New Orleans *Delta* affirmed "Modesty is the most remarkable trait of Hays. . . . Indeed, I question whether there is a man in Taylor's army who has so poor an opinion of the merits and services of Hays as he himself."

The men who rode with Hays knew him best. "There never lived a commander," stated the *Delta*, "more idolized by his men." Worth watched Hays's Rangers fight under various conditions and declared they were "the best light troops in the world."[36] Of Hays, he often said. "Jack Hays is the tallest man in the saddle in front of the enemy I ever saw."

WEDDING BELLS

GENERAL TAYLOR expressed his obligation to Hays and "his satisfaction with the efficient service rendered . . . particularly in the operations around Monterrey."[1] Hence Hays was somewhat embarrassed by a Ranger's shooting a lancer who was riding along a street. The Colonel was near and heard the report of the gun. He rushed into a building opposite where the lancer had fallen and found a single occupant, a Ranger. Hays asked him if a shot had been fired from that house. The soldier denied knowing anything about the shot. But Hays examined the fellow's revolver and promptly arrested him, charging that he was guilty or knew who was. He turned the man over to the custody of the proper military authorities.[2] The Texas troops neither tolerated nor defended atrocities of their own or other troops. [3]

After Hays had made preparations for departure, General Worth, the military governor, requested that the regiment appear at his headquarters. When the command was formed in front of the house, the general bade them farewell in a short speech of appreciation. Then he asked them to partake of wine with him. The men formed in line, passed alongside a huge table where they drank wine being poured for them, and slowly moved toward an exit. Worth, Hays, and their staffs stood near this door, and as the Rangers filed by, the General shook hands with each man. Sergeant J. B. Barry of Captain Eli Chandler's company chronicled that Worth told Hays: "It was the untiring, vigorous bravery, and unerring shots of your regiment that saved my division from defeat." [4]

Hays's departure was delayed by his official reports, but after a couple of weeks he and the remaining Rangers were ready to ride toward the Rio Grande. A major from Ohio who watched them go wrote: "Gifted with the intelligence and courage of backwoods hunters, well-mounted and skilled in arms, they were excellent light troops. Had they remained and given their whole attention to the guerrillas, they might have been ex-

ceedingly useful. . . . we saw them turn to the blood-bought
State they represented, with many good wishes and the hope
that all honest Mexicans were at a safe distance from their
path." [5]

This annotator could hardly have known that many of the
departing Rangers had been fighting for years some of these
same guerrillas who, before the war, were simply banditti invaders, nor that there were educated men among the Rangers
who also had the courage and intelligence of woodsmen and
hunters. The presence of Indians as depredators near their
homes was reason enough for them to return home. [6]

Hays's arrival in San Antonio generated an outburst of welcome. The people had read the statement of a New Orleans
officer: "In scaling heights, storming batteries, and clambering
over walls and housetops, the voice of the gallant Colonel, and
the reports of the unerring rifle of the Rangers, were ever
heard in the van. The courage and constancy, and subordination of this corps is the theme of admiration in the army." [7]

Innumerable letters from Taylor's camps, items in newspapers throughout the nation, and magazines sought to apprise
the American people of "who and what this famous 'Jack Hays
and his men' really are." Readers of the war news clamored for
more information concerning this unique regiment, "led by
such an officer." [8]

Now the most popular man in Texas and lauded throughout
the country, Hays could have claimed high political or military
honors. Instead, he accepted modestly the congratulations
pressed upon him and looked forward to retiring to private life.
Scarcely had he reached Texas before he was informed by
Governor Henderson that the government hoped he would
recruit another regiment.

The Colonel was en route to Mississippi on a business visit
and wrote from Houston to Major Chevaille, who had decided
to take a furlough:

> Sir: By authority vested in me by the Governor of this State,
> to raise and organize a regiment of mounted volunteers, to hold
> themselves in readiness to march to the U. S. Army, I hereby

authorize and appoint you to raise and organize the said regiment, as though I were present in person.[9]

Several days later Chevaille announced that he was at San Antonio, where he would receive companies of eighty men. The regiment was not to be called into the field for service unless the prospect of active hostilities became imminent.

On the morning of November 5, Hays and Sam Walker arrived at Galveston from Houston on board the steamer *Sabine*. The Galveston *Civilian* carried a lengthy, eulogistic article in which it stated the two Rangers were "distinguished before and since the beginning of the war between the United States and Mexico . . . and though in the morning of life, when honors most elate men, they wear their laurels as modestly as if unconscious of their existence."[10] The city authorities entertained them with a fine dinner followed by a ball.

Hays and Walker sailed to New Orleans, where the news of their coming had preceded them. The papers had narrated Hays's deeds of daring for a half dozen years. When the steamer docked, a crowd was present. As the conservative *Picayune* asserted: "The arrival of these gentlemen yesterday from Texas created a sensation throughout the city. . . . They were warmly greeted by thousands, and they will pardon us for saying we heard repeated exclamations of surprise that such brave hearts and authors of such bold deeds were found in gentlemen so unpretending in appearance and so totally free from assumption of manner or thought."[11]

The New Orleans authorities wished to tender them "some mark of public distinction," but Hays explained that Walker must hasten to Washington on business, while he was en route to a county nearby in Mississippi and thence must return hurriedly to see about his prospective regiment. This explanation afforded the reporters an opportunity to add that he probably would "draw from the city a large unmber of recruits, proud to serve under such a soldier—the hero of a hundred fights."[12]

In accepting General Ampudia's agreement to evacuate Monterey with a temporary cessation of hostilities, General Taylor had violated his orders. President Polk believed, "It will only enable the Mexican army to reorganize and make another stand." With Santa Anna now at the head of the military party in Mexico and apparently preparing for a determined war, more troops must be sent to Mexico. On November 23, 1846, Secretary of War Marcy wrote General Winfield Scott, the highest officer in the service, "to go to Mexico, take command there and set on foot a Gulf expedition." Veracruz was to be taken as the base and dominant place in the furthering of the campaign to conclude the war by marching on the capital. Taylor, who throughout the summer and fall of 1847 maintained his headquarters at Monterrey and then Matamoros, was to send every man he could spare to the Gulf coast, whence they would be forwarded to assist Scott in carrying through the Veracruz–Mexico City expedition.

Hays returned to San Antonio in December. On January 1, 1847, he conferred with Governor Henderson relative to his regiment. Hays was of the opinion that the President and the War Department would grant every reasonable request the volunteers might make. There was an intimation in the newspapers that prospects were uncertain as to whether crusty General Taylor would remember to discharge the volunteers when active operations ceased or would require them to serve for the duration of the war. There was, however, "no man around whom the Texans would rally with greater alacrity than Colonel Hays. His services have endeared him to the people." [13] There were still indications that recruits preferred to enlist for a definite period, say six or twelve months. [14]

Hays preferred experienced border-warfare men who had been at San Jacinto, Mier, or Monterrey. These now were slower to enlist because they had been in the service so long that they had neglected their civil business. Already, since annexation approximately a year before, one man in every six of legal age had served Texas in a campaign against Mexico. During the summer of 1846 Texas had three regiments in the field. If "the other states had been represented in one half that proportion," the war would have been terminated and no new troops would have been needed in 1847. [15]

When only enough recruits arrived at San Antonio to organize four companies, Hays discerned that a specific term of service would within a few days have secured the necessary frontiersmen. Wearied, therefore, with the delay, he went to Austin to confer with Governor Henderson. The governor had received news that about ten thousand Indians from various tribes west of the upper Rio Grande had come into Texas and had scattered themselves along the headwaters of the Colorado. Some of these intruders, whose numbers later were discovered to have been greatly exaggerated, were reported to be within eighty miles of Austin. Henderson became so uneasy that he wrote an urgent entreaty to the Secretary of War, requesting permission for Colonel Hays to raise a regiment of mounted troops for the protection of the frontier.

When Hays arrived at the governor's office, he outlined his desire to go to Washington to obtain a modification of the existing war enlistment instructions. Henderson mentioned his uneasiness about the frontier and the delay in conducting military affairs by correspondence; whereupon, Hays suggested his proposed mission to the capital should embrace a portrayal to President Polk and the War Department of the situation along the three frontiers of Texas. The governor agreed, and on February 18, 1847, he sent Hays as his personal representative on the mission. The Colonel sailed from Texas to New Orleans on the *Galveston,* and then proceeded to Washington by steamer and rail on the interior route.

Though Hays had some friends and acquaintances in Washington, the military reports and newspaper accounts of his achievements in Mexico had aroused discussion in various circles there. According to the Little Rock *Arkansas Banner* of April 14, "The appointment of Col. Hays formerly announced as Major of Infantry, had been withdrawn previous to his arrival, as no one acquainted with this veteran of a hundred fights and skirmishes would believe that he could be induced to enter the regular army at the expense of rank already attained by services of unparalleled hardships and danger." Now the Georgetown and the Washington press hailed his visit and purpose.

Hays's representations to the President and the War Department resulted in an order, issued on March 20, for him to raise the proposed regiment. He was directed to employ as many of the companies as he deemed essential along the Texas frontier and to use the others in ridding the lower Rio Grande country of guerrillas. The term of enlistment for service in the war should be one year.

In Washington it was talked openly that the Administration expected, as soon as feasible, to use Hays's skill below the Rio Grande. Taylor's line of communication, which he had left exposed to the enemy by his choice of position for his troops, was a matter of concern to Secretary Marcy. During Hays's stay in Washington, the Mexican guerrilla leaders made repeated attacks on Taylor's supply trains. Destroying or capturing the contents of 150 wagons, killing 100 wagoners and troops, these cavalry bands of Generals José Urrea and Antonio Canales cut off entirely for weeks Taylor's communication between Monterrey and Camargo. Canales, "the Chaparral Fox," boasted that he had killed 161 Americans during February, 1847. Colonel Samuel R. Curtis, senior officer on the Rio Grande and in command at Camargo, had dispatched a special messenger to Washington requesting fifty thousand volunteers. Curtis also appealed to Governor Henderson for volunteers and received an immediate response.

Since no obstacle to the accomplishment of his visit was presented, Hays felt that he had gained the time to look over Washington and to pay his respects to Mrs. James K. Polk before setting out for home. As an engineer, Hays admired the well-planned city, though its chief trade—politics—stifled his enthusiasm. Nor could the capital, he thought, match New Orleans, say, in population, gaiety, or historical interest. Willard's Hotel, where he stayed, was pretentious, but lacked the charm of the St. Charles.

When he called upon Sarah Childress Polk, the First Lady received him very graciously, inquired about his relatives in Tennessee, who were her old friends, and drew from him a portrayal of Susan, his fiancée. Then they talked of the approaching wedding of William Carey Jones of New Orleans and Eliza Preston Carrington Benton, daughter of Senator Thomas Hart Benton, to which ceremony Hays had received an invitation. Mrs. Polk suggested that since the President would leave the Bentons early for a conference, Hays should join them and be her escort.

Hays was at the White House a few minutes before eight on the evening of March 18. He was greeted cordially by the President, Mrs. Polk, and other ladies of the Presidential mansion. They all left at eight for the home of Senator Benton, where the wedding was to be held. Among the guests from Washington official society, Hays saw Secretary of the Treasury Robert. J. Walker and others whom he knew.

After the ceremony, President Polk "waited on the bride to the supper table," while Hays in the stately procession through the assemblage silently prepared to follow—for the only time in his life his social poise then threatened to forsake him—as "the escort of the mistress of the White House, the lady of President Polk." The guests had nearly ceased talking and had shifted to form an aisle, their attention first upon the bride. and the President, when Hays followed with Mrs. Polk. He was keenly aware of the focusing of a battery of eyes on him and the quietude which accompanied his automatic steps throughout the long walk to the dining room.

On March 21, Hays left Washington for Texas, taking the river route.[16]

Back at home, Hays began to enlist six months' volunteers for the purpose of resisting the peril feared by Curtis. By emphasizing the short period of enlistment, he was enabled to make rapid progress; meanwhile he dispatched Chevaille to report to Taylor with the men collected at San Antonio before Curtis's call was received.

Taylor ordered Chevaille to explore the country between China and Matamoros, and Chevaille soon reported that Urrea had left the region. After Chevaille's detachment had frightened the guerrillas away and had escorted important provision trains through the dangerous section, General Taylor reported nonchalantly to the adjutant general that escorts could now be reduced.[17]

Since Hays had returned from Monterrey, he was able to visit Susan more often. Still there were always numerous demands on his time, and the months passed along into 1847. At last a day was set for the wedding, the 29th of April. Ever an active youth in a world of army men and frontiersmen, this was— though he never talked of women and sex even in masculine company—the love of his life.

Months before, Hays had directed a carpenter in plans for the building of a house for his bride. It was in San Antonio's two hundred block on South Presa Street, the first two-story home there. He also had arranged his business so that in the event of his death all technicalities would be cleared in handling his lands. Three hundred and twenty acres of this land was located on the Frio River. The papers bearing on several other pieces of land were placed in the care of Judge Calvert and Susan for the duration of the war. His modest savings of money had been realized largely from some lands conveyed in Guadalupe County in 1845.

Only once during their period of engagement did the course of true love run a bit irregularly. This was caused by Susan's acceptance of an invitation by a young man to help gather flowers a few miles from town. Texas wild flowers in the spring were so beautiful and profuse that she could not resist. While they were plucking bluebonnets, Indians tried to capture them, and only their fast horses enabled the two to escape. The Colonel was not a little displeased at her disregard of his admonitions not to venture where the Indians might capture or murder her.[18]

On the day before the wedding, which was to be at the home of the bride's parents, Hays organized a small cavalcade of his San Antonio friends to ride to Seguin with him. Susan's cousin Mrs. Riddle, who had lost her husband and had remarried, was the only woman in the party. Chevaille and Acklin were along. Since friends from various communities were to be present, in addition to all Seguin and special guests from Austin, Houston, San Antonio, and Washington-on-the-Brazos, it was decided to have the ceremony read at the Magnolia Hotel. Even the most capacious room there, which provided the largest auditorium in the town, could not accommodate the attendance; the crowd overflowed into the street. All managed, however, to catch a glimpse of the handsome couple. The bride wore her mother's wedding dress, a beautiful gown of exquisite materials from Paris. The Reverend Doctor Anderson, a Presbyterian pastor,[19] read the ceremony before a bower of native flowers from her parents' and neighbors' gardens. The honeymoon was to be in San Antonio.

Next day a large escort of friends, who had come to the wedding and had remained overnight in Seguin, rode with the couple to San Antonio. At the Salado River numerous friends from that city, including fourteen carriages of ladies, met them. The San Antonians had a lunch spread, and, true to plans made with Chevaille, the newlyweds arrived on schedule. After the music, feasting, and toasts, the crowd filed into town.

Colonel Sam Sims, in command of the northern Texas frontier regiment, had formed his men in two facing ranks under the Alamo Plaza trees and awaited the coming of the wedding party. Hays and his bride alighted from their carriage and walked under the crossed rifles of the regiment and were saluted with military honors as they entered the Alamo gates. [20] Bells from every church within hearing joined with the town's alarm bell in chiming the joy of the occasion. After the day's festivities, the young couple went to the home of the Lockmars', on Soledad Street, because their house was not yet completed. Next evening the groom was host at a grand ball and supper which was, according to report, a courtesy of Hays's friends. Monsieur Guilbeau, the French consul, later gave a party that saw the beauty and chivalry of San Antonio welcome the Colonel and his bride. [21]

Hays expected to leave for Monterrey with his six months' volunteers at the end of two weeks. During this time he and Mrs. Hays were the recipients of many social courtesies from the Elliots and other gracious families of the city. It was also during these days that the Colonel arranged for his bride to remain with Mrs. Elliot Howard on Soledad Street during his absence. To counteract the softening effects of the numerous parties, the Hayses went for long buggy rides into the country. As they turned cityward, Hays would dismount and run alongside the fast-moving trotters for miles.[22] The Colonel wished to keep in condition to lead his men.

Hays's "Regiment of Texas Mounted Volunteers," which enlisted for six months in response to Colonel Curtis's cry of distress, left San Antonio for Monterrey on May 14. Unaware that Curtis had exaggerated Taylor's peril, Hays marched toward the Rio Grande.[23] He planned to cross the river at Laredo.

On the day after the departure of the regiment, Taylor issued an order to the effect that any men not mustered for the duration or twelve months should return to their points of rendezvous and be discharged. "Old Rough and Ready" was ignoring the instructions of Curtis, Henderson, and even Marcy, under whom Hays was working in good faith.[24] Curtis had, of course, made the call and the six months' order.

With Chevaille's four companies and Captain H. W. Baylor's company, Taylor had five companies of horse from Texas. This was his allotment of men from that state under the instructions of April 26 from the War Department. Provided with this additional reason and now referring specifically to Curtis's call for volunteers from Texas, Taylor sent a messenger to meet the regiment enlisted for six months and turn it back.

Taylor's messenger met Hays's command at the Nueces River.[25] The Colonel returned with his regiment to San Antonio, inasmuch as Taylor's manifesto of a year's enlistment or no service did not appeal to the men, who were responding to Curtis's proposition.[26] The volunteers were discharged at San Antonio and afterwards were paid. Secretary Marcy upheld Curtis's requisition made in good faith, and in a letter to Taylor reminded the general that "these companies have not been taken into calculation." [27]

This change of plans which necessitated Hays's going back to San Antonio may have been momentarily embarrassing to him, but likely he was not too unhappy, for the end of the march had brought him again to his sunny-spirited and beloved Susan.

GUANAJUATO

Xichu

luis de la Paz

Xicha de Lalons

Pozos

S. Mig.

Pucan

Xilitla

Huejutla

Aquilica

chap

Tolanlo

Penamilleo

Sonano

Huelula

Texaya

ALIJNUE

QUERETARO

CHELALA

Cadereyta

Buena-vista

Cimapan

Mextitlan

ncalepec

Tenango

Huimilpan

S. JUAN

del R.

Doctor

Tecozautla

Huichapa

Jilotepec

Acoxno

El Monte

Tulancingo

Zac

de

ago

La Zanja

Coronco

Nopala

Pachuca

Tula

onimo

Salvali

aste

Acambaro

Cahlalapa

Tesontepe

Jp

inzunzan

S. Morio

Tomascutingo

Zunpango

Axapusco

Tlaxco

Huevotlipan

S. Felipe

del Obraje

Curutitlan

Tlanepantla

Ixtlahuaca

Taxcuco

Ayotla

TLAXCALA

Co

Ne

C

Tiricato

S. Felipe

Grande

Fernando

TOLUCA

Tenango

MEXICO

Tlalpan

Lerma

Popocatepec

CHALCO

Puncingo

S. Pueb

PU

TEF

Temascal

-tepec

Tenango

CUERNAVACA

Sta Isabel

Purunguan

Tejupilca

Acatitlan

Sultepec

Zacualpan

Morelos

Allixco

TER

Zacapuata

Sta Ma

Taxco

Nexpa

Igualdeo

Quetzio

Luca

Yutzamala

Iguala

MATAMOROS

Sirandaro

Cutzamala

Cocula

Rio

Tehui

cingo

Oh

Suchitlan

Rio Mexcala

Zoctepec

Chiautla

Acatlan

Tecomatlan

Mexcala

va

Sta Barbara

M

Zopilote

Apango

Totolcingo

Olinana

CHILAPA

Izcaliuan

Tlacot

Santiago

Chilpancingo

Tixtla

TLapa

Juslan

S. Cristobal

Tlacuapa

oquillas

Uecpan

Alavac

Nacinila

Pascala

S. Mig.

Luis

Dos Caminos

Tase

Chacalintlo

Jitilltepe

Coyuca

Tlaxcatlixtlahuaca

REGIONS AND PLACES INTO WHICH HAYS'S RANGERS PURSUED GUERRILLAS.

Raids by predatory bands upon Scott's line were practically stopped by the Rangers. *After* General P. G. Conde's *Carta Geografica General De La Republica Mexicana.*

ALAMO PLAZA TO MEXICO CITY

ON July 6, 1847, Hays succeeded Captain M. S. Howe as commander of the Texas frontier with orders to place the frontier line in a state of defense. Two days later an order, dated June 2, arrived from the Secretary of War directing Hays to take whatever portion of his command that could be spared from the Indian frontier and report for duty to General Taylor at Monterrey.

Hence Hays completed recruiting a regiment which would serve for twelve months or for the duration of the war. He was elected to its colonelcy without opposition, and on July 10 was mustered into Federal service. Immediately there came wide congratulations through the press and numerous letters.

From his headquarters at San Antonio, in a letter signed *Colonel Commanding the First Texas Mounted Volunteers,* Hays wrote to General Taylor on July 13. He mentioned the number of troops on the frontier and referred to the order to report.[1] The Colonel stated a fortnight would be required to assemble his new command and asked for direct orders. This letter and accompanying papers were started by express to Taylor. The bearer, Captain G. K. Lewis, was attacked and wounded by Indians on the Nueces River. Having learned through one of his Mexican spies of the attack upon his messenger, Hays immediately transmitted copies of the papers and a note of instruction to Lewis, in case he was able to proceed.[2]

Taylor received Hays's dispatches on July 21. The General's reply ordered Hays to leave whatever force the protection of the frontier required and to come with the remainder—say, five companies—to Mier.[3] Taylor had received no authentic news from Mexico City for a month and nothing from Veracruz for a longer period. Other than establishing a camp of instruction and trying to decrease the rate of sickness among the troops at Mier and Buena Vista, his army now stood idle. The guerrillas

were enjoying good health, judging from their growing boldness in attacks upon Taylor's wagon trains.

Hays therefore found it necessary to spend some time in ar-
ranging matters relating to the frontier. The Indians were
threatening again. Four of a party of five surveyors working on
the Llano River for Robert Hays, the Colonel's younger brother
from Mississippi, were attacked and killed. The Colonel dispatched a messenger to Robert S. Neighbors, Special Indian
Agent, requesting him to ascertain the facts.[4] Captain Lewis had
been ambushed on the Laredo Road; so the Colonel sent Captain
G. M. Armstrong with forty men on a hurried scout to the
Medina River.

If an approach to adequate frontier defense were to be secured, a line of Ranger stations must extend from the Rio
Grande to the Red River. After conferences with the governor
and the Indian agents, Hays made a long and detailed report
to R. W. Jones, adjutant general, at Washington. He not only
explained the location of the forces and their commanders [5] but
also emphasized the importance of the more strategic posts.
Colonel Peter H. Bell of Hays's regiment was to be left in
charge of the frontier during the Colonel's stay in Mexico.

Hays declared that he regretted having "to speak in terms
of reprehension of an officer," but stated the Ranger companies
along the frontier line had been "kept in a state of almost total
uselessness, whilst in the pay of the United States" under the
command of Howe. It is the only indictment made by Hays
against another officer, and it is obvious that he was pained in
making it. The charges were unanswerable; even the adjutant general's department characterized the reproach as
"interesting." [6]

The inefficiency of Howe burdened Hays with many unexpected last minute details. There were such matters as correspondence with physicians and visits of inspection to hospital
stores and patients at Austin and elsewhere.[7] There were con-
tracts to be made with surgeons, distribution of medicines to
the frontier posts, and at the last moment he had to send Captain Jacob Roberts's company out to the Pedernales to protect

the German settlements from threats of Indian raids. Then it was necessary to remind the adjutant general that the government was "considerably in arrears" to the Rangers employed upon the line.[8] The Colonel assigned two companies of his regiment to frontier service.

On August 12 Hays started to Mier with five companies. Roberts's company was to join him after resting their horses following recent scouting. The march to Laredo revealed that numerous members were rather raw material for Rangers. Hays was aware that, man for man, these recruits were not the equal of those he had commanded during the first months of the war.[9]

General Scott had captured and occupied Veracruz on March 29, 1847. Then he advanced toward Mexico City. Enemy armies could not stop his progress, but guerrillas were making Scott's rear a nightmare to him. Soon only large forces of men and supplies dared try to go from Veracruz to the advancing army ahead. Usually the wounded or sick left on the road or in villages were murdered. On June 4 Scott wrote that he feared he could not protect his hospitals in the large cities.

The Mexican government invoked its long-discussed "system of guerrillas"[10] on August 16, 1847. All the people within eighty miles of every point occupied by the Americans should rise and attack the enemy. One band routed a force of three hundred Americans, captured 121 wagons loaded with provisions, and 137 pack mules carrying clothing. Scott had to abandon communication with Veracruz. Secretary of War Marcy wrote Scott that the guerrilla system was "hardly recognized as a legitimate mode of warfare, and should be met with the utmost allowable severity."[11] On October 6 Marcy ordered Scott to destroy the rendezvous of the guerrillas.

President Polk was disturbed about Scott's having closed his line of communications. He discussed the subject with Marcy at great length. "I suggested," wrote Polk, "that the mounted Regiment from Texas under the command of Col. John C. Hays, who has a high character as an officer, be ordered to proceed without delay to Vera Cruz."[12] Marcy and the President prepared "a letter to Col. Hays to that effect."

Next day Marcy wrote Taylor, transmitting a note of instructions to Hays which required the Colonel to proceed to Veracruz "with such of his command as can be spared for the purpose of dispersing the guerrillas which infest the line between that place and the interior of Mexico."[13] Marcy's order was received by special express on August 13.

On September 13 General Scott's columns crashed into Mexico City, and by next morning the Americans possessed the capital. This loss compelled General Santa Anna to renounce the Presidency of Mexico on the 16th. The office devolved upon Manuel de la Peña y Peña, who established a recognized government at Querétaro, the temporary capital of Mexico. He was supported by the moderates, who were eager for peace. Some factions opposed to him determined to prolong the war into an endless guerrilla conflict. Numerous American officers could see no signs of peace—Mexico would neither fight nor treat.

While Scott was issuing his "martial law order" and assisting the American envoy, N. P. Trist, in attempting to negotiate a satisfactory peace treaty, small American forces in the interior of Mexico were confronting serious military difficulties. Santa Anna, boasting eight thousand men, was besieging Colonel Thomas Child's command of four hundred able-bodied soldiers at Puebla. Brigadier General Joseph Lane—a political general who had commanded the Indiana Volunteers at Buena Vista— en route from Veracruz to Mexico City with the first brigade to arrive from Taylor's army in northern Mexico, heard of the siege on September 27. Gathering reinforcements as he marched, Lane set out to raise the siege. Meanwhile, the lordly Santa Anna took twenty-five hundred men and left General Joaquin Rea to carry on the siege. But Santa Anna received an order, dated October 7, from the government at Querétaro which deposed him as head of the army. He turned over his command to General Isidro Reyes and then set off to join his family at Tehuacan, seventy miles southeast of Puebla. When Lane neared Puebla, Rea fell back to Atlixco, twenty-five miles distant.

Any definite American policy concerning the occupation of Mexico seemed to be an insoluble problem. But the Administration determined to occupy the capital, retain the main ports, extend its holdings, and maintain the line of communication to Veracruz. Secretary Marcy advised Scott to use his own judgment as to military occupations.

General Scott described future military operations between Mexico City and the seacoast as "disinfesting" the road of robbers and guerrillas. Because of the extreme difficulty in communicating with Veracruz, once a letter was baked in a loaf of bread and entrusted to a daring courier who traveled in disguise. Padre Celedonia Jarauta, most active of the guerrilla leaders, aroused great hopes among the Mexicans. It was necessary to oppose such activity with greater activity if Scott's line of communications and supply were to be kept open.

J. P. Henderson, governor of Texas, received a communication from Washington that Hays was being directed to go to the mouth of the Rio Grande and from there to secure transports to Veracruz. The government's order to Hays, forwarded by Henderson, was intended to reach him somewhere on the Rio Grande.[14] Upon his arrival at Mier, Hays received his new orders and marched to Camargo, where he rested his horses for four days. After a week's slow march to Matamoros, and an eight-day stay there, the force moved to Point Isabel about ten miles from the Gulf. While Hays arranged transportation to Veracruz, the regiment encamped several miles below Point Isabel. From Point Isabel Hays marched his regiment to Brazos de Santiago, and the first detachment embarked immediately for Veracruz.[15] Others sailed on October 5, but Hays, who voyaged with the last of his men, did not reach Veracruz until the 17th.[16] Two days later he drew the first of two consignments of Colt revolvers from the Veracruz depot.

While awaiting equipment at Vergara, the Ranger camp three miles from Veracruz, Hays made several scouting expeditions—once toward Santa Fe. When a band of two hundred guerrillas tried to ambush the Colonel and twelve men and then sought to ride over the Texans by sheer weight of numbers, Hays and his men dismounted and, aiming their guns across their saddles, awaited the onslaught. When the charging horsemen were within thirty yards a dozen rifles volleyed, and riderless horses galloped by on either side of the Rangers. Again the Mexicans charged, this time meeting a rain of lead from six-shooters which emptied more saddles. They withdrew: courage alone was not sufficient.

A New Orleans newspaper reporter wrote: "The Rangers are the very men for these guerrillas, and are worth four times their number of any other mounted men I have seen here. Col. Hays looks quite well, except that the end of his nose is shedding its skin, and his face is pretty sunburnt all over. Jack Hays is a remarkable man, as useful to his country as he is modest and independent." [17]

Numerous officers of the Army and Navy at Veracruz sought Hays's acquaintance. Adjutant J. S. "Rip" Ford avers that they soon prized the Colonel's friendship. Troops from the other states attempted to catch a glimpse of him. Ford records in his memoirs:

They would rush from their tents and "Hurrah for Col. Hays." It was amusing to witness the mistakes made on such occasions. Col. Hays was a rather small man, and wore no uniform. Some large, good looking Ranger would be taken for him. One man humored the notion, and gave it encouragement. Major Chevaille saw him, and registered a vow of vengeance. Not long afterwards Chevaille gave the fraudulent colonel a terrible drubbing. He never repeated the act.

Hays enjoyed the calls of Commodore M. C. Perry and other notables, but as he was very busy drilling his command, was seldom to be found in his tent. His orderly, John Buchanan, taking advantage of his superior officer's absences, often made merry—particularly one day when Colonel J. M. Withers, of the Ninth Regiment of Infantry, sent over to Hays a half-barrel of fine whisky. This time the amiable orderly decided to hold open house. Only two hundred yards distant were boys from General Caleb Cushing's Massachusetts Volunteers who streamed over to pay their respects. Decorum reigned, however, and

Buchanan gave little attention to any details other than serving refreshments. As the callers drifted away, there came to the tent "a Massachusetts semi-official." Glancing about the quarters, he saw an article he fancied, picked it up, and started to leave. There was a slender, nontalkative, young man sitting at the far end of the tent, who had just come in. Dressed in very plain civilian clothes, he was ignored by the caller, who deemed him of little significance until the seated man ordered:

"Put that down, sir!"

The Boston man allowed contempt, disgust, and indignation to register on his countenance. Then he "beat the long roll of profanity" and shouted: "You don't know who I am, sir!"

By this time Ford and others were standing at the entrance, quietly enjoying the scene, and they laughed until the sergeant stepped from the tent and bellowed for his guard. This was too much for Ford, who thundered:

"What! Put our Colonel in the guardhouse! Don't you try it!"

The seated man was Colonel Hays, and he had taken enough. "Ford," he said, "order a file of men here."

A squad of Ranger guards came on the double. In an instant the sergeant was disarmed and placed in their midst. As he was marched away, his features registered his thought: punishment, reduction to the ranks, court-martial. After a few days he was released, since Hays placed no charges against him. He never again accepted an invitation to one of Buchanan's parties. [18]

On October 26 Scott's local ordnance supply officer delivered to Hays another lot of the scarce Colts. Target practice was a daily requirement at Vergara. Some of the raw men had never handled the long-barreled six-shooters which were as accurate as Mississippi rifles and carried to a greater distance; yet at the end of two weeks they were using six-shooters effectively.

Hays was the only field officer in the regiment when an order was obtained to elect a major. Captain A. M. Truett was elected. Had Chevaille, who had resigned his command in General John E. Wool's brigade to rejoin Hays, been present he probably would have been chosen.

Frequently the Colonel sent out his officers in charge of scouting parties to develop initiative. Captain Jacob Roberts led a scout in the direction of Medellin River. When Roberts returned, he requested Hays's adjutant to write up his report to the Colonel. The captain hesitated about the loss of the enemy killed, but finally stated the number as five. The adjutant was doing the report cheerfully, but wanting facts, he asked:

"Look here, Jake, I want the truth. How many did you kill?"

"Not more than twenty-five," Roberts replied.

It was difficult to restrain some of these men who had suffered unnecessary domestic bereavement at the hands of outlaw raiders.

When there came an order to advance, Hays and his officers construed it to mean they should report to Scott. Immediately some of the staff suggested to Hays that they make the march alone. Hays listened to their compliments, smiling at the reminder that no force so small—five hundred and eighty men— had made the trip from Veracruz, and ignored the argument that the feat would secure distinction. The Colonel expressed his appreciation of their confidence in themselves and in him, but thought it would be more prudent to march with Major General Robert Patterson's convoy. The subject was never revived.

As Hays swung his regiment into line on November 2 with Patterson's column, it was some satisfaction to know that the guerrillas in the neighborhood were causing less annoyance. Bands were more circumspect around old Antigua, and no longer did certain archpredators haunt their strongholds and ambush passing trains.

Only Captain G. M. Armstrong was inclined to straggle. He rode along with some officers of another command. Hays noticed this, but did not admonish him, because he knew Armstrong was moody over his failure to be elected major. Circumstances at last took care of the matter before Hays had to. One day there came the sudden reports of several Mexican *escopetas.* Armstrong and his comrades dug in their spurs and raced for the regiment while their attackers scampered into the brush.

Some delay and trouble was also occasioned by an Englishman brought along as a regimental musician. This man, Self, was the fellow Hays had once treated to a mock Indian attack. Now, in an effort to atone for his part in the escapade, the Colonel showed him every consideration, but Self occasioned him much worry by lagging and taking frequent pulls at the bottle. Once Hays missed him when they encamped for the night and sent a company early next morning to look for him. Violin music guided the Rangers to a camp where the player was the only Anglo-Saxon. All the guerrillas were captured, but the frightened Self had become so oblivious to everything that he fiddled on and on. Finally the captain of the rescuers brought him to recognition of his surroundings by a hearty slap on the shoulders.

Hays slept the next night on the ground under the national bridge. Late in the evening Adjutant Ford was startled to see a stranger sitting on a horse in the midst of their cooking equipment. The intruder asked many questions. Ford's answers angered the man, who strung several oaths together and exclaimed:

"I am wagon-master, and if you get sick, I'll see you in hell before you can ride in on my wagon." And then the visitor further inquired in a derisive tone:

"Whose camp is this anyhow?" When Ford answered, "It is Colonel Hays's," the rider used quirt and spurs vigorously to get out of it. [19]

Since Hays was in command of the division's escort, he placed some Rangers in advance of General Patterson and his staff, followed with a majority of his men next, and distributed Rangers at intervals along the column. On November 4 Jalapa was reached[20] and camp was made two miles beyond. More than three thousand men had made the march without accident. "The presence of Col. Hays and his . . . Texas Rangers acts like a charm upon the rascals [guerrillas]," wrote the *Picayune's* field correspondent from El Encero.

Troops encamped near Jalapa stationed themselves along the road to watch their arrival. A member of a regiment of Pennsylvania Volunteers wrote in his diary: "We gave him [Hays] three cheers; they are a fine body of men and well mounted, with six-shooting rifles." [21]

American military governors and garrisons were being established at Puebla, Perote, and Jalapa. These officials realized the war had assumed a guerrilla character.[22] Rangers now were to be used not only to keep the line of communication open but also to pursue the guerrillas into their mountain retreats.

While the majority of his men rested themselves and their horses at Jalapa, Hays took the companies of Armstrong and Roberts and marched on to Puebla. There was little excitement at Jalapa, though a momentary flurry was caused when a guerrilla whom the Rangers had captured en route from Veracruz committed suicide in the guardhouse on November 13.[23]

When Hays and the two companies of Rangers rode into Puebla, hundreds of General "Jo" Lane's brigade watched them pass along the main street. Albert Brackett, a lieutenant in the Fourth Regiment of Indiana Volunteers, wrote:

They certainly were an odd-looking set of fellows, and it seems to be their aim to dress as outlandishly as possible. Bobtailed coats and "long-tailed blues," low and high-crowned hats, some slouched and others Panama, with a sprinkling of black leather caps, constituted their uniforms; and a thorough coating of dust over all, and covering their huge beards gave them a savage appearance. Their horses ranged from little mustangs to large American full-bloods, and were every shade and color. Each man carried a rifle, a pair of pistols, and . . . two of Colt's revolvers; a hundred of them could discharge a thousand shots in two minutes, and with what precision the Mexican alone can tell. I watched them closely as they went silently by me, and could distinguish no difference between the officers and men. They carried no sabers.[24]

Each Ranger also carried a knife, a hempen rope or hair lariat, and a rawhide riata.

Lieutenant Colonel Ebenezer Dumont, of the same command as Brackett, wrote home a description of the Rangers' entrance into Puebla.

They rode, some sideways, some standing upright, some by the reverse flank, some faced to the rear, some on horses, some on asses, some on mustangs, and some on mules. Here they came, rag-tag and bobtail, pell-mell, helter-skelter. The head of one covered with a slouched hat, that of another with a towering cocked hat, another bareheaded whilst twenty others had caps made of the skins of every variety of wild and tame beasts. . . .

A nobler set of fellows than these same Texian tatterdemalions never unsheathed a sword in their country's cause or offered up their lives on their country's altar. Young and vigorous, kind, generous, and brave, they have purposely dressed themselves in such a garb, as to prove to the world at a glance that they are neither regulars nor volunteers common, but Texas Rangers—as free and unrestrained as the air they breathe, or the deer in their own native wildwood.

Many condemned them on sight, for the world is prone to judge a man by his coat. But by correct deportment and marked propriety during their stay at this place they won rapidly upon the esteem of those who had condemned them in advance.[25]

Hays greeted Lane,[26] with whom he had formed a friendship early in the war. When they heard that a body of Mexican troops with several American prisoners were at Izucar de Matamoros, they set out for the place. Hays commanded one hundred and thirty-five Rangers, Lieutenant H. B. Field of the Third Artillery had one gun and twenty-five men, and Captain Lewis was in charge of the Louisiana Dragoons. The marchers were pelted with a hard, cold rain, but reached Matamoros at sunrise.

Hays led a charge which drove the pickets back upon the main body thence all in a rapid flight into a forest back of the place. There were from four to six hundred in the company. Among the seventy-five killed and wounded of the Mexicans, were Colonel Piedras, the commander, and several officers. None of the Americans were lost; twenty-one of their countrymen were freed, mounted on captured horses and armed for service. The remainder of the day was devoted to destroying all materials taken, with the exception of the munitions.[27]

Hays now ordered all captured horses belonging to noncombatants to be returned to any who could prove ownership. Some of the Mexicans attempted to claim animals not theirs.

Chaplain Samuel H. Corley owned a very spirited black horse which was one of the most noted steeds in the regiment. This animal had bolted at Monterey with Captain Robert H. Taylor on his back and upset the decorum of a funeral procession by jumping over the hearse. He often would stampede with Corley and disturb that gentleman in a manner highly mortifying; yet the horse was intelligent, and the parson valued him highly. A Mexican claimed the horse, said he had raised him, and brought witnesses to support his claims. Those who knew the horse were amazed at the claimant's effrontery, but were amused by Corley's excitement and his declaration that he would not surrender his property without a fight.

Early next morning the expedition began its return march. Twenty-five Rangers led the advance guard while one company formed the rear guard. About five miles from Matamoros the force came to a difficult pass called Galaxara. Here the column was extended, and the artillery and four heavily loaded captured wagons soon were far behind. Lane was with them, trying to accelerate their progress.

In this formation a squad of scouts beyond the advance guard retreated under the sudden attack of two hundred lancers. Hays spurred forward and led the guard in a charge to meet the enemy, who broke and retreated. The Colonel, with thirty-five men, pursued them across a wide plain.

Hays, now spurring, then jockeying a bit more speed, occasionally settled in his saddle and half turned as he swung his rifle in a sweeping gesture to his men to come on! Sometimes he jerked the stock of his gun to his shoulder and fired, but was not wasting his lead. Across the prairie and up the long foot of the mountains, the enemy fled. The fugitives found their horses almost exhausted, and midway the hill, made a stand. Into the face of their final shots charged Hays. Alongside him Adjutant Ridgely was shot from his saddle. Captain Roberts's horse was killed under him, and the officer was thrown. The lancers fled over the summit with the Rangers terrifyingly close behind them.

But Hays was not surprised when five hundred lancers spilled from a ravine and moved to meet the Americans. Since the latters' rifles and revolvers were empty, the Colonel gestured for retreat. As they went, they recovered the bodies of Ridgely and Private William Walpos, who also had fallen in the ascent of the hill. When Roberts's men came by him he seized George White's stirrup, and, gathering momentum, swung up behind.

As Hays moved down the height, he was trying to reload while looking backward at the lancers. He could trust Roberts to keep the men moving toward the pass. The Colonel served as their rear guard now.

After he saw that his men had reached the plain, Hays whirled his horse to face the lancers and "deliberately shot two of them dead." At intervals he slowed down, faced about in the saddle, and shot at the nearest pursuer. Every time the Colonel did this, the enemy reined in a zigzag movement to make an irregular target. This slowed their advance. Hays covered the retreat until the Rangers entered the pass. Lane reported: "Never did any officer act with more gallantry than did Colonel Hays in this affair of the 24th." [28]

Upon rejoining his men, Hays found them with their guns reloaded and in position to command a view of the plain. The lancers had been checked, and when the remainder of the Rangers and the Dragoons arrived and charged, the enemy ran for the mountains.

Thus were General J. Rea's five hundred lancers defeated and his total force of twelve hundred scattered and rendered comparatively harmless. General Lane estimated the enemy killed and wounded at fifty. Two Americans were killed and two were wounded. The round trip had covered a distance of one hundred and twenty miles. The enemy was forced to abandon Matamoros and Atlixco. Lane was so delighted with the work of the Rangers, and "particularly of Colonel Hays," [29] that he hoped to have their service in the future.

There was an incident connected with the retirement from Izucar de Matamoros which embarrassed Hays. It had to do with the conduct in battle of a volunteer recruited after the Rangers had arrived at Veracruz. Hays noticed the terror he suffered on the battlefield and during the next fight sent him on an errand which would keep him away until the battle was ended. After the command had returned to camp, Hays talked privately to the soldier. He kindly advised him not to attempt a military life if his condition were not suited for it. Perhaps, he suggested, the man should return home. He counseled with the youth tactfully regarding marriage, suggesting that if he married he should select a woman whose nervous system appeared to be different from his own; preferably a mate with the blood of heroes in her veins.

A few days later, Lieutenant Brackett was in downtown Puebla and stood looking out of a second floor window. A slender young man spoke to him from the pavement and asked, "Could you please direct me to Colonel Dumont's quarters?"

"Colonel Dumont's quarters?" Brackett replied. "Certainly, just walk up those stairs." Whereupon Brackett met him and took him to Dumont's office. Dumont introduced the visitor to Brackett as Colonel Jack Hays. Brackett chronicled:

I could scarcely realize that this wiry-looking fellow was the world-renowned Texas Ranger. Jack was very modest, and, sitting down on a mess-chest, commenced conversing. He was very plainly dressed, and wore a blue roundabout, black leather cap, and black pants, and had nothing about him to denote that he belonged to the army or held any rank in it. His face was sun-browned; his cheeks gaunt; and his dark hair and dark eyes gave a shade of melancholy to his features; he wore no beard or mustache; and his small size—he being only about five feet eight—made him appear more like a boy than a man. . . . Hays was no great talker, appeared to avoid speaking as much as possible; still he was very kind, and did not seem to put on any unnecessary airs. He spent the afternoon with Dumont, and we supped together.[30]

Hays and his men at Puebla rejoined their unit when the column arrived. As the Colonel had received an order for assignment of duty at Mexico City, he marched his five companies out ahead of Patterson's command.[31]

XV

NEAR MONTEZUMA'S HALLS

WHEN Hays and his Rangers moved on toward Mexico City, followed by Major F. T. Lally's Ninth Infantry and Patterson's column, they had been anxiously awaited for a month by General Scott. To be able to occupy Mexico Scott needed another force as large as that which he now had. His troops numbered about six thousand, with over two thousand sick. After the arrival of all reinforcements expected, Scott would have only eleven thousand effectives and three thousand sick.[1]

General P. F. Smith organized a military police. Marauders or peaceful soldiers found on the streets after eight in the evening were taken to the guardhouse. The city was overflowing with escaped felons and *léperos,* and the life and property of the inhabitants and the Americans depended upon the military police.[2]

From the moment of their entrance into the outskirts of the city, Hays's Rangers became increasingly the object of marked attention. For some distance the column was not molested; then a Mexican on the sidewalk of a suburban street threw a stone at one of the hated gringos and knocked his hat to the ground. Retaliation was instantaneous; a flash, and the assailant fell dead. The Ranger, replacing his pistol and reaching down from the saddle, picked up his hat and rode on without a word from anyone. A few blocks farther another stone thudded into the ranks: another mestizo had tossed his last rock. Except the two gun reports, the sound of horses' hoofs, and the creak of saddle leather, no noise was heard and no disturbance was caused as the column marched on, its ranks unbroken.[3]

Hays had no intention of producing a sensation or creating a ripple of disturbance, but the news of the arrival of the Rangers ran ahead of them along the avenue. "The greatest curiosity prevailed," Ford wrote, "to get a sight of *Los Diablos Tejanos*— The Texas Devils."[4] The streets of the city were paved with smooth, round stones. A trooper accidentally let one of his pistols fall from his belt. When it struck the pavement, it was discharged, the ball ricocheting off a civilian's leg. The unfortunate Ranger was accused of attempted murder.

Brigadier General E. A. Hitchcock, acting as inspector general on Scott's staff, recorded in his diary on December 6: "Hays's Rangers have come, their appearance never to be forgotten. . . . All sorts of coats, blankets, and head-gear—but they are strong athletic fellows. The Mexicans are terribly afraid of them." [5]

Colonel Dumont, who was conversant with the Rangers' recruiting of weapons and mounts in the fighting around Puebla, also described their entrance into Mexico City. "Hays's men," he wrote, "entered the city of the Aztecs and approached the Halls of Montezuma . . . the subject of universal curiosity. The sides of the streets were lined with spectators of every hue and grade, from a major general of the North American Army to a Mexican beggar. Quietly they moved along. Not a word was spoken. They seemed unconscious that they were the observed of all observers. The trees in their own native forests would have attracted as much of their attention as they seemed to bestow upon anything around them. They seemed to say, 'We have seen men, and have been in cities before.' " [6]

The New Orleans *Picayune's* correspondent reported:

As the gallant Rangers filed through the streets, covered with mud and dust accumulated on their long journey, it would have done you good to see the Mexicans stare, particularly when they were informed that these were the much dreaded Texans or *Tejanos*. Dressed as Rangers always are, in anything that comes to hand—some with blankets wrapped around them, and some in their shirt sleeves—but all well mounted and well armed, they presented a sight never before seen in the streets of Mexico, and the usually noisy léperos were as still as death while they were passing. The gallant Jack Hays appeared to be the object of peculiar interest, and the better informed class of Mexicans were particularly anxious to have pointed out to them the man whose name has been the terror of their nation for the past twelve years.[7]

Facetiously, this reporter wondered why anyone should fear soldiers who could fire only seventy-five hundred shots to every five hundred men within a few minutes. His conclusion was: "They have got a name. ... We have several times been asked if the Texans will be allowed to go into the streets without a guard over them. It is really surprising that men with such a reputation should be among the very best disciplined troops in our army, and not disposed to commit outrages or create disturbances in any way."

Hays halted his Rangers in the Grand Plaza with the center of the column opposite the cathedral. The officers went to see about getting assigned to quarters while the men waited quietly. As they sat their horses, one of them beckoned to a candy vendor nearby. The Texan took a piece of candy and ate it; then he consumed a second and a third piece in the same deliberate manner. The Mexican decided he was being robbed. He seized a stone, hurled it at the rider, and missed; the horseman pulled a pistol and shot him. Ten thousand heard the shot and, being already apprehensive, stampeded. Men ran over each other, blocked one another into sewers, and fought to put distance between themselves and *los Tejanos sangrientes*. The customer would have paid the vendor. Hays's men did not respect a thief; they once had drummed one out of their regiment despite his fighting ability.[8]

On the same evening, as several Rangers were about to file into a theater, a thief stole a valued handkerchief from one of the men and ran. The owner leveled a six-shooter upon him, pulled the trigger, recovered his handkerchief, then calmly rejoined his friends. After that episode the Texans learned hand-kerchief snatchers were numerous and safeguarded their bandannas by pinning them to their pockets. When a rogue snatched and missed, they caught him and applied corporal punishment to that portion of his anatomy which he customarily used most.[9]

Some of Hays's officers engaged board at the Inn of the National Theater. They appeared for their first meal and were greeted very pleasantly. The waiter at their table studied them in an attempt to determine their branch of service and their rank. He asked questions as he laid the silver. He yearned to know from which *de los Estados Unidos* the men came, and began a roll call of the states. One of the officers who resented his impertinence said,

"*Somos Tejanos*—we are Texans."

The waiter's eyes dilated; he gaped at his customers and, dropping his tray, dashed from the room.

Within a few minutes another waiter came to their table laughing. An officer interrupted him to ask,

"Where is the other waiter?"

"Gone! You will see him no more. If you are Texans, you are my countrymen," replied the second waiter.

He remained, although it was obvious that any revelation of a threatening gesture from one of his "countrymen" would have sent him off at a record-breaking exit.[10]

Colonel Dumont was of the opinion that the Rangers were adaptable. He saw in their entry into Puebla and their military campaigns more courage than conduct. In Mexico City he discerned "both courage and conduct." The prankish appearance and mounts of the Texans at Puebla suggested freakish individuals among them, but their behavior in Mexico City indicated that "in each place they acted their part well." While their commander was known for his modesty, even shyness, his quietness was not weakness.

For instance, when General Scott heard that two Mexicans had been killed as the Rangers entered the city, he sent an orderly requesting Hays to report to him. Within a few minutes the Colonel stood before his commander in chief. Saluting, Hays said:

"I, sir, am Colonel Hays, commander of the Texas Rangers and report myself to you in accordance with an order just received."

General Scott replied: "I have been informed, sir, since the arrival of your command in this city, two Mexicans have been killed. I hold you, sir, responsible for the acts of your men. I will not be disgraced, nor shall the army of my country be, by such outrages. I require you, sir, to say whether my information is correct, and if so, you will render me a satisfactory explanation."

Colonel Hays rejoined: "Your information is correct. General, the Texas Rangers are not accustomed to being insulted without resenting it. They did kill two Mexicans as I entered the city, and I, sir, am willing to be held responsible for it."

Hays's bearing and the manner in which he spoke were so frank and unabashed the general could not doubt the Colonel's belief that his men were justified.

General Scott's wrath abated, and he invited Hays to be seated and give a full statement of the facts. After Hays had given the simple details, he added a succinct explanation as to why many of his men had volunteered for service. He described the fall of the Alamo, the butchery at Goliad, and the execution of the prisoners from Mier. At the conclusion of the interview, Hays was dismissed courteously, and nothing was said about punishment for the offenders.[11]

Léperos promoted disorder. Looting their own people, assassinating the Americans, these turbulent ruffians were an increasing menace.[12] They enjoyed pretending to pass an American officer simultaneously and in the collision knocking him into the sewer. When Texans sauntered along the sidewalks, these mischievous villains usually found they had something urgent to attend to on the opposite side of the street.

One time Van Walling and Pete Goss, two of the Rangers, were passing quietly along a street. A crowd of léperos ambushed them and threw stones at them. Then they charged upon their intended victims with knives, but the Rangers had their six-shooters under their coats. Four léperos were killed and several others were wounded before they could escape.[13]

In Mexico City, as in other towns occupied by Americans, there had occurred only an external revolution. There was scarcely a night that some American was not killed or a morning without three to five soldiers being found dead in the streets. American patrols and local police were unable to stop these murders. Ordinarily léperos sought out drunken soldiers and

[184]

stabbed them. The Texans wished to check these killings before too many of their comrades paid the price of a surprise attack. After they had been in the city about a month, an incident occurred which almost stopped the nightly assassinations.

Adam Allsens, of Captain Roberts's company, who was riding through the section of the city called "Cutthroat," was surrounded and attacked. He was finally able to spur his horse through the mob and escape—literally cut to pieces, with the pulsations of his heart visible through the slashes. He lived for eight hours and gave useful details concerning the locality and his assailants.

The very silence of Allsens' company indicated that revenge would be taken. Still Hays could not arrest men in anticipation of vengeance they might be contemplating. Day retired and night chimes registered ten o'clock, yet no disturbances had been reported.

At 26 Doncella Street, the Colonel was in his quarters conversing with Ford and Captain Parry W. Humphreys, a visitor. Suddenly when some shots were heard Humphreys asked, "Were not those shots from six-shooters?"

Hays changed the subject, and the conversation continued. Again shots, which now sounded like firing by platoons, rang out, and Humphreys expressed the opinion they were from six-shooters. Hays suggested that the Horse Marines, who had been drilling outside the walls, probably were responsible for the shooting.

"They are always making a noise," he added.

In about two hours the firing ceased. A few minutes later Humphreys remarked,

"I wonder why the commanding general's orderly is coming here?"

He was looking out a window as he asked the question, and Hays seemed to be worried. He rose from his chair and started walking toward the rear of the building. As he walked away, he said over his shoulder,

"Ford, if he comes, tell him I am not in."

Humphreys had tried to get Hays to say what he really

thought. Humphreys had seen no orderly when he looked out the window. The three men, he knew, had heard six-shooters being fired. When Humphreys left for his quarters at one o'clock Hays had not yet returned. The adjutant found him asleep in a spot where even a curious orderly would have hardly thought to look.

Next evening Humphreys told Ford that the Mexican police had more than eighty bullet-riddled bodies in the morgue. They were found in the streets and no one had claimed them. The military patrol had not stopped the firing. After all, over a period of three months hundreds of American soldiers had been assassinated.[14]

Some of the soldiers evaded the eight o'clock curfew and appeared at fandangos, where many were assassinated by the guerrillas and léperos. The Rangers devised a plan to protect themselves from their enemies and to destroy them at the same time. One or two would present themselves at the fandangos and shortly afterwards pretend to become very drunk. When an assassin advanced with a knife upon an intended victim, a six-shooter would appear and one more misguided murderer would be ready for the morgue.

On one occasion six Mexicans were killed in a single collison. General Scott, according to Ford, inquired,

"Colonel Hays, is it so that your men have killed six Mexicans recently?"

"Yes, General," Hays replied. "The Mexicans piled rocks on a house and began stoning my men, and they used arms in self-defense."

The general agreed that they had done right, and nothing more was said about the matter. But after their first month's stay the Rangers were kept busied with expeditions pursuing guerrillas.

Quartered in the southern edge of the city near San Angel, Hays and a detachment of his men went in search of guerrillas when two American soldiers were found murdered near the Contreras battleground. They scoured the vicinity, but the assassins had escaped.

During the Christmas holidays reports came that the notorious Padre Jarauta was heading an aggressive band in the vicinity of Otumba. When he heard that Hays was to patrol the Veracruz-to-Mexico road he changed his locality. Even Mexican authorities detested the type of men Jarauta used.

Hays conferred with a middle-aged American, who knew the surrounding regions, to secure him as a guide. This man, called Juan el Diablo (John the Devil), had once been employed as a stagecoach driver in the Valley of Mexico. With Juan as a guide for his sixty-five Rangers, Hays marched from the city on the evening of January 10. Efforts were made to leave as secretly as possible.[15] After some hours of riding, it seemed to Hays that the guide had been misinformed about the road. The Colonel led the column back to the familiar Veracruz road. Here the force rested until daylight, then rode to a large plantation where care was exercised throughout the day to avoid being seen by others than those living there.

At nightfall Hays broke camp and by daybreak was in Otumba. Hays was told that Jarauta was at San Juan Teotihuacan, approximately twelve miles to the west, but nearer to Mexico City. Within three hours the Rangers were in the plaza, which was very large and entirely surrounded by stone buildings. The most important building—the one which the Rangers chose as headquarters—occupied almost one side of the square and had lots and stables attached.

After the horses were fed nearly every man went to sleep, only to be awakened by shots and firing. Captain E. M. Daggett and five men nearest the largest door repulsed the first onslaught. When Hays reached the door, he saw that men on the tops of neighboring houses were firing at the building while seventy-five mounted Mexicans were attempting to storm the doors by charging across the plaza. The Colonel directed several Rangers to make their way under cover to the top of the building, and two squads to be ready to dash through the door to meet the next charge.

The leader led another charge, but one of his officers outrode him. The Rangers rushed through the large door and distributed themselves in front of their building. On came the lancers, and when Ford fired the hard-riding Mexican officer fell from his horse.

The guerrillas halted before they reached the dismounted Texans and thrust their lances in front of them, as if expecting the Rangers to impale themselves upon the long weapons. Instead of advancing, the Americans took unhurried aim and knocked several from their saddles. One officer charged obliquely almost alone. Chevaille's heavy six-shooter ball lifted the rider over his saddlebow and his horse's head. The lancers judged it was safer to retreat.

The guide and some others present identified the enemy leader as Padre Jarauta. Now he prepared for a charge that would parallel the building held by the Rangers. His intent was obvious: to ride down the dozen Rangers in the street and to prevent others from coming through the door. Meanwhile Hays was directing the housetop fighters so that the Mexicans on several roofs could not aim carefully at the Texans in the streets. With horses aligned, lances poised, and Jarauta in front with sword extended, the enemy spurred into a gallop.

Jarauta's men were blasted from their saddles when almost riding down the defenders. Falling lancers and frightened mounts saved the Texans from being crushed by numbers. After the charge had thundered past the defenders, Jarauta was seen to fall from his horse. Some of his men dismounted and tried to carry him into a building, but were either killed or wounded. Successive relays of rescuers finally took him under cover. At last the lancers galloped away, and the Mexicans on housetops disappeared. The fight was over, but the Rangers' horses had neither finished eating nor were rested sufficiently for Hays to follow in pursuit.

Hays and some of his men rode out to see whether the attackers had left the town. When they returned, others had examined the results of the fight. Fifteen dead guerrillas and five wounded were found; several severely wounded men were able to ride away. None of the Rangers were injured. The officer knocked from his horse by Chevaille lay critically wounded and unconscious. Hays directed that he be taken to a house whose occupants promised to look after him. Jarauta's horse had several bullet wounds, and the saddle upon it was splattered with blood. It was evident that the leader had been carried off with the wounded. The Colonel was informed later that four hundred infantry were on the tops of the houses.

In the afternoon Hays set out with his men to Mexico City. A detachment of Mexicans moved parallel with them for more than an hour, but every time Hays advanced with a group of the Rangers and challenged them, they retreated. Mexico City was reached at ten in the evening. During the last thirty hours the force had marched a distance of one hundred and ten miles and defeated the enemy whose numbers were, conservatively, five times that of the Rangers.[16]

XVI

SECRET EXPEDITION

ON January 18 Hays with four companies of his Rangers and Major Polk with two companies of the Third Dragoons and one company of the Mounted Rifle Regiment were detailed to work with General Lane. These picked troops were to scour the country for guerrillas, particularly in the neighborhood of Puebla and Oaxaco. The force totaled only three hundred and fifty men, but orders were to clear all roads of predatory bands.

Innumerable spies about caused these officers to attempt a secret departure. Their plans were laid so carefully that not even the troops were told of the expedition. Hays ordered Lieutenant Josiah Pancoast, commissary, to provide himself with funds for a month's march with six hundred men.[1] In the early morning all rode quietly from the city to a point five miles from Rio Frio, to meet Brigadier General Thomas Marshall's wagon train which was en route to Mexico City. Marshall reported that a band had been threatening his rear guard; so Lane detached two companies of Rangers to guard the wagons.

In Puebla, Doctors Brower and Wooster, Colonel Dumont, and Major W. W. McCoy—all of the post—went along with the expedition to see what would happen.[2] Instead of continuing toward Veracruz, they turned left at Amazoque in order to deceive the natives, then shifted abruptly to the right and traversed a ravine leading to the mountains. Throughout the night they endured a sleety, pelting rain, which soon saturated and chilled even the most hardened riders.

The almost impassable route extended over a distance of forty-five miles. Much of the time the troops were obliged to ride in single file, and frequently the trail compelled them to lead their horses. Daybreak found them in a bleak and lonely region in which they saw two large adobe haciendas. Hays's and Polk's men seized the residents and also a few passersby for fear they might betray the presence of the Americans. The horses were concealed near the haciendas and the men were ordered to remain inside the patios during the day. Some girls in the cookeries told the Rangers that they were the first white men *las muchachas* had seen.[3]

At dark the forces marched toward Tehuacán. Lane now revealed that a trusted guide had informed him General Santa Anna with a force of a hundred regular cavalry and a much larger number of guerrillas was residing in that town.[4] After traveling five miles, the column suddenly met a showy coach drawn by four mules in ornamented harness. The vehicle, accompanied by a dozen armed guards, was occupied by the driver and one man. Hays immediately disarmed the escort and arrested the passenger. Whereupon, the occupant of the coach stated that he had a safe-conduct from General P. F. Smith, commanding the district. Striking a light, the Mexican showed his pass, which proved to be authentic. An informal and friendly discussion arose between Lane and Hays as to whether, under the circumstances, it should be literally respected.[5]

Lane stated that he had no alternative. Hays insisted somewhat urgently the group should not be released until a little later. If they were released now, Hays said, Santa Anna might learn of the approach of the troops. There were many miles yet to go, and, if warned, the ex-dictator and his followers would almost surely escape. The Mexican had acknowledged that he had just left Santa Anna at Tehuacán.

The gentlemen from Puebla, who dubbed themselves Lane's "volunteer staff," were chatting among themselves in undertones and unanimously agreed that the Mexican should be detained. Whether Lane overheard them and became piqued is problematical. Anyhow, he now spoke in a different tone and more seriously than during the several minutes of previous conversation:

"Do you know, Colonel Hays, the penalty for violating a safe-conduct? It is death."

"That's all right," responded Hays. "I'll take the chances."

"I would rather that you set him at liberty," said Lane.

"If you order me to do so, General, of course I shall obey."

"Well, then, if you prefer it in that form, Colonel Hays, I order you to let the Mexican re-enter his carriage and go undisturbed." [6]

Hays directed the column to move to one side of the road. The men watched silently by the dim starlight as the carriage passed to the rear and out of sight.

Hays signaled his officers and resumed the march. Lane evidently realized that if he were wrong he would miss an opportunity to achieve a splendid climax to the second conquest of Mexico, for he tendered no objection when the Colonel set the pace at a steady gallop wherever the trail permitted. For more than forty miles they followed the narrow, rocky excuse for a road, then at dawn learned they were within two miles of town. A halt was made and those at the head of the column conferred. If the enemy were encountered, everyone should fight in his own way. Speed, determination, and skill must succeed, because the horses were too tired for a retreat. The guide explained the position of the sentinels as he had last seen them, a fraction of an hour before.

As the troops neared the town, signal lights were flashed, and a single gun sent a bullet whistling over their heads. Hays led his men in a charge into the plaza while Polk's troopers encircled the village. Some of the Rangers' horses were so exhausted at the conclusion of the hard gallop that they fell in the streets. The first thing seen at the plaza was a white flag, but Hays, not trusting appearances, sent his men dashing from street to street. [7] Not a living object was in sight; the only sounds were the creak of their saddles and rifle scabbards and the beat of the horses' hoofs.

It was easy to ascertain the house in which Santa Anna had been quartered. The long dining table had not been cleared, and candles still burned upon it. Seventeen abandoned packed trunks were found in a room adjoining the patio, and on all sides evidences of hasty flight were visible.

Some of the junior officers and men began to collect souvenirs from the possessions of the fugitives; others began to open the trunks. Dr. Wooster, who had secured for himself a white satin mat as a souvenir, narrated:

The trunks contained everything . . . dresses by the hundreds, which General Lane gallantly had forwarded to Doña Santa Anna with the expressed hope that when next he found her dresses, he would find her in them. A coat of Santa Anna's . . . embroidered and embossed with solid gold. This was given to the State of Texas. There was a resplendent gold bullion sash of immense proportions and weight. This was sent to some other state. Then there was a lifesize oil portrait of Santa Anna.

But marvel of all, a Texan lieutenant, and perhaps some privates, drew forth from the bottom of a trunk a long, tapering, green velvet-covered case. This was quickly opened, and from its satin cushions was taken a cane of wondrous splendor. Its staff was of polished iron. Its pedestal was of gold, tipped with steel. Its head was an eagle with blazing diamonds, rubies, sapphires, emeralds—an immense diamond in the eagle's beak, jewels in his claws, diamonds everywhere. The cane was a marvel of beauty!

The Texans cried with one accord: "Give it to Colonel Jack!"

The finders instantly assented, and joined in a chorus, "Give it to Colonel Jack!"

There was an adjournment of the young treasure-seekers to the room occupied by the headquarters. General Lane was lying on a small bed in one corner, Colonel Hays was resting near on a cane chair, and a few other officers were lounging around.

The presentation was made and accepted in the most informal manner, and while all were admiring the imperial bauble, in came the redoubtable Major William H. Polk—late minister to Naples—who asked to inspect the cane. While looking at it with beaming admiration, he said,

"I should like such a thing as this very much, to give to my brother."

Hays replied promptly, "I have no use for such an ornament. Take it, Major, and give it to the President, and say it is a present from the Texans." [8]

Daylight afforded opportunity for Lane and Hays to confer with the alcalde and priests. Lane ascertained that "a courier had preceded me [Lane], arriving about two o'clock in the morning, with information for General Santa Anna that I was approaching with my command . . . this courier was one of the escort I had met in the early part of the preceding evening . . . and further confessed that he had been sent by a direct route to warn General Santa Anna of the impending attack." [9] Lane's official report thus does not refer to Hays's warning that Santa Anna would receive information of the approach of the Americans, but Dr. Wooster and others have recorded the facts.

Following a day's rest in Tehuacán, the force advanced northward toward Orizaba, crossing the mountain range near the snow line at an altitude of more than fifteen thousand feet. The horses staggered along at a slow walk, and many of them panted painfully; men bled at the nose. Misty rain was encountered, and clouds around them so obscured their vision for a time that they could not see farther than twenty feet. Hays, dressed lightly as usual, wished for Santa Anna's heavy military coat, but it was in the possession of Captain Daggett.

Descending to the valley, they camped in a hamlet at the base of the mountain, where they bought and consumed a wagonload of oranges. A messenger brought an announcement from Orizaba that a deputation would meet the command to discuss terms of capitulation. He was told that the committee would be informed regarding the terms, the implication being that guns might assist in framing the provisions.

Three miles from the gates of the city, the column was met by a procession of priests, followed by a long, irregular throng of citizens. Hays halted the troops as the priests came and kneeled before them. On a large silver platter the padres tendered the keys of the city and asked that life and property be spared in return for its peaceful surrender. Lane, who had dismounted, immediately returned the keys and instructed the churchmen to rise and put on their hats. He assured them that private and church property would be respected.

The American force, flanked by the priests and thousands of citizens, entered Orizaba and took possession of it without firing a gun. Its garrison of nearly two thousand had just evacuated, leaving one long unmounted brass cannon in the center of the main street. Hays and Lane exchanged significant looks when they passed this big gun. It was plain to them that the commandant had used the reception committee as a ruse to gain time while fleeing from the gringos.[10]

Hays was appointed commander of the military, and Major Polk was made governor of the city. Polk's chief task was to ascertain whether the municipal authorities had encouraged the guerrillas. There was ground for distrust when it became known that much tobacco and cigars were being removed from the Mexican government warehouse without authority. Hays advised Lane to turn the tobacco, which was valued at more than a quarter million dollars, over to the alcalde and take that official's receipt for the property. Lane followed Hays's advice and forwarded the receipt to Colonel James Bankhead, who was coming from Veracruz to take permanent possession of Orizaba.[11] Neither Hays, Polk, nor Lane ever secured a dollar from these valuable spoils. They were, however, tendered whatever cigars they cared to put into their pockets.

Hays took three companies of the command and escorted Lane to receive the capitulation of Córdova. During the march several armed Mexicans were seen crossing the road in advance of the column. Hays pursued the force, killing one soldier and wounding the leader, but their familiarity with the country enabled the remainder to escape. At Córdova six American prisoners who had been captured in various regions were rescued. This mission consumed only one day, since the round trip was less than forty miles.

After a week's occupation of Orizaba, Hays and his men, accompanied by Lane, set out on their return to Puebla. Polk and his troops joined them that evening at Acatzingo. Through a region considered hostile and along a route never before trod by United States troops, the Mexicans offered no threat or resistance. Every town sent out its deputies to assure the column of a peaceable reception, and necessities for the animals and men were furnished promptly and liberally. More than a dozen cities and large towns chose to submit to American demands rather than to question the capabilities of Hays and Lane.[12]

Although there had been a dearth of fighting, the excursion afforded compensations. The scenery was picturesque, the variety of food was appetizing, and many amusing incidents diverted them. For instance, there was the Englishman at Córdova who bantered Mike Chevaille for a trade of saddles. Chevaille was willing, but from some misunderstanding the men came to blows. Whereupon, the Englishman took the matter to Lane. According to Adjutant Ford, the following conversation took place:

> Englishman: General, Maj. Chevaille has been beating me!
> General Lane: Did he beat you very badly?
> Englishman: Yes, quite badly.
> General Lane: Keep a sharp lookout, or he will beat you again.

Apparently there was no further trouble.

Another episode drew shoulder-shaking laughter from some of the boys. Ford wrote:

> Hardy Stockman, one of our interpreters, while passing around in a town, saw a large number of chickens in a yard. About nightfall he conducted some of the men to the place. The owner was told that the Texas boys had come to buy some chickens. The Aztec asserted he had none.
> "Where are those I saw here today?" Stockman asked.
> "The soldiers stole them," the owner replied.
> "Then, sir, if there are any chickens on your premises, they do not belong to you?" Stockman inquired.
> "No, sir, they do not," the owner answered.
> Stockman went into the back yard, gathered a handful of gravel, and made what the Irishman called a "slinging shot." Some of the gravel struck a large bake-oven, and very unluckily for his master and himself, a rooster told where he was. The boys went for him and his whole family. The hidalgo was terribly exercised. He told a tale of poverty and declared he would be ruined unless he got pay for his chickens.
> "Your chickens! You lying old rascal! You have no chickens. Should we pay you for them, you would swindle the rightful owner out of the money. Come, none of your tricks, Old Sharpy," warned Stockman.
> The old simpleton saw his last darling pullet as she squalled a final adieu to him and his.[13]

Hays sent Major Truett forward on February 5 with a portion of the Dragoons and some Rangers to guard the wagon trains from Puebla to Mexico City. He and Lane left with the remainder of the force at midnight for Tlaxcala, which they passed through at ten o'clock the next morning. Taking a scenic and little known route, the Americans after a long and exhausting ride neared the town of San Juan de Teotihuacán, about thirty miles from Mexico City. Scouts brought the news that Colonel Manuel Falcón and his force were stationed here. Hays thereupon raced forward to seize the town, and if the enemy fled, Polk was ordered to pursue.

Hays captured Falcón's papers, two hundred and fifty muskets, as many lances, numerous *escopetas,* and a large quantity of ammunition and uniforms. This property had to be destroyed because no wagons were available to carry it. Seventeen of the enemy were killed and several were wounded.

Next day the expedition rode into Mexico City, after an absence of three weeks and two days. During the excursion one private was killed by mishap and three received accidental wounds. The march, as a whole, was one of the most rapid and strenuous of the war.[14]

XVII

LAST CONFLICT

AFTER the horses had rested a week, Hays received orders to move against guerrillas infesting the country northeast of Mexico City. He directed his officers to prepare two hundred and fifty Rangers for the expedition, and his commissary to take two thousand dollars. Polk with one hundred and thirty Dragoons and Rifles and a Lancer company of contraguerrillas commanded by Colonel Dominguez were added to the command. Lane was in charge of these combined units.

Starting out for Tulancingo—the mountainous country north of Rio Frio—they progressed slowly at the beginning because of the necessity of conserving the strength of the horses and deceiving the ever-present spies. During the first day, February 17, only twenty miles was covered. On the second and the third nights as they were approaching Tulancingo, they rode all night, hoping to surprise General Mariano Paredes, J. N. Almonte, and even the treacherous guerrilla chieftain, C. de Jarauta.

During the march Hays sent Ford with orders to the rear of the column. There the latter found some of the dragoons had neglected to watch their saddle girths as their mounts' bellies shrank, and that the riders had been thrown. "The dismounted men were swearing at a terrible rate," Ford chronicled later. Several horses were completely exhausted, and a few had died under the saddle. Their owners recruited animals from the haciendas passed because no man wanted to be left long in the rear in that country![1]

At daybreak the Rangers, who were leading, came to a hill overlooking a long valley and saw Tulancingo, approximately ten miles distant. Although they had ridden seventy-five miles, Hays led his men to the foot of the height and spurred his horse into a gallop. Lane thought five hundred men were in the town and hoped the column could surprise them.[2] They were unsuccessful in that information had somehow preceded the expedition; Padre Jarauta had been gone two days, and Paredes escaped on a fast horse at the last moment. Major Polk opened the jail and released all prisoners. He then atttempted to find some Mexican who knew the whereabouts of Paredes, whom he was especially eager to capture.

It was decided to rest the horses for a day or more, which Hays spent in buying some horses to replace the worthless native animals which the dragoons had been forced to "borrow" along the way. Lane turned his attention to the locating of Jarauta's retreat. The men employed themselves in various duties, and several amusing incidents took place. For example, Ford was trying to sleep when he was aroused by much shouting and laughter among the Rangers nearby. He hurried to them.

"What is the matter?" he inquired.

"We drove up a beef," a soldier answered, "that the contractor had bought, and we were going to shoot it. A Mexican woman came and asked us to let her kill the animal as bull-fighters do. She took the sword, and aimed to plunge it into the creature's neck just behind his horns. She missed her aim, and the bovine tossed her about twenty feet into the air—and she didn't go up head foremost."

"Where is the woman?" Ford asked.

"I reckon she has not stopped running yet," the soldier answered.[3]

It was learned that Jarauta and his force were at Sequalteplan, in the mountains about seventy-five miles north of Tulancingo. Sending the sick—most of whom were riflemen and contraguerrillas—back to Mexico City in charge of Dominguez, Hays and other officers set out with the command in further search of the bandits. Nightfall found them in camp near a hacienda, whose owner was reputed to be quite wealthy. In strolling idly about, one of the junior officers found a barrel of wine in a room attached to the *iglesia*. Senior officers, including Lane, Hays, Captain Alex Hays of Pennsylvania—West Point friend of U. S. Grant and Lane's aide—and some lesser officials were informed of the discovery. Private G. M. Swope—popularly known as "Old Frazzler" and deemed the authority on drinks—was brought to judge. He pronounced the contents of the barrel to be superior Madeira wine. His confident diagnosis caused most of the officers, who had provided themselves with glasses, to sip with relish. Just when the liquid regalement was progressing pleasantly, the lord of the manor stalked in, tremendously excited.

"He informed us," remembered Ford, "he was a poor man, and if we drank that wine, it would bankrupt him."

Alex Hays rejoined: "But, my friend, we will pay you for the wine we drink."

Our host changed tactics: "Oh, do not drink that wine. It belongs to the priest."

"We will pay the priest," said Alex.

The Mexican was full of resources: "I implore you not to drink that wine. It is consecrated."

Alex came back with a clincher: "Then we will drink it for the love of God."

The discomfited Don departed in deep disgust. The barrel and its lessened contents were left in good order.[4]

The troops moved at midnight with Hays leading a forced march despite the nature of the road. The fatigued condition of Polk's horses and some of his dragoons scattered the column considerably; yet the head of the formation was at the outskirts of Sequalteplan about sunrise. Hays, Truett, and Lane rode forward cautiously to a point where they had a clear view of the town. On becoming convinced that the enemy was at hand, they waited for the last of the Rangers to be brought into column. The men were riding single file along a mule path.

Hays ordered an advance toward the suburbs. Here a Mexican officer stepped sleepily through a front door of a house and was quickly seized. He was astonished at the presence of the Rangers, who rode on at a fast trot. There was one plan of battle: find the guerrillas and fight them.

A guard was seen standing by a large open gate in a wall which surrounded some barracks. He saw the column, but moved too slowly to close the gate. Hays was leading such a fast charge that his horse struck the gate with a crash and knocked it wide open. When Rangers poured through, there was no room for fighting on horseback. A dozen sprang from their horses and met the guerrillas as they tried to leave the buildings, killing and wounding several of them. From the adjoining lot, Colonel Montagna and sixty men opened a heavy attack upon the Texans. But Hays decided that Truett and Chevaille could battle this *cuartel*. With the four other companies Hays raced to the main plaza, while from both sides of the street bullets whistled past him and his men. He discovered, in a street to the left, "a strong detachment of the enemy, lancers and infantry, coming forth from a large barrack." [5] In another street there was also to be seen an additional body of the enemy; so Hays sent fifteen men under Lane against this smaller group while he himself led at the same time a charge upon the barracks.

"With my immediate force," reported Hays, "I attacked those of the enemy who had shown themselves on the left. After firing at us from within and without the walls, a running and mixed fight took place, which was continued so long as the enemy was visible, and over a space of road equal to half a mile." [6] Hays's report, as usual, was modest and brief. The hostiles outnumbered him more than two to one and gave him, as Lane said later, "a very busy fight for half an hour." Lane could not "commend in terms too strong Colonel Hays."

As Hays knew that it was useless to try to overtake the remaining lancers, he wheeled back to the plaza. Here he met Adjutant Hays, sent by Lane to seek reinforcements, and he dispatched Captain Daggett to Lane's assistance.

Lane was outnumbered, and his opponents were well sheltered. He dismounted the Texans, and the combatants fought at distances of from thirty feet to muzzle-to-muzzle. In a desperate effort the Texans forced the doors. Thirty of the enemy were killed, and several prisoners were taken, many escaping through a rear passage which was unknown to the Americans. [7]

Having routed the main forces of the enemy, Hays, directing from the plaza, sent reinforcements again to Lane and to Truett. He then devoted his efforts to pursuing any scattered and fugitive Mexicans who had escaped their attacks. Soon Colonel Montagna and twenty of his men surrendered, most of the remainder being killed or wounded, shot, usually, through the eye.[8] The Rangers were very deliberate in their firing after the first few minutes of the conflict had converted the struggle into a siege. Hays learned, while chasing some guerrillas in the western part of town, that Jarauta's quarters were in the large church fronting the plaza. Search of the premises revealed that the chieftain had escaped a few minutes before any of the American troops had arrived at the building.[9] Jarauta's force consisted of four hundred lancers and fifty infantrymen. Hays's loss was five men wounded, three of them severely, while the enemy had one hundred and twenty killed.[10]

The American force left Sequalteplan the next morning, February 26, and traveled most of the night following. Some incidents occurred on the return journey of about one hundred and fifty miles which gave much amusement. For instance, a Mexican had followed the column and had overtaken the command when a stop was made. Queried as to his motive, he said that he had a grievance to report. He was taken before Lane to tell his story which, in brief, was:

"Señor, I am a peaceable man and have taken no part in the war. My two daughters went to Tulancingo on a visit. The Texans stole their horses."

Lane replied: "Well, sir, if you will point out your horses, they shall be returned to you."

Then the general escorted the citizen to a balcony of the second story of the house in which the ranking officers were quartered. Below them every horse could be seen, including a fine animal which Chevaille had presented to the general several weeks before. The Mexican looked carefully at the horses and then pointed to Lane's horse and said,

"There is one of them."

Lane swung an astonished gaze upon his visitor, and then "Old Gritter Face," as the men called him, lost his temper and yelled:

"Get out of here, you infernal liar, or I will have you hung in fifteen minutes!" [11]

That evening the march was halted while the column was once more the unwelcome guest of the master of the hacienda in the mountain valley. Again there was an unpleasant incident, precipitated by a few of the younger troops who were attempting, against all orders, a little quiet foraging.

Bill Hicklin's presence was disclosed by a squawking hen which he was trying to kidnap. Another young daredevil threw a stone at a pig which he planned to stun, but the missile ricocheted from the shoat, bounced around a corner, and struck "Old Gritter Face" on the shin. At this instant, the proprietor came hurrying up to complain about his chickens and pigs being disturbed. The general, now hopping mad from the effect of the stone, used strong language in avowing "his willingness to see the landlord, the hens, and the pigs settled" in hell. [12] His orders promptly ended the foraging.

As Hays led his Rangers into the heart of Mexico City, eyes were focused on the Mexican lance which each man carried as a souvenir of his recent battle. The expedition had consumed fourteen days and covered more than five hundred miles. Including the four hundred of the previous excursion, these partisans had traversed more than nine hundred miles in thirty-five days. Much of the riding was over country that was barely passable. During this last six weeks of being "quartered" in or near Mexico City, they had been marching and fighting throughout five of them. [13]

XVIII

PARTISAN GREETS DICTATOR

AFTER the American and Mexican commanders in chief ratified an armistice on March 4, any subsequent revolts were to be checked by the armies of both nations. Such men as Paredes and Almonte remained quiet, and Santa Anna was preparing to leave the country. There were still some active guerrillas, but as Hays had just disciplined the most daring and energetic of these, Padre Jarauta, he directed his operations after March 1 chiefly toward minor leaders who preyed on wagon trains along the Veracruz road.

Hays next received an order to move his regiment down the road toward Veracruz, to patrol the road as he marched slowly toward the coast, and send detachments at will against any robbers found. It was circulated early throughout the command that the regiment was soon to be at the coast, where the men would be mustered out.[1]

Twenty miles from Mexico City, Hays and several of his officers and men paused upon an elevation near Rio Frio to gaze back upon the valley. The distant capital looked like a white spot, but recollections magnified vision. Nonchalance soon possessed most of the soldiers, and they rode on undisturbed by care. Among these last was a youth who served as Hays's hostler. He rode a fine horse and led another, and was expected to be where the Colonel could signal him if in a hurry for a fresh mount. He persisted often in loitering behind the column, whenever Hays was not about, and then galloping by the force with the excuse that Hays, ahead with scouts, might need him. Every time he passed Ford and Chevaille, their horses became excited and a disturbance took place all down the line. These officers remonstrated strongly with him, but the heedless youth only laughed. Major Chevaille even wished that the guerrillas "would catch and kill him."[2]

Midway between Mexico City and Puebla the Rangers came to Rio Frio, a scenic place Hays always enjoyed so much that encampment for the night was made there. For once, he did not order his horses brought near him in readiness for a possible emergency. Probably all concerned were so delighted with the beauty of the spot that the hostler was forgotten.

At dawn Hays ordered camp broken, and the column swung onto the road. Chevaille and Ford were leading. They came to an abrupt halt when they found a mutilated body in their path. Both dismounted and Ford knelt to ascertain if life lingered, but the guerrillas had done a thorough job. Ford stood up after a hasty examination of the corpse and, detecting an interesting expression on Chevaille's face, inquired,

"Mike, what are you thinking of?"

"I'll be damned if I ever make such a wish about a man while I live," vowed Mike.[3]

Hays said nothing about the two good horses which had been entrusted to his hostler. The Colonel left Major Truett with the companies of Daggett and Handley in this section for a while.

As the regiment moved on toward Veracruz, it camped in localities where there was evidence of too much boldness on the part of robber bands. Hays sent out troops of Rangers to administer chastisement in liberal doses. In the community of San Carlos, the sergeant major demonstrated thoroughness in his art by standing in his tracks and killing with a six-shooter three skeptical guerrillas at a distance of more than one hundred and twenty yards.

The Rangers paused for a couple of days at Tepejahuilco. Hays's spies, Miguel and Vicente, reported to him that a band of guerrillas was at San Juan de los Llanos, sixteen miles away. The Colonel directed Ford to take fourteen men to search the village.

Ford and his detail rode into the plaza of San Juan just at dusk. When he demanded quarters and provisions for men and horses, the deputy of the prefect of police conducted the Rangers to a large stone building but stated that the prefect could not furnish rations for mount or man. Whereupon Ford and Pete Goss, who served as interpreter, called upon the prefect and inquired the reason for his refusal. Ford stated his name, rank, and regiment, but the Mexican was plainly unimpressed. Finally Ford mentioned Hays as commander of the unit. Instantly calling his deputy, the prefect gave orders to provide for the needs of "Devil Jack's" men, and at the same time extended an invitation to come and bring any friends he wished to dine. Ford accepted the invitation.

Still the adjutant was uneasy. There were enough men around the Americans "to knock us on head with stones." [4] Should he attend the dinner? What would Hays do under these circumstances? Ford knew there would be no faltering on the Colonel's part in such a situation. He was received cordially and enjoyed a sixteen-course dinner served on fine silver in luxurious surroundings. Indeed there was magic in a name!

After his narrow escape from capture at the hands of Hays, Santa Anna so feared being made a prisoner that he decided to leave the country. The authorities of both Mexico and the United States granted permission for his departure.[5] Passports were received, but Santa Anna and his family had to await the arrival of a vessel. In correspondence with Colonel George W. Hughes, governor of the American occupation at Jalapa, the former president stated that he wished to reside in the meantime near El Encero, where he owned an estate. He inquired whether Hughes would provide a safeguard. Hughes replied that when the general was ready to move, he would be greeted with honors, furnished with the safeguard, and later given an escort to the coast.[6]

Meanwhile Hays and his men, traveling by easy marches to Veracruz, encamped about two miles before reaching Jalapa, the most delightful place Hays had ever seen. This camp promised to afford a few days of rest from the exacting pursuits of the loitering bands.

At Jalapa, on the morning of March 28, Hughes and his staff left with three companies of Maryland mounted volunteers commanded by Major John R. Kenly to meet Santa Anna and his entourage at San Miguel. Kenly was in charge of the escort, and led out along the Perote road to the village, which was only six miles distant. Here the convoy halted at the house of General José Durán to await the arrival of Santa Anna.

Santa Anna's procession was preceded by a small force of well-mounted and well-equipped lancers. Next came an eight-mule carriage occupied by the ex-president, his wife, and his daughter, and followed closely by a company of lancers. When the general's carriage came to Durán's residence, the procession halted, and the ex-dictator and his family alighted. Immediately Hughes and his staff were presented to the guests.

Antonio Lopez de Santa Anna's second wife was often called the "Flower of Mexico." Apparently only twenty years or younger, she was of middle height and attractive figure, and rather Anglo-Saxon in appearance. Her eyes were hazel and her hair dark, but her skin was unusually fair. Her beautiful mouth disclosed perfect teeth. Dignified and gracious in manner, she exhibited as much poise in this unhappy situation as if she were entertaining in the president's palace at the capitol. Seño-rita Santa Anna, a child of her father's first wife, was entirely different from her young stepmother in appearance and demeanor. About fifteen years of age, she looked much older. She had no English, she explained, as they were always traveling or moving, which circumstances interfered with her education.[7]

Hays had been informed by Hughes of Santa Anna's plans. It was about four miles to Durán's, where Santa Anna was stopping for dinner; hence the Colonel and several of his officers went to meet the defeated leader and pay their respects to him. Truett and Ford decided, about the same time, that they would ride into Jalapa and watch the Mexicans greet their former foremost general.[8]

At General Durán's the distinguished guests, host, and various military officers sat down to dinner at half past two o'clock. Señora Santa Anna sat at the head of the table, her husband to her right, Hughes and Señorita Santa Anna on her left; Kenly was placed at the opposite end of the table, with the other guests seated next to Hughes according to rank.

After dinner Santa Anna, passing a case of fine cigars, invited

Kenly to smoke. In a moment the resultant conversation pro-
voked much hearty laughter, especially from the general. With
several officers standing alert and stiff behind his chair, the food,
wines, and tobacco were mellowing the former dictator. Even
as Santa Anna was expanding almost to the point of reveling
because of his combined enjoyment of himself and the impression he was creating, Kenly was becoming more uneasy. He was
apprehensive of the Ranger camp located on both sides of the
main road, between San Miguel and Jalapa, along which
General Santa Anna's procession had to travel. Rumors had
reached him that Santa Anna should not pass alive through their
camp. The reports of the threats had caused Kenly to inquire
of Hays about the situation. Hays told him that he believed there
was no danger of any act of retaliation. Evidently Kenly was not
well acquainted with the Colonel or his men. Not satisfied with
Hays's reassurance, he kept worrying, aware of his distraction
and occasionally glancing at the American officers crowded
about the door.

Among the throng he noticed a man without insignia. This
individual was an American, dressed partly in the Mexican fashion, but quite plainly. He wore a silk sash around his waist, a
round, skirtless, sleeved coat, and a Mexican hat. In this person
devoid of badges of authority, Kenly recognized Hays. Immediately the major arose from the table and went to the Colonel
and greeted him, saying,

"Suppose you let me present you to General Santa Anna."

Hays replied, "Well," and they moved toward the dinner
table.

As Kenly and Hays approached Santa Anna, "There was,"
Kenly narrated, "general suspension of conversation, a movement of alarm perceptible among the Mexican officers of the
escort, and a silence very painful to me. Santa Anna was as yet
eating fruit. I said, 'General, pemit me to present to you'—when
I had got thus far, he turned his face toward us and was in the
act of rising—'Colonel Jack Hays.' When I pronounced this
name, his whole appearance and demeanor changed, and if a
loaded bombshell with fuse burning and sputtering had fallen

on that dinner table, a greater sensation would not have been caused. The Mexican officers arose from their seats; standing and motionless they looked at me. Señora Santa Anna turned very pale; the General resumed eating fruit, with his gaze on the table. Colonel Hays, gentleman that he was, bowed politely and withdrew from the room." [9]

Apparently Santa Anna's appetite was satisfied instantly, as he approached Kenly immediately after Hays's withdrawal and stated that they were ready to march. Kenly acceded to the request instantly, although he records that he had the opportunity to speak to Hays, implying he tendered his regrets.

Kenly's apprehension was based upon his slight but impressive knowledge of the former relations of the "Napoleon of the West" with some of the Rangers. He was unaware that Truett and Ford were back in camp in an effort to prevent any possible attack upon the cavalcade.

Upon reaching the Ranger encampment, Ford and Truett "appealed to reason and to honor. . . . 'He [Santa Anna] is virtually a prisoner of war. He is in his own country, and is traveling under safe-conduct granted by our commanding general; to take his life would be an act the civilized world would brand as assassination. You would dishonor Texas!' They [the men] answered, 'Then we will not do it.' The men then wanted to talk to Santa Anna, but were advised to remain silent. They were stationed on the side of the road." [10]

In San Miguel, Kenly placed a company of his troopers on either side of the carriage. A sergeant at the head of each of the single-file companies carried a United States flag. The escort of Mexicans was just in front of the carriage, and Kenly's third company closed the column.

As the procession neared the encampment, Kenly galloped to the head of the column and placed himself in front of the carriage mules. His movement focused the attention of the Mexicans on the Rangers, who were seated on the stone fences on either side of the road. Though the hundreds of Texans were quiet and motionless, the Mexicans became alarmed. Carriage drivers shouted at their mules, whistled shrilly, and plied their whips so vigorously that the teams broke into full speed, the escort doing likewise, perforce.

Kenly states that he now saw a lone mounted Texan riding toward them in the middle of the road. So the major "made right at him, struck the side of his horse's head," chronicled Kenly, "with the flat of my sabre, he swerved, and we were past horse and rider before either I am sure was aware of what was the matter." [11] Kenly's excuse for this act was that there was no time for explanation or warning.

Adjutant Ford's account of the Rangers' review of Santa Anna's party does not mention the incident of the lone Texas horseman's treatment at the hands of Kenly. Nor does his chronicle agree in other details with that of the commander of the escort. Ford concluded: "The un-uniformed representatives of Texas stood motionless and silent. . . . There were no salutations, no ungraceful remarks. . . . The Texans broke ranks and returned to camp." [12]

Hays commended his officers on their direction of the men in this incident, and through them the Rangers learned how pleased he was with their conduct. The experience changed Santa Anna's opinion of Texans. Hughes and some of his officers visited him at his hacienda. The general talked freely concerning the war. When someone mentioned Hays's men, Santa Anna remarked: "A Texan would think he had made a bad shot if he did not hit a Mexican's eye at a hundred yards."

On April 4 Santa Anna left Mexico. Hays was one of his escort to La Antigua, where he was to embark on a Spanish ship for Venezuela. Major General W. O. Butler, who had succeeded Scott, complimented the Colonel in assigning him to this task.[13]

XIX

GOING HOME

HAYS's next encampment was at El Encero, fourteen miles below Jalapa. A few of his men began to catch homesickness from the army that daily passed their camp, nor was their nostalgia reduced by hearing the Pennsylvania Volunteers march by singing a stanza from "We Are Coming Home":

> We are coming! Adieu, ye daughters of a royal line.
> We own ye held our hearts in thrall awhile;
> But now fair maids in other lands we find,
> Who will greet the soldier with a smile.

Soon all the troops were at Veracruz except the Rangers. The Colonel visited the port on April 10 to arrange for the discharge of his regiment and to apply for transportation to Texas for most of the men.[1]

General Santa Anna's lands were so extensive on either side of the Veracruz road that the Rangers were practically on the grounds of his hacienda. In fact Lieutenant Pancoast bought beef for the force from the general's majordomo. This meat would become so vitiated soon after it was obtained that Pancoast complained, but the Mexican protested that he could obtain no better. It was revealed later that Santa Anna's majordomo had been systematically swindling them by charging top prices for beef which he had bought at a bargain because it had been in the market so long.[2]

With a commissary to purchase supplies, Hays did not approve foraging, and thievery and robbery were instantly and severely punished. Few of the Rangers, however, were guilty of such crimes. Dislike of the Mexican was one thing; violation of regulations which could bring criticism upon Texas was another. Regardless of a soldier's background, Hays would not tolerate lawlessness even when approached with distressful appeals.[3]

[211]

Hays took a detachment of his command and made an inspection tour back to Mexico City to ascertain whether the road was comparatively free of guerrillas. His recent efforts had enabled the stagecoach to resume its schedule between the capital and Puebla. As Hays made the return trip, he counseled with the garrison commanders at Rio Frio and Puebla concerning means of circumventing the guerrillas.

Back at El Encero, Hays became even more aware that any day might bring orders to march his men to Veracruz and muster them out of the service. While the opportunity presented itself, however, various matters were consummated, both trivial and beneficial. Arguments were settled as to whether Colt's latest model six-shooter would throw a ball farther than a Mississippi rifle. Thorough trials proved to all that the Colt secured the greater distance.[4] During their stay here both officers and men joined in presenting the chaplain with a memento of their association—five hundred dollars in gold as a practical token of their respect and affection. Months later, in a letter to Ford, Corley wrote: "God bless Hays's regiment, but for them I could have never paid my debts."[5]

A few days after his return from Veracruz, Hays received orders to march his regiment to that city. Serving as an escort for a train of wagons, they arrived at the coast on April 29, and again camped at Vergara. They celebrated the anniversary of their enlistment by marching into Veracruz and being mustered out. All except Hays and Ford were leaving the service. In Texas these officers were rejoining the Rangers engaged in guarding the long frontier. Hays's leadership had engendered a fraternal regard between men and officers, and it was in harmony that adieus were exchanged.

Hays had become one of the most popular military leaders in America, and it was as a leader of men that he now was being greeted everywhere. Ford, whose position entitled him to speak authoritatively, wrote:

He [Hays] expressed no feeling of jealousy towards his subordinate officers. He gave them opportunities to distinguish themselves, and was outspoken in his commendations of good conduct. He was lenient to the erring, unless the offense had involved a taint of dishonesty; then he was immovably rigid. He was almost idolized by many. He was modest and retiring; an expression of admiration of his acts would cause him to blush like a woman.

As a commander he trusted a great deal to the good faith of his officers. He went among his men, patiently heard their complaints, and redressed abuses. He knew how to conduct marches requiring toilsome endurance, and to prevent his men from becoming despondent. On the battle field he saw everything, and readily took advantage of the errors of the enemy. He was cool, self-possessed, and brave; a good shot, and the man who singled him out in a fight came to grief.

Had the Mexican War lasted longer, another brigadier-general would have been appointed. It was understood in the City of Mexico that Col. Hays had an excellent chance to receive the appointment. . . . A county in Texas was named in honor of him soon after annexation.[6]

Hays, his officers, and some of the troops embarked on the steamboat *Maria Burt* and landed at Powder Horn, Texas, on Lavaca Bay amid much cheering and applause from the people of the community.[7] After a cannon salute, a speech of welcome, and a dinner, the Rangers were invited to be honor guests at a ball in the evening. Even men eager to be on the road to their homes could not decline such generous hospitality.

Hays, Truett, Ford, and Daggett stayed at the same house. They agreed that an effort should be made to improve their appearance, for their clothing was tattered and besmeared with travel stains, but they soon found that the village afforded few facilities for replenishing wardrobes. Since Daggett was especially unfortunate in that he was over six feet tall and proportionately large, the nearest approach to a fit that he could obtain was a suit with coat sleeves and trouser legs almost six inches too short. He had Santa Anna's regimental coat, expensive and pretentious by any standard, but it was made for a medium-sized figure. So he compromised by buying one of the ready-made New York creations for men of large size.[8]

Hays wore Santa Anna's coat, valued at a thousand dollars. The garment of coarse blue cloth was padded throughout. The body was lined with black satin, the skirts with white satin, and all back seams and borders of the skirt were covered with bands of heavy gold lace; weighty gold-lace epaulets were on the shoulders. Ornamented with heavy gold ball buttons and embossments of gold on the front, the coat weighed fifteen pounds. Although it was gaudy, too narrow in the shoulders, and tailored for a pigeon-breasted figure, Hays wore it in lieu of adequate clothing and also on a dare from his comrades. His enjoyment of the evening was no whit dampened by the attention which his borrowed finery attracted.[9]

This reception was merely the first tendered to Hays and his men. Population was sparse—the settlements neither numerous nor large—but every town through which they passed en route to San Antonio showed its appreciation by bestowing honors and proffering entertainment. When the party reached Salado Creek they were greeted by a citizens' delegation and most of the townspeople.[10] Five evenings later, neighboring towns joined with San Antonio in staging a congratulatory ball to welcome the returning Rangers. The festivities would have complimented a town larger and more pretentious.[11]

Among the more than three hundred persons assembled after eight o'clock were many whose "manners, dress and accomplishments would grace any similar assemblage in any city in the Union."[12] The ballroom was appropriately and tastefully decorated with flags, flowers, and evergreens. Upon a conspicuous transparency was the inscription:

> Texas!
> Honor to the Brave,
> And Welcome To The Return of
> Soldiers and Patriots.
> San Antonio, May 20th, 1848.

A large flag hung in the center, and at the ends of the room the words ALAMO and BUNKER HILL, suggesting remembrance of Travis and Warren, covered the walls.

At nine o'clock the committee on arrangements ushered in the distinguished guests. Dancing continued until midnight when refreshments were served; then the dancing was continued until an early hour of the morning. A local correspondent of the New Orleans *Delta* stated: "Of course, the beautiful and amiable lady of Colonel Hays was the bright and particular star of the evening, the cynosure of all eyes and the constant recipient of the most marked attention. . . ." [13]

Everyone in the city seemed delighted with the cordial reception tendered Hays. No man in Texas was more popular, or more widely spoken of throughout the states. Texans would have enjoyed giving him any gift within their power if he had merely indicated his desires. Many supposed that he would resume command of the frontier battalion, but Hays had other plans.

A week after the San Antonio ball, Hays and Colonel Bell conferred with state officials in Austin, and Hays indicated he soon was to visit Washington to settle his war accounts with the government, then retire from the service. The Austin *Democrat* of June 10 explained:

. . . Circumstances of a private nature are said to have induced this determination on his part. He has spent the prime of his life in active service on the frontier and in Mexico. Any one at all conversant with the military life is aware how difficult it is to save much of army earnings.

The security of the frontier and the probability of peace with Mexico, precludes the possibility of the entertainment of an idea that the Colonel retires at a time when his country requires him in the field. . . .

When the news of Hays's plan to retire reached New Orleans, the *Picayune* of that city carried a long story concerning the "Retirement of Col. Hays" and commented: "The gallant Hays, who has carried his life in his hand for the last ten years, and perhaps braved death oftener in that time than any other man —whose services in the field have been more ardent and valuable to Texas than those of any other citizen, is at length about to retire, and reposing on his laurels, which he seems to wear unconsciously, so modest is his bearing, to seek in the bosom of his family the repose and enjoyment to which he is so well entitled." [14]

The citizens of San Antonio had permitted him only a few

days' rest before they presented him with their ideas of a road-exploring project. He wished to resume surveying, and yet he realized the service to the city, state, and nation that would be done by opening a route from San Antonio to Chihuahua. Perhaps there was also the thought of an all-weather overland route to the Pacific. Hays agreed to mention the road enterprise at the proper time in Washington.

During this unsettled period he was not disinterested when a young counselor from Virginia suggested that they go to California. The proposal was discussed at Mrs. Elliot's where the Colonel and Mrs. Hays were guests. Mrs. Hays would have to be left in Texas until after her husband had become established. Thoughts of the long journey facing the Colonel, the tedious wait until she could join him, and the fact that it would be a venture at best, caused Susan to give way to tears. Mrs. Elliot scolded him kindly, but disapprovingly. Hays for the time dropped the idea.[15]

In June he journeyed to Washington. Through every city he traversed, someone recognized him, and he was lionized. At the capital he made satisfactory settlement of his claims against the government and resigned from the army. Then he consulted the authorities about opening the San Antonio-El Paso road. Not only did they authorize his proposed exploration of the area, but they also approved his use of Rangers from an outpost.

EPILOGUE

AFTER the Mexican War, Jack Hays answered the call of the West, moving on to the Gold Rush country of California. Before 1849 expired, he was enroute to the western state, where he lived in the San Francisco region through the days of the silver era as well. His thirty-three years there covered some of the state's most turbulent decades. Although his reputation as a military man lived on in California, his civilian life appears in retrospect to be just as important. Again his fearlessness and integrity contributed to his success, first as sheriff of San Francisco County and then as U.S. surveyor general of California. He briefly interrupted his business career to lead a successful campaign against a Paiute uprising in Nevada.

His ability and reputation for honesty helped him become one of the most important ranchers and real estate developers in the region — founder of Oakland and liberal philanthropist; a civic leader active in the promotion of utilities, banks, wharves, and railroads; mainstay of the California Democratic party; and generous supporter of academic institutions and education in the state. He was representative of the wholesome, successful man of his times, and more typical of the state's admirable leaders than its most ambitious politician, distinguished orator, or wealthiest squatter, for he succeeded in combining the active and the contemplative life to a degree rarely equaled.

After 1870 Hays lived a semiretired life as a stockman and capitalist on his ranch in Alameda County. His health declined gradually during his last years, yet in spite of ailments — especially rheumatism — he often bestirred himself to assist some guest in his community or to attend an important meeting.

He died in 1883 — on San Jacinto Day — at the age of sixty-six.

NOTES

PREFACE

[1] Arneson, E. P., in the *Southwestern Historical Quarterly*, Vol. 29, No. 2 (Oct. 1935), 96; Stuart, B., in the *Galveston News*, May 8, 1910.

[2] The most complete publication about Hays is a pamphlet [Hunter, J. Marvin (Editor)], *Jack Hays, The Intrepid Texas Ranger* (1928?).

CHAPTER 1

[1] Caperton, J., Sketch of Colonel John C. Hays, Texas Ranger, MS.

[2] Gorgas, Miles C., to Mrs. H. T. Hays, Sept. 6, 1915.

[3] Gorgas, Miles C., A "Roughshort" of some of the descendants of Colonel Robert Hays and Jane Donelson, prepared Sept. 5, 1915.

[4] Copy of Extract from Robert Dyas, Huntsville, Ala., to Miles C. Gorgas.

[5] Putnam, A. W., *History of Middle Tennessee* . . . (1859), 638; Gorgas, as cited.

[6] Williams, S. C., *Early Travels in The Tennessee Country* . . . (1928), 338.

[7] Abernethy, T. P., *From Frontier to Plantation in Tennessee* (1932), 203.

[8] Heitman, F. B., *Historical Register and Dictionary of the United States Army* (1903), 516.

[9] West, E. H., "John Coffee Hays," *Dictionary of American Biography*, VIII (1932), 463.

[10] Betty Hays, daughter of Colonel John C. Hays, statement in the addenda to [Hunter], *Jack Hays, The Intrepid Texas Ranger*, 46.

[11] West, as cited.

[12] Betty Hays, as cited, 51; Wood, M. W. (Pub.), *History of Alameda County, California;* . . . (1883), 898.

[13] Wood, M. W., *History of Alameda County, California* (1883), states that Work, who became Sonoma County's first sheriff, "used to tell this story."

[14] Betty Hays, as cited, 51.

[15] Affleck, J. D. History of John C. Hays (n.d.), MS.

[16] Caperton, as cited.

[17] Brackett, A. G., *General Lane's Brigade in Central Mexico* (1854), 196.

[18] Affleck, as cited.

[19] For the colonization of Texas, the revolution, and the beginning of the Republic of Texas, see Barker, E. C., *The Life of Stephen F. Austin* (1925).

CHAPTER 2

[1] *Laws of the Republic of Texas*, 1836, I, 53.

[2] Caperton, Sketch of Colonel John C. Hays, Texas Ranger, MS.

[3] Smith to W. S. Fisher, Sec. of War, San Antonio de Bexar, Mar. 27, 1837; *Telegraph and Texas Register*, Apr. 11, 1837.

[4] Rockwall, R. R., *A Noble Company of Adventurers* (n.d.), 86–89.

⁵ Richardson, R. N., *Texas, The Lone Star State* (1943), 147.

⁶ Wright, J. W., *San Antonio de Bexar, Historical, Traditional, Legendary* (1916), 72; DeShields, J. T., *Border Wars of Texas . . .* (1912), 264.

⁷ Caperton, as cited.

⁸ *Ibid.*

⁹ Looscan, Adele B., "Miles Squier Bennett," The *Quarterly* of the Texas State Historical Association, VII (July 1903-April 1904), 166.

¹⁰ Gulick, C. A., and Allen, W. (Eds.), *Papers of Mirabeau Bonaparte Lamar,* Vol. 4, part 1, p. 230. Cited hereafter in this chapter as the *Lamar Papers.*

¹¹ DeShields, as cited, 265.

¹² *Lamar Papers,* as cited, 230.

¹³ Also spelled Flaco.

¹⁴ The Indians and Mexicans of this area of the Southwest called the Rio Grande the Rio Bravo.

¹⁵ Wood, *History of Alameda County, California, . . .*, 899.

CHAPETR 3

¹ Caperton, Sketch of Colonel John C. Hays, Texas Ranger, MS.

² Green, R. M. (Ed.), *Memoirs of Mary A. Maverick* (1921), 29.

³ Barker, E. C., Potts, C. S., Ramsdell, C. W., *A School History of Texas* (1912), 166.

⁴ Morrell, Z. N., *Flowers and Fruits in the Wilderness . . .* (1872), 113.

⁵ Webber, C. W., *Tales of the Southern Border* (1887), 55. Webber served in Hays's company during the time of which he writes in this work.

⁶ *Ibid.*, 56.

⁷ Green, as cited, 29.

⁸ *Texas Telegraph and Texas Register,* Sept. 4, 1839.

⁹ See Green, as cited, 30.

¹⁰ Wilson, Mrs. M. A. C., *Reminiscences of Persons, Records and Documents of Texan Times* (1882), 3-4.

¹¹ *Lamar Papers,* Gulick and Allen (Eds.), IV, pt. 1, 231-232.

¹² Statement of Hays. See the *Lamar Papers,* as cited, 232.

¹³ Smithers, H. (Ed.), *The Papers of Mirabeau Bonaparte Lamar* (1927), V, 409-410.

¹⁴ *Ibid.*, 233.

¹⁵ Morrell, as cited, 129.

¹⁶ Sowell, A. J., *Early Settlers and Indian Fighters of Southwest Texas* (1900), 19; DeShields, *Border Wars of Texas,* 324.

¹⁷ Barker, Potts, Ramsdell, as cited, 163-164.

¹⁸ See the *Record of Surveys,* Surveyor's Office, Bexar County.

CHAPTER 4

¹ This was the expressed opinion of Bigfoot Wallace, an authority on the subject. See Sowell, *Early Settlers and Indian Fighters of Southwest Texas,* 57.

² *Laws of the Republic of Texas,* 3 Cong., 1 Sess. (1839).

³ Caperton, Sketch of Colonel John C. Hays, Texas Ranger, MS.

⁴ *Ibid.*

NOTES

5 DeShields, *Border Wars of Texas,* 329; Wilbarger, J. W., *Indian Depredations in Texas* (1889), 74.

6 Sowell, as cited, 334-335.

7 Hays to Branch T. Archer, Secretary of War, in the Austin *Sentinel,* Apr. 22, 1841.

8 Caperton, as cited.

9 *Lamar Papers,* IV, Part 1, p. 233-234; Caperton, as cited; Hays to B. T. Archer, Secretary of War, July 1, 1841, in the Austin *Sentinel.*

10 This account is drawn chiefly from Sowell, as cited, 20 ff.

11 *Lamar Papers,* as cited. Vol. IV, Part 1, pp. 234-235; Caperton, as cited.

12 Hays to B. T. Archer, Sec. of War, Aug. 19, 1841.

13 The detail consisted of Sam Walker, Bigfoot Wallace, William Powell, and Chapman Woolfork.

14 Austin *Gazette,* Sept. 1, 1841.

15 Caperton, as cited; Wilbarger, as cited, 74-75; DeShields, as cited, 369-370. The account given here is far more conservative than the better-known versions.

CHAPTER 5

1 Green (Ed.), *Memoirs of Mary A. Maverick,* 55, 59.

2 *Ibid.*

3 Caperton, Sketch of Colonel John C. Hays, Texas Ranger, MS.

4 Smith, S. C., *Chile Con Carne: Or, The Camp and the Field* (1857), 268.

5 Caperton, as cited.

6 *Ibid.*

7 Morrell, *Flowers and Fruits . . . ,* 176.

8 Army Papers, Archives of the Republic, Texas State Library.

9 Later Atascosa County.

10 Sowell describes this fight which may also be found in the Colonel J. S. Ford Papers, State Library, Austin.

11 Brown, J. H., *History of Texas from 1685 to 1892* (1892), II, 211.

12 Brown, as cited, 213.

13 They were ambushed and captured on the Nueces River.

14 He also was captured.

CHAPTER 6

1 Brown, *History of Texas . . . ,* II, 213-215.

2 This incident was referred to locally as the "runaway of 1842." See Wright, *San Antonio de Bexar . . .* (1916), 75.

3 *Telegraph and Texas Register,* June 15, 1842.

4 *Ibid.,* June 29, 1842.

5 Report of the Secretary of War, Nov. 12, 1842; *Telegraph and Texas Register,* Jan. 4, 1843.

6 Organized as Guadalupe County in 1846.

7 "Hutchinson's Diary," Texas State Historical Association *Quarterly,* Vol. 13 (1909-10), 294.

8 *House Journal Appendix,* 7th Cong., Republic of Texas, p. 16.

9 *Ibid.,* 21-22.

NOTES

[10] See address of San Antonio citizens to the citizens of Gonzales County, Sept. 10, 1842 in *Ibid.*, 18-19.

[11] See *Sen. Ex. Doc.* 32, 31 Cong., 1 Sess., Report of the Sec. of War.

[12] Brown, as cited, 222.

[13] Morrell, *Flowers and Fruits in the Wilderness* . . . (1882 edit.), 166.

[14] *Ibid.*, 167.

[15] Matthew Caldwell to Sec. of War of the Republic, Sept. 18, 1842, in *Appendix to House Journal,* as cited, p. 16.

[16] Morrell, as cited, 168.

[17] Brown, as cited, 224.

[18] More conclusive evidence indicates that Hays's eyes were hazel or a deep blue but looked black when gleaming, while his hair was reddish-brown and looked black against a fine clear complexion which was gradually blackened by the Texas sun.

[19] Caperton, Sketch of John C. Hays, Texas Ranger, MS.

[20] Caperton, as cited.

[21] This incident is from Caperton, as cited.

[22] Morrell, as cited, 174; Caperton, as cited; Sowell, *Early Settlers and Indian Fighters,* 24-25.

[23] Sowell, as cited, 26.

[24] Smither, H. (Ed.), "Diary of Adolphus Sterne," *Southwestern Historical Quarterly,* Vol. 34 (Austin, 1931), 260.

[25] Caldwell, as cited, 17-18.

[26] Morrell, as cited, 179 ff.; *Telegraph and Texas Register,* Oct. 26, 1842.

[27] *Telegraph and Texas Register,* Jan. 15, 1843.

CHAPTER 7

[1] Hendricks, S. B., "The Somervell Expedition to the Rio Grande, 1842," *Southwestern Historical Quarterly,* XXIII, 115, 118.

[2] Williams, A. W. and Barker, E. C., (Eds.) *The Writings of Sam Houston, 1813-1863* (1941), IV (Sept. 1821- Feb. 1847), 144.

[3] Hamilton, M. C., Secretary of War & Marine, to Brig. Gen. A. Somervell, Nov. 19, 1842, in *Appendix to House Journal,* Republic of Texas, 7th Cong., pp. 7-9.

[4] Richardson, *Texas, The Lone Star State,* 163.

[5] Anson Jones, Secretary of State, to Isaac Van Zandt, Chargé d' Affaires of Texas, Feb. 16, 1843 in Garrison, George (Ed.), *Diplomatic Correspondence of the Republic of Texas,* II (1), Part 2, p. 127.

[6] *Appendix to House Journal,* 7th Cong., as cited, pp. 3-4.

[7] See Hamilton to Somervell, Nov. 19, 1842, in *Appendix to House Journal,* as cited, 7-9.

[8] Army Papers, Texas State Library.

[9] Brown, *History of Texas from 1685 to 1892,* II, 236.

[10] Hendricks, as cited, 116, 117, 120.

[11] Green, T. J., *Journal of the Texian Expedition Against Mier* (1845), 52.

[12] Green, as cited, 52-53; Hendricks, as cited, 118-119; Brown, II, 235-236.

[13] See Hendricks, as cited, 121.

[14] Brown, as cited, 237.

[15] Hendricks, as cited, 123.

[16] The negligent guard was said to be William Alsbury. See Brown, as cited, 237.

NOTES

17 Hunt, Memucan, in the *Telegraph and Texas Register,* Jan. 18, 1843.
18 Brown, as cited, 239.
19 Green, as cited, 48-49.
20 Brown, as cited, II, 241-242.
21 *Ibid.*
22 Vestal, S., *Bigfoot Wallace* (1942), 127.
23 Hendricks, as cited, 137.
24 Report of the Secretary of War, Nov. 25, 1843.

CHAPTER 8

1 *Morning Star* (Houston), Apr. 20, 1843.
2 *Telegraph and Texas Register,* May 10, 1843.
3 Jones, Anson, *Official Correspondence Relating to the Republic of Texas* (1859), 214.
4 *Morning Star,* May 11, 1843; *Telegraph and Texas Register,* May 17, 1843; Binkley, W. C., *The Expansionist Movement in Texas, 1836-1850* (1925), 105-106.
5 *Telegraph and Texas Register,* June 21, 1843.
6 *Morning Star,* Sept. 21, 1843.
7 Yoakum, H., *History of Texas . . . 1685 to . . . 1846* (1856), II, 413-414.
8 New Orleans *Bee,* Dec. 5, 1843.
9 Report of Secretary of War.
10 *Laws of the Republic of Texas,* 8th Cong. (1844), p. 3.
11 Webb, W. P., *The Great Plains* (1931), 173. This volume contains an authentic and readable account of the six-shooter.
12 *Telegraph and Texas Register,* Mar. 6, 1844.
13 *Laws, 8th Congress,* as cited, pp. 31-32.
14 The company was to patrol from the county of Bexar to Refugio.
15 *Telegraph and Texas Register,* Mar. 6, 1844.
16 *Ibid.,* Mar. 20, 1844.
17 Brackett, *General Lane's Brigade in Central Mexico,* 196.
18 *Telegraph and Texas Register,* Apr. 17, 1844.
19 Wilbarger, *Indian Depredations in Texas,* 66.
20 *Ibid.,* 290-295. Wilbarger's account of the riding match was quoted from an unpublished manuscript which later appeared as Duval, J. C., *Early Times in Texas* (Austin, 1892).
21 Sweet, G. H., *Texas: Her Early History . . .* (1878), 37-38.
22 Chabot, F. C., *The Perote Prisoners . . .* (1934), 82.
23 *Texas Democrat,* May 15, 1844.
24 *Morning Star,* May 9, 1844.

CHAPTER 9

1 Sowell, *Early Settlers and Indian Fighters of Southwest Texas,* 319.
2 This account is from that given by Tom Galbreath in Sowell, as cited, 319-322.
3 *Morning Star,* May 9, 1844.
4 Dallas *News,* May 14, 1893.
5 Hays to Secretary of War and Marines, June 16, 1844, in *Texas National Register* (Washington, Texas), Dec. 14, 1844; *House Journal,* Republic of Texas, 9 Cong., 38.

⁶ The Pinto Trace or Trail was an old Indian trail between southwest Texas and Nacogdoches.

⁷ Hays, as cited.

⁸ Wilbarger, *Indian Depredations in Texas,* 78; Morphis, J. M.,*History of Texas, from Its Discovery and Settlement; . . .* (1875), 429.

⁹ All accounts of this fight are more detailed and "readable" than the account given here. See, for instance, Reid, S. C., Jr., and Wilbarger.

¹⁰ *Morning Star,* as referred to in the text.

¹¹ This was the opinion of President Lamar. See Thrall, H. S., *A History of Texas . . .* (1876), 118.

¹² See *House Ex. Doc.* 2, 28 Cong., 2 Sess., p. 27. Ser. No. 464.

¹³ See Hill to Jones, Aug. 6, 1844, in *Ibid.,* pp. 25-26.

¹⁴ See Jones to Howard, Aug. 6, 1844; Howard to John C. Calhoun, Aug. 7, 1844, in *House Ex. Doc.* 2, 28 Cong., 2 Sess., pp. 24-25.

¹⁵ Bell, a native of Virginia, served six years as a Ranger under Hays. He was Governor from 1849 to 1853 and was re-elected in 1857.

¹⁶ Jones, as cited, 374.

¹⁷ Castro's Diary. Part III. Quoted in Sowell, as cited, 131. See, also, Sowell, pp. 148-154.

¹⁸ Also quoted in DeShields, *Border Wars of Texas,* 396.

¹⁹ Wilbarger, as cited, 72.

²⁰ *Morning Star,* Dec. 11, 19, 1844.

²¹ *Laws . . . Ninth Congress . . . Republic of Texas* (1845), 101.

²² Four new stations were created.

²³ See H. A. Alsbury to President Anson Jones, Feb. 23, 1845, in Jones, as cited, 436.

²⁴ *Telegraph and Texas Register,* Apr. 30, 1845.

²⁵ *Morning Star,* May 15, 1845.

²⁶ *Telegraph and Texas Register,* May 21, 1845.

²⁷ *Texas National Register* (Washington, Texas), Sept. 4, 1845.

²⁸ Smith, J. H., *The Annexation of Texas* (1911), 374-376.

²⁹ *Ibid.,* 448.

³⁰ Wm. G. Cooke to Anson Jones, June 21, 1845, in Jones, as cited, 472.

³¹ B. Sloat to T. G. Western, Supt. of Indian Affairs, Aug. 18, 1845, in Texas Indian Papers.

CHAPTER 10

¹ A. J. Donelson, Spec. Rep. of U. S., Austin, Texas, to James Buchanan, Sec. of State, U. S., July 6, 1845, in *Sen. Ex. Doc.* 16, 28 Cong., 2 Sess., p. 84.

² *Telegraph and Texas Register,* Sept. 3, 1845.

³ *Ibid.*

⁴ Taylor to Jones, Aug. 16, 1845, in *Sen. Ex. Doc.* 337, 29 Cong., 1 Sess., pp. 92-93.

⁵ Taylor to Adjutant General, Sept. 14, 1845, in *Sen. Ex. Doc.* 337, 29 Cong., 1 Sess., pp. 97-98.

⁶ *New Orleans Daily Picayune,* Oct. 8, 1845. This paper will be cited hereafter as the *Picayune.*

⁷ *Telegraph and Texas Register,* Nov. 15, 1845.

⁸ *Picayune,* Nov. 28, 1845.

⁹ *Picayune,* Jan. 6, 1846, quoting the *Texas National Register* (Washington, Texas).

[10] Major Joseph Daniels to Anson Jones, Dec. 31, 1845, in Jones, as cited, 508.

[11] Roemer, Ferdinand, Dr., *Texas mit Besonderer Rucksicht auf Deutsche Auswanderung* ... (1849), 162-164.

[12] *Texas Democrat*, May 6, 1846; also in *House Ex. Doc.* 60, 30 Cong., 1 Sess.

[13] Catlin, G., *North American Indians* (1891), 495-496.

[14] Webb, *The Great Plains*, 68.

[15] Harrison, F. M., in "Battle at Painted Rock," in addenda to [Hunter], *Jack Hays, The Intrepid Texas Ranger*, 42.

[16] By all these names and more was Hays known among the Comanches.

[17] [Hunter], as cited, 43.

[18] This account is based chiefly on that of Harrison, as cited, 41-44. Published in [Hunter], the story probably was obtained from Affleck.

[19] Caperton, Sketch of Colonel John C. Hays, Texas Ranger, MS.

[20] Hendricks, George C., in the *Austin Statesman*, Dec. 7, 1903.

[21] *Ibid.*

[22] *Ibid.*

CHAPTER 11

[1] Smith, J. H., *The War With Mexico* (1919), I, 154-155.

[2] *Ibid.*, 149-150; Taylor to Adjutant General, May 11, 1846, *Sen. Pub. Doc.* 337, 29 Cong., 1 Sess., p. 125.

[3] Webb, W. P., *The Texas Rangers, A Century of Frontier Defense* (1935), 94.

[4] Greer, James K. (Ed.), *A Texas Ranger and Frontiersman* (1932), 33.

[5] *Picayune*, June 8, 1846.

[6] Captains C. B. Acklin, S. L. S. Ballowe, E. Chandler, F. S. Early, J. Gillespie, T. Green, C. C. Herbert, and J. B. McCown were in command of the eight companies. McCulloch and R. A. Gillespie were on detached services with their companies. Walker was doing special service with a mixed company. See also, Special Order No. 113, July 28, 1846.

[7] *Texas Democrat*, Jan. 27, 1847.

[8] Kenly, J. R., *Memoirs of a Maryland Volunteer* (1873), 53.

[9] *Texas Democrat*, Jan. 27, 1847.

[10] *Picayune*, Aug. 14, 1846.

[11] Webb, as cited, 96, 98.

[12] King, W. H., "The Texas Ranger Service," in Wooten, D. G. (Ed.), *Comprehensive History of Texas* (1898), II, 338.

[13] In *House Ex. Doc.* 60, 30 Cong., 1 Sess., pp. 676-677. Ser. no. 520.

[14] *Picayune*, Sept. 10, 1846.

[15] *Ibid.*

[16] Reid, S. C., Jr., *The Scouting Expeditions of McCulloch's Texas Rangers* (1847), 108-109.

[17] Charles A. Harper, Hays's Adjutant, and a lawyer by profession, in the *Texas Democrat*, Jan. 27, 1847.

[18] *House Ex. Doc.* 60, 30 Cong., I Sess., Orders No. 119, 120, Sept. 17 and 18, 1846, p. 506. Ser. no. 520.

[19] Harper, as cited.

[20] Pioneer, A, "Recollections of the Mexican War," *The Pioneer* (San Jose, Calif.), XV, No. 8, p. 125 (Aug. 15, 1900). Under the anonymous signature of "A Pioneer" there appeared a series of articles under this title. The articles are authentic.

[21] [Giddings, Luther], *Sketches of the Campaign in Northern Mexico by an Officer of the First Ohio Volunteers* (1853), 143.

NOTES

22 *Ibid.,* 143-144.

23 *Ibid.,* 154. These brief descriptions of the Monterey defenses have been drawn from Giddings, and Kenly, as cited, 102-103.

24 Smith, as cited, I, 238, 496.

CHAPTER 12

1 General Worth to Major W. W. S. Bliss, Asst. Adjt. Gen., Army of Occupation, Sept. 28, 1846, in *House Ex. Doc.* 4, 29 Cong., 2 Sess., p. 102. Ser. no. 497.

2 [Giddings], . . . *Campaign in Northern Mexico* . . . , 158.

3 "Recollections of the Mexican War," by "A Pioneer," in *The Pioneer,* Oct. 15, 1900, p. 152. Cited hereafter as "Recollections."

4 *Ibid.; Picayune,* Nov. 19, 1846.

5 *Picayune,* Oct. 23, 1846.

6 Greer (Ed.), *A Texas Ranger and Frontiersman,* 34.

7 *Ibid.,* 34-35; *Picayune,* Oct. 23, 1846; Caperton, Sketch of Colonel John C. Hays, Texas Ranger, MS.

8 Greer, as cited, 34-35.

9 Hays to Gen. J. Pinckney Henderson, Commanding Texan Division, Sept. 24 (?), 1846, Papers of Mirabeau Bonaparte Lamar, p. 139. This was a copy of the report handed to Worth.

10 Adjutant C. A. Harper in the *Texas Democrat,* Jan. 27, 1847.

11 Clairborne, J. F. H., *Life and Correspondence of John A. Quitman* (1860), I, 399n. James L. Freaner, native of Maryland, came to Louisiana as a mere youth. He went to Texas with the Louisiana regiment and there joined the Rangers.

12 Caperton, as cited.

13 Reid, *Scouting Expeditions of McCulloch's Texas Rangers,* 157.

14 Harper, as cited.

15 Hays, as cited, 139. Colonel Hays detached the companies of Green, McCown, R. A. Gillespie, Chandler, Ballowe, and McCulloch.

16 Hays, as cited, 139.

17 *Ibid.*

18 [Giddings], as cited, 193.

19 "Recollections," as cited, No. 8 (Oct. 15, 1900), p. 153; Worth, as cited; *Picayune,* Nov. 19, 1846; Greer, as cited, 37; Giddings, 195.

20 Kenly, *Memoirs of a Maryland Volunteer,* 121, 158. The enemy lost about two hundred killed and wounded; the Americans six killed and fifteen wounded.

21 Morphis, J. M., *History of Texas* . . . (1875), 450-451.

22 Hays, as cited, 140.

23 Four companies of the 7th Infantry commanded by Captain T. H. Holmes accompanied Hays; four companies of the 8th Infantry and a reserve of four companies of the Artillery Battalion followed Walker. There was a howitzer with Hays's party and two 6-pounders with that of Walker. Lt. Col. Childs was senior officer.

24 Smith, *The War With Mexico,* II, 258.

25 Greer, as cited, 38-39.

26 *Ibid.,* 39.

27 *Picayune,* Nov. 19, 1846.

28 "Recollections," as cited, No. 11 (Nov. 15, 1900), p. 169.

29 *Ibid.,* 170.

30 Quoted in *Niles Register,* Nov. 21, 1846, p. 181.

31 Smith, *Chile Con Carne* . . . , 93-95.

NOTES

32 "Recollections," as cited, No. 11, p. 171.

33 See *Gen. Orders No. 24*, Headquarters Camp, Near Monterey, Oct. 1, 1846.

34 Riddell, T. W., Napa, Calif., to Murgotten, A. P., San Jose, Calif., Jan. 18, 1901, in the *Pioneer* (San Jose, Calif.), Feb. 15, 1901.

35 Bosqui, E., *Memoirs* (1904), 34n.

36 Caperton, as cited.

CHAPTER 13

1 Taylor's orders no. 124, Oct. 1, 1846, *House Exec. Doc.* No. 60, 30 Cong., 1 Sess., p. 508. Ser. no. 520.

2 Signed statement of Lieut. W. B. P. Gaines, Hays's regiment, and of Hays, Monterey, Oct. 6, 1846, in *Ex. Doc.* 60, 30 Cong., 1 Sess., pp. 431-432.

3 Statement of Senator Jeff Davis, Mississippi, Aug. 5, 1850, in Rowland, D. (Ed.), *Jefferson Davis . . . Letters, Papers and Speeches* (1923), I, 459-460.

4 Greer (Ed.), *A Texas Ranger and Frontiersman . . .* , 41; Ford, J. S., Memoirs, MS.

5 Giddings, *Sketches of the Campaign in Northern Mexico*, 221-222.

6 Webb, *The Texas Rangers*, 110.

7 *New Orleans Picayune*, Nov. 13, 1846.

8 *Ibid.*

9 *Texas Democrat* (Austin), Nov. 11, 1846.

10 Galveston *Civilian* quoted in the *Picayune*, Nov. 13, 1846. Hays was never a prisoner of the Mexicans, although Walker once was before the war.

11 *Picayune*, Nov. 13, 1846.

12 *Ibid.*

13 *Texas Democrat*, Jan. 6, 1847.

14 *Picayune*, Jan. 24, 27, 1847.

15 *Texas Democrat*, Mar. 6, 1847, quoting the Galveston *Civilian*.

16 *Picayune*, Mar. 31, 1847.

17 Taylor to Adjutant General, Apr. 21, 1847, *House Ex. Doc.* 60, 30 Cong., 1 Sess., p. 1131. Ser. no. 520.

18 Hays, Betty, "Family History," in addenda to [Hunter, (Ed.)], *Jack Hays, The Intrepid Texas Ranger*, 57.

19 John C. Hays, Division of Veterans Records, the National Archives.

20 Galveston *News*, Feb. 17, 1887.

21 *San Antonio Express*, July 3, 1904.

22 Hays, B., as cited.

23 See the *Picayune*, May 29, 1847; Wilcox, *History of the Mexican War*, 693.

24 Taylor's Orders, No. 60, May 27, 1847, *House Ex. Doc.* 56, p. 336, 30 Cong., 1 Sess.

25 Taylor to Adjutant General, June 8, 16, 1847, *House Ex. Doc.* 56, 30 Cong., 1 Sess., pp. 365-368.

26 Ford, Memoirs, MS.

27 Marcy to Taylor, June 26, 1847, *House Ex. Doc.* 56, 30 Cong., 1 Sess., pp. 382-383.

CHAPTER 14

1 Hays to Taylor, July 13, 1847, in the Peter Hansborough Bell Papers.

2 Hays to Taylor, Hays to Gen. M. B. Lamar, Hays to Capt. G. K. Lewis, July 19, 1847.

NOTES

3 Taylor, Camp near Monterey, July 27, 1847, to Adjutant General of the Army, Washington, in *House Ex. Doc.* 56, 30 Cong., 1 Sess., p. 376. Ser. no. 520.

4 Hays to Neighbors, July 15, 1847, I. O., N 31; Neighbors to Medill, Aug. 5, 1847 in *Sen. Ex. Doc.* 1, 30 Cong., 1 Sess., pp. 897-898.

5 See Hays to Jones, Aug. 9, 1847, in the Peter Hansborough Bell Papers. This reference will be cited hereafter as the Bell Papers.

6 Hays wrote in part: . . . "Although I regret the necessity compelling me to speak in terms of reprehension of an officer,—a desire to do justice to the brave men he kept in a state of almost total uselessness, whilst in the pay of the United States demand a statement of facts."

7 See Hays to Dr. J. W. Robertson, Aug. 10, 1847; Hays to Surgeon General, Aug. 11, 1847, in the Bell Papers.

8 Hays to Adjutant General, U. S. A., Aug. 11, 1847, in the Bell Papers.

9 Smith, S. Compton, *Chile Con Carne* . . . , 291-294. Smith was an active surgeon with General Taylor's division.

10 Alcaraz, Ramon, *The Other Side* . . . (1850), 439-442.

11 *Sen. Ex. Doc.* 52, 30 Cong., 1 Sess., p. 138.

12 Quaife, M. M. (Ed.), *The Diary of James K. Polk* . . . (1910), III, 89.

13 *House Ex. Doc.* 56, 30 Cong., 1 Sess., p. 385.

14 Henderson to Lamar, Aug. 17, 21, 1847, in the *Lamar Papers*, IV, 176-178.

15 *Picayune*, Oct. 10, 1847.

16 *Niles Register*, Oct. 30, 1847.

17 *Picayune*, Oct. 29, 1847.

18 This story is from Ford's Memoirs, MS.

19 *Ibid.*

20 *Picayune*, Dec. 9, 1847.

21 Oswandel, J. J., *Notes on the Mexican War, 1846-47-48* . . . (1885 edit.) 382.

22 Taylor to Adjutant General, Oct. 4, 1847, in *House Ex. Doc.* 56, pp. 390-391.

23 Oswandel, as cited, 95.

24 Brackett, *General Lane's Brigade in Central Mexico*, 173-174.

25 Dumont, Ebenezer, Lieut.-Col., Fourth Regiment Indiana Volunteers, "Letters of," published in the *Indiana Register* and quoted in the *Democratic Telegraph and Texas Register* (Columbia, Texas), Feb. 24, 1848.

26 Brigadier-General Joseph Lane had entered the war as Colonel of the second Regiment of Indiana Volunteers.

27 Lane's report to Adjutant General, U.S.A., from Puebla, Dec. 1, 1847, in *House Ex. Doc.* 1, 30 Cong., 2 Sess., p. 86. Ser. no. 537.

28 Lane, as cited, 88.

29 Brackett, as cited, 192.

30 *Ibid.*, 194-195.

31 Oswandel, as cited, 401.

CHAPTER 15

1 Smith, *The War With Mexico*, II, 183-184.

2 *Ibid.*, 226; M'Sherry, R., *El Puchero: or, A Mixed Dish from Mexico,* . . . (1850), 162-163. M'Sherry was an acting surgeon of marines with the medical department of Scott's army.

3 Dumont, E., "Letters of," in the *Indiana Register* and quoted by the *Democratic Telegraph and Texas Register*, Feb. 24, 1848.

4 Ford, Memoirs, MS.

[5] Hitchcock, E. A., . . . *Fifty Years in Camp and Field* (1909), 310. General Scott to Marcy, Dec. 10, 1847, mentions the date of arrival as the 7th, but Ford and others agree with Hitchcock.

[6] Dumont, as cited.

[7] *Picayune*, Dec. 29, 1847, quoting their correspondent's letter of Dec. 7.

[8] Greer (Ed.), *A Texas Ranger and Frontiersman* . . . , 41-42. The story of the candy vendor is drawn from Ford, as cited.

[9] Ford, as cited.

[10] *Ibid.*

[11] This account is taken from Dumont, as cited.

[12] Smith, as cited, 166-169, 226.

[13] Ford, as cited.

[14] This anecdote is drawn from Ford, as cited.

[15] Oswandel, *Notes on the Mexican War*, 449.

[16] Scott to Marcy, Jan. 13, 1848, in *House Ex. Doc.* 60, 30 Cong., 1 Sess., p. 1067; Scott, W., *Memoirs of* . . . (1864), 567-568; Ford, as cited; Oswandel, as cited, 457; *Picayune*, Jan. 29, 1848; *Niles Register*, Feb. 19, 1848. The above account of the fight at San Juan is drawn chiefly from Ford who was a participant.

CHAPTER 16

[1] See the "Josiah Pancoast Letters" in Chabot, F. C. (Ed.), *Texas Letters* (1940), 97.

[2] Wooster, D., "Santa Anna . . . A Reminiscence of the Mexican War," in *The Vidette* (Washington), 1896.

[3] Chabot, as cited.

[4] Lane, Brigadier General, Report of, in *House Ex. Doc.* 1, No. 9, 30 Cong., 2 Sess., Ser. no. 537. See also, W. L. Marcy to President Polk in this same document.

[5] Wooster, as cited.

[6] *Ibid.*

[7] Chabot, as cited, 98.

[8] Wooster, as cited.

[9] Lane, as cited, pp. 90-91.

[10] Wooster, as cited.

[11] *Ibid.*; Lane, as cited.

[12] Wooster, as cited.

[13] Ford, Memoirs, MS.

[14] Oswandel, *Notes on the Mexican War*, 480.

CHAPTER 17

[1] Ford, Memoirs, MS.

[2] "Report of Brigadier General Lane," March 2, 1848, in *House Ex. Doc.* 1, 30 Cong., 2 Sess., Ser. no. 537. See, also, "Josiah Pancoast Letters," in Chabot (Ed.),*Texas Letters*, 99; Ford, as cited.

[3] Ford, as cited.

[4] *Ibid.*

[5] "Report of Colonel Hays," March 1, 1848, in *House Ex. Doc.* 1, 30 Cong., 2 Sess., Ser. no. 537.

[6] *Ibid.*; Lane, Joseph, Autobiography of Joseph Lane (1878), MS.

NOTES

7 Lane, "Report of," as cited.

8 "Report of Major Truett," March 2, 1848, to Adjutant John S. Ford, in *House Ex. Doc.* 1, 30 Cong., 2 Sess., Ser. no. 537.

9 Hays, as cited.

10 Hays, as cited; Lane, "Report of," as cited.

11 This anecdote is from Ford, as cited.

12 *Ibid.*

13 Chabot, as cited, 100; Oswandel, *Notes on the Mexican War*, 508-509.

CHAPTER 18

1 "Josiah Pancoast Letters" in Chabot (Ed.), *Texas Letters*, 100.

2 Ford, Memoirs, ms.

3 *Ibid.*

4 *Ibid.* This story is drawn from Ford's Memoirs which, although incomplete, is the best account of Hays and his men in the war with Mexico.

5 Smith, *The War With Mexico*, II, 181.

6 Kenly, *Memoirs of a Maryland Volunteer*, 391; Oswandel's *Notes on the Mexican War*, 524.

7 These brief descriptions are drawn largely from Kenly, as cited, 393, 394.

8 Ford, as cited.

9 Kenly, as cited, 395.

10 Ford, as cited.

11 Kenly, as cited, 396.

12 Ford, as cited.

13 New Orleans *Delta*, Apr. 27, 1848.

CHAPTER 19

1 New Orleans *Delta*, Apr. 24, 1848. Cited hereafter in this chapter as the *Delta*.

2 Ford, Memoirs, ms.

3 Photostat in possession of the author.

4 Ford, as cited.

5 *Ibid.*

6 *Ibid.*

7 *Delta*, May 29, 1948.

8 Ford, as cited.

9 *Ibid.; Delta*, July 3, 1848; Chabot (Ed.),*Texas Letters*, 98; *Niles Register* (Baltimore), Feb. 26, 1848.

10 *Delta*, July 3, 1848.

11 *Ibid.*

12 *Ibid.*

13 *Ibid.*

14 *Picayune*, June 28, 1848.

15 Watson, M. L., in the Galveston *News*, Feb. 17, 1887.

INDEX